The Insider's Guide to Santa Fe, Taos, and Albuquerque

The Insider's Guide to Santa Fe, Taos, and Albuquerque

FOURTH REVISED EDITION

Bill Jamison and
Cheryl Alters Jamison

The Harvard Common Press
Boston, Massachusetts

For Heather

The Harvard Common Press
535 Albany Street
Boston, Massachusetts 02118

Printed in the United States of America

Library of Congress Cataloging-in-Publication Data
Jamison, Bill.
   The insider's guide to Santa Fe, Taos, and Albuquerque /
Bill Jamison and Cheryl Alters Jamison.—4th rev. ed.
      p. cm.
   Includes index.
   ISBN 1-55832-113-6
   1. Santa Fe (N.M.)—Guidebooks. 2. Santa Fe Region
(N.M.)—Guidebooks. 3. Taos (N.M.)—Guidebooks.
4. Albuquerque (N.M.)—Guidebooks. I. Jamison, Cheryl
Alters. II. Title.
F804.S23J348 1996
917.89'5—dc20   95-26180

Special bulk-order discounts are available on this and other Harvard Common Press books. Companies or organizations may purchase books for premiums or for resale, or may arrange a custom edition, by contacting the Marketing Director at the address above.

Maps by Charles Bahne
Cover illustration by Jackie Schuman
Cover and interior design by Joyce C. Weston

10 9 8 7 6 5 4 3 2 1

Contents

Part Four: ALBUQUERQUE   191

Part Five: OFF THE BEATEN PATH   241

Maps

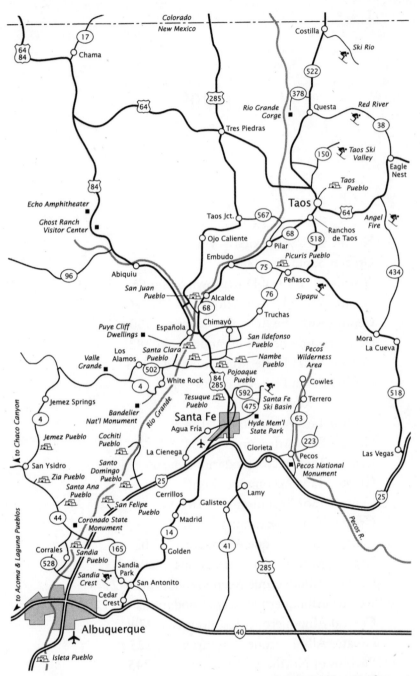

Northern New Mexico

Publisher's Foreword

THE HARVARD COMMON PRESS is honored to publish *The Insider's Guide to Santa Fe, Taos, and Albuquerque*, the oldest continually updated, nationally distributed guide to northern New Mexico. First released as *Santa Fe, An Intimate View* in 1982, the book has established a track record that few guides to any place can match.

Bill and Cheryl Jamison are the main reasons for the success. Residents of the area, who update each edition personally, the Jamisons couldn't be more perfect for the assignment. As authors of other respected guides to the Caribbean, Mexico, and Hawaii, they know the travel turf; all three books, part of Houghton Mifflin's *Best Places to Stay* series, deal with accommodations, giving the Jamisons keen insight and expertise about lodging anywhere, including northern New Mexico.

Just as important, the Jamisons understand food, another critical element in a good travel experience. Authorities on American regional cooking, they have written five acclaimed cookbooks. Their *Smoke & Spice* (Harvard Common Press, 1994), which celebrates the American barbecue tradition, won the prestigious James Beard award.

Another reason for the success of this guide is its honesty and impartiality. No one pays to be mentioned in the book or receives any special consideration. The Jamisons make all the judgments on their own, offering an informed individual perspective that's not swayed by favors or fawning.

We won't claim that the book is totally free of errors. No guide is. The Jamisons and Harvard Common Press make a concerted effort to ensure the accuracy of information about even the smallest details, but changes do occur in everything from historical interpretations to today's prices. We cannot accept responsibility for errors that may appear occasionally. Always verify any facts that affect your plans in a significant way.

Please let us know about your experiences in northern New Mexico, pleasant or unpleasant. The Jamisons update information and evaluations regularly in preparation for the next edition of the book, and they always appreciate feedback of any kind. Send your letters to *The Insider's Guide to Santa Fe, Taos, and Albuquerque,* Harvard Common Press, 535 Albany Street, Boston, MA 02118.

Dancing Ground of the Sun

*T*HE PUEBLO Indians established a village near the site of Santa Fe six or seven centuries ago, long before any Europeans arrived in the area. According to legend, they called the village "the dancing ground of the sun," a splendid description of northern New Mexico's natural aura.

If you approach the area from the south, as most visitors have for four hundred years, the vast Southwestern desert gradually and reluctantly yields to the forested peaks of the Jemez Mountains to the west and the Sangre de Cristo Mountains to the east. Interstate 25 from the Albuquerque airport, the entry route for most modern travelers, follows the valley of the Rio Grande between the mountains, parallel to the old Spanish route from Mexico City. The founders built Santa Fe, Taos, and other early towns on high plateaus right under the towering shelter of the eastern range.

Now as then, the expansive sky overhead dominates the perspective. The desert below, like a great ocean, takes an infinity to reach the horizon. The mountains above, and those beyond in all directions, rise proudly and primordially over the arid land, daunting in their massiveness and seeming indifference. The Spanish wanted the elevated view from their towns primarily for protection against invaders, but their priests must have also noticed that the sin of human pride would be hard to maintain in such a setting.

Many writers have strained for language that would match the grandeur of the scenery. D. H. Lawrence, who lived just north of Taos in the 1920s, made one of the noblest efforts.

> For greatness of beauty I have never experienced anything like New Mexico. All those mornings when I went with a hoe along the ditch to the Cañón, at the ranch, and stood, in the fierce, proud silence of the Rockies, on their foothills, to look far over the desert to the blue mountains away in Arizona, blue as Chalcedony, with the sage-brush desert sweeping grey-blue in between, dotted with tiny cube-crystals of houses, the vast amphitheater of lofty, indomitable desert, sweeping round to the ponderous Sangre de Cristo Mountains on the east, and coming up flush at the pine-dotted foothills of the Rockies! What splendour!*

The land is a magnificent stage for the dazzling performance of the sun. When Lawrence tried to describe the place of the sun in the local environment, he stretched even further for an apt image.

> Never is the light more pure and overweening as there, arching with a royalty almost cruel over the hollow, uptilted world. It is so easy to understand that the Aztecs gave hearts of men to the sun. For the sun is not merely hot or scorching, not at all. It is of a brilliant and unchallengeable purity and haughty serenity which would make one sacrifice the heart to it. Ah, yes, in New Mexico the heart is sacrificed to the sun and the human being is left stark, heartless, but undauntedly religious.

The sun's intensity in northern New Mexico results from a combination of circumstances. Its warmth reflects the region's southern latitude, about the same as Atlanta's. Winter days are

* The D. H. Lawrence quotes are from *Phoenix: The Posthumous Papers* (Penguin, 1936).

milder for skiing than anywhere else in the Rockies, though ski vests and sweaters remain useful all year, even on summer evenings, because of the contrasting coolness of the mountain air.

The brightness of the sun comes from the clarity of the air. At the 7,000-foot altitude in Santa Fe and Taos, its rays avoid the last mile and a half of the earth's dust-laden atmosphere. The desert aridity keeps the humidity low and the air relatively free of the misting effect of water particles. These factors combine to give the sun more rein than it has anywhere else in the United States.

It's the play of the sun and its shadow on mountain, desert, and adobe that has lured so many artists to the region. Robert Henri and Marsden Hartley, who spent months in New Mexico on several different visits, were fascinated with the brilliance of the color. Hartley said the area "is of course the only place in America where true color exists, excepting the short autumnal season in New England."

John Sloan, a leading figure in the "ashcan school" of American art, made a summer home where there were no ashcans, just off Canyon Road in Santa Fe. His subject matter shifted to the local population, but what was most notable in his work was the shimmering glow of the sun. Andrew Dasburg, probably the greatest of the American cubists, moved permanently to New Mexico, first to Santa Fe and then to Taos. Dasburg said, "I felt as though I had come upon the Garden of Eden; everything was pristine."

The first people to appreciate the amplitude of the place, long before the artists arrived, were those who called it "the dancing ground of the sun." In the complex pantheistic beliefs of the Pueblo peoples, their natural surroundings assume sacred dimensions. Everything, animate and inanimate, has a spirit, which is benevolent or malevolent depending on how well humans respect it.

Most settlers who succeeded the Pueblos were less concerned about maintaining religious harmony with the environment than with using it. The Spanish wanted the mountains to yield gold, and the Americans looked to them for furs, coal, timber, and now upscale residential developments. Something may have been lost over time, particularly as a result of the population growth and commercial exploitation of the 1980s and '90s, but most residents and visitors still feel elements of the spiritual power that the Pueblos attribute to their land. D. H. Lawrence is not a very representative case for much of anything, but many new arrivals do share his first impression of the place. He came to the area after years of traveling the world, jaded by the expectation of monotony.

> Superficially, the world has become small and known. Poor little globe of earth, the tourists trot round you as easily as they trot round the Bois or round Central Park. There is no mystery left, we've been there, we've seen it, we know all about it.
>
> We are mistaken. I realized this with shattering force when I went to New Mexico. The moment I saw the brilliant, proud morning shine high up over the deserts of Santa Fe, something stood still in my soul and I started to attend. In the magnificent fierce morning of New Mexico one sprang awake, a new part of the soul woke up suddenly, and the old world gave way to a new.

PART ONE

The New Mexico Heritage

CHAPTER ONE

The Pueblos

*T*HE ANCESTORS of the Pueblos, the Anasazi people, settled in the Southwest several thousand years ago, but no one is certain of their origins. The Pueblo explanation is the most tantalizing. They believe their ancestors came from an underworld beneath the earth's surface, a place that was dark, ugly, and damp, the very opposite of the South-west. They struggled to climb out and, after many vicissitudes, finally emerged through the earth's navel, onto the land and into the light. The point of emergence is represented by the small opening, or *sipapu*, in Pueblo *kivas*, their sacred ceremonial chambers.

The Anasazi were nomadic hunters and gatherers until they began cultivating corn, about 2000 B.C. Archaeologists have unearthed hundreds of tiny cobs from that ancient period, as thin as a pencil and less than two inches in length. Over the next millennium the Anasazi refined their agricultural methods, added the protein of the bean to their repertory, and learned how to support cities from their farms. In their first permanent settlements they lived in pit houses, large holes in the ground covered with logs. The Anasazi developed these circular, underground structures originally as granaries for storing corn, but later found them suitable for housing as well.

The Pueblos have never forgotten the importance of corn in the development of their civilization. They use cornmeal and corn pollen as Catholics use holy water, to bless the newborn and the dead and to prepare for important rituals, and they celebrate its spiritual power in some of their most striking ceremonial dances. Their underground kivas have remained very similar in structure to the original corn granaries, long after their ancestors began building houses aboveground.

Anasazi Architecture and Life

The Anasazi were impressive architects. After leaving their pit houses, about the time that Europe was entering the Dark Ages, they constructed some magnificent cities. One of the oldest was in Chaco Canyon, a dry, hot valley in the desert canyonlands of northwestern New Mexico. In their prime, in the twelfth century, the Chaco residents built eight large stone structures capable of housing at least five thousand people. Pueblo Bonito, the grandest of these communal dwellings, rose four stories high and contained eight hundred rooms and thirty kivas. It was the largest housing structure built in the Western Hemisphere until a New York City landlord topped it in the 1880s. The forty-foot-high walls, some of which are still standing, had to be massive at the base to support the building, but the Anasazi laid the stones with delicate and intricate artistry, as effectively as any modern mason could with much more sophisticated tools.

Life in Chaco Canyon was probably as pleasant as possible for the Stone Age. The residents had an elaborate naturalistic religion that entailed frequent and splendid community ceremonies. They engaged in trade that ranged as far as the Pacific Ocean and brought them, among other things, various shells and gems for jewelry. The Anasazi knew basket weaving before coming to Chaco and developed pottery after they settled in the canyon. They wove cotton blankets and colored them with vegetable dyes. Some of their possessions were so precious that the

Anasazi hid them in cleverly concealed wall crypts that have been discovered only by chance.

The Anasazi left Chaco for unknown reasons, possibly drought, during the thirteenth century. Most residents moved east to the Pajarito Plateau, overlooking the Rio Grande Valley. The major settlement, among many, on the 8,000-foot plateau was in Frijoles Canyon, an excellent home site. Six miles long and a half-mile wide, the canyon is crossed by a small, spring-fed stream that carries ample water to irrigate the valley floor. Berries grow wild along the creek and tall pines, good for lumber, cover the canyon's southern slope. The sheer north wall is dotted with natural caves, which some of the residents dug out and walled in for homes. Other people lived in a circular communal structure, three stories high, near the creek.

The ruins of the settlement are now a part of Bandelier National Monument, named for Adolph Bandelier, the first archaeologist to study the Pueblos. In a novel about the Frijoles people, *The Delight Makers* (Harcourt Brace Jovanovich, paperback edition, 1971), Bandelier speculated that they left the canyon largely because of feuds and witchcraft within the community.

The Rio Grande Pueblos

By the time the Spanish arrived in the area in 1540, most of the local inhabitants had moved down from the Pajarito Plateau into their present-day villages along the Rio Grande Valley. Currently, there are sixteen Pueblo communities in the valley, in an area stretching about 75 miles both north and south of Santa Fe. The other three Pueblo villages in New Mexico, and the Hopi villages in Arizona, are farther west.

The Spanish named the people of all of these towns *Pueblo*, meaning "community" or "village," because of their settled life. Actually each community, or *pueblo*, is a separate tribal group, with its own traditions and local laws. The people share a common cultural background and are still known generically as

Pueblos, but they speak six different languages, which vary considerably in some cases, even between villages in close proximity.

In many respects life in the present-day pueblos is similar to what the Spanish encountered over four centuries ago. The Spanish, and later the Americans, tried to introduce changes in Pueblo life, and did succeed to some degree, but on the whole ancient Pueblo traditions have prevailed. The extent of change differs substantially from one community to another, since each is fully independent and self-governing, but generally the Pueblos have accepted concepts and practices they found useful and rejected anything that seemed likely to destroy the continuity of their way of life.

In government, all the villages have retained the ancient form of council rule. The Spanish forced the Pueblos to choose a governor for each community, to act as a spokesman and liaison to the outside world, but a council of experienced leaders representing the most significant interests in the pueblo still makes the important decisions. In council, now as in the past, unanimity is the goal in taking action, even when this requires holding interminable meetings or leaving a vital matter unresolved for a considerable time. Religious leaders, *caciques,* continue to influence decisions, but they no longer dominate councils in the way they did in previous centuries.

Pueblo Religion

Both the Spanish and the Americans attempted to eliminate the native religion. The Spanish tried diligently to convert the Pueblos to Catholicism, and later the Americans arbitrarily assigned all Indians to various Christian churches. One Baptist missionary sent to Laguna Pueblo was so zealous in his efforts that he caused a major split in the village that has never fully healed. The Spanish, who were usually more patient and persistent, were slightly more successful.

Most of the Pueblos accepted Catholicism to the degree that it did not interfere with their own ancient beliefs. Saints were easy to adopt because they were similar to the sacred beings known as *kachinas*. Prayer and mass seemed sensible to the Pueblos, analogous to their own rituals, and the Christian calendar offered a few refinements over their own in tracking the important changes in the seasons. Other Christian concepts were more often tolerated than endorsed.

When the Pueblos adopted elements of Christianity, they regarded them as supplements to their existing religion, not as replacements. At first this was frustrating to the Spanish, but they learned over time that efforts to suppress the old beliefs could be even more frustrating. The peaceful Pueblos killed overly righteous priests and eventually organized the most effective mass routing the Spanish Empire ever encountered in the New World in response to an attempt to quash their religion. After a century of struggle the two peoples reached a compromise. The Spanish began looking the other way and the Pueblos went underground—literally—with their religion. They banned the Spanish, and later the Americans, from their kivas, where they continued their most sacred ancient rites in seclusion.

In more ordinary and practical matters, the Pueblos have been less resistant to change. They have traded housing concepts freely, teaching the newcomers their adobe methods while adopting Spanish building technologies and modern innovations as well. Some Pueblos still live in large communal dwellings and reject electricity and piped water, but most today own houses that look conventionally suburban.

Herding livestock was an even easier adjustment. Cattle and sheep provided the same necessities as deer and buffalo and didn't have to be hunted. Besides, sheep supplied wool, which was simple to weave and much warmer than cotton.

Pueblo and Navajo Crafts

The Pueblos quickly adopted Spanish weaving techniques and then passed them along to the Navajos, who had settled in the

Southwest just a couple of centuries before the Spanish. A Navajo legend claims that Spider Man and Spider Woman taught them to weave, but the evidence is clear that their real benefactors were the Pueblos, whom they raided for a lot more than ideas and with whom they have maintained some enmity to the present.

The Pueblos colored their wool with impermanent vegetable dyes, developed much earlier for their cotton cloth. The Navajos, however, experimented with durable and bright dyes introduced by the Spanish and soon surpassed their teachers in weaving skills. By the early nineteenth century the Spanish and Pueblos were acknowledging the proficiency of the Navajos and trading for their blankets. Some Pueblos continued to weave after that time, but they never made an effort to emulate the artistic and commercial success of their students.

The situation was somewhat similar with jewelry craftsmanship. The Pueblos mined turquoise in the Southwest, and made it into jewelry, before either the Spanish or the Navajos arrived in the region, and they continued to work primarily with turquoise and other stones even after the Spanish introduced metalsmithing. Some contemporary jewelers, particularly ones from Santo Domingo and Zuni, have achieved artistic and financial success with traditional materials and styles, but as with weaving, the Navajos on the whole were more adaptable and commercially successful.

Navajo artisans convinced the Spanish to teach them smithing around 1850 and began copying and modifying Spanish silverwork. They were making squash-blossom necklaces and silver *concha* belts by the 1870s, using design ideas borrowed from Spanish silver bridles. In the next decade they discovered a technique for setting turquoise in silver, taking a precut stone and molding the metal to fit it.

For over a century now, Navajo silver work has been in high demand with traders and collectors. One Pueblo group, the Hopi, began producing exceptional metal jewelry in recent decades, but most Pueblo artisans maintain their historic attachment to turquoise.

Pueblo Pottery

In pottery the Pueblos preserve tradition with similar dedication. They still make pots by hand, as their ancestors did, without the use of a potter's wheel. Coiling ropes of clay on top of one another to build up the walls of a piece, they then smooth the surface to eliminate any trace of the coils. The pots are fired outside in the open, instead of in a kiln, with dried dung cakes frequently used as the fuel.

Pottery has been the most refined Pueblo craft for hundreds of years, and it is the only one that the Navajos haven't borrowed. Skills declined around the turn of the century—after the railroad brought enamelware, tin pails, and other manufactured kitchen products to the area—but a significant renaissance began in the 1920s and has continued since.

Much of the stimulation for the renaissance came from the village of San Ildefonso, just north of Santa Fe. The most famous residents of the pueblo, Maria and Julian Martínez, developed a distinctive style of black pottery that was inspired by old fragments discovered in an archaeological dig. Maria was already an accomplished potter in 1919 when Julian worked out the technique for producing matte black designs on her polished black pots. The style became an immediate success, to such a degree that Maria began signing her work in 1925, something Pueblo artists had never done before.

The black-on-black style is still popular among San Ildefonso potters, but many of the best have branched out in different directions. Rose Gonzales introduced intaglio techniques in the 1930s, carving designs on the surface of the vessel. Later, Blue Corn revived the polychromatic style that had been common in the village in the nineteenth century. Her work influenced Popovi Da, Maria and Julian's son, to do some similar pots, even while he was assisting his mother at her work and developing a new firing technique of his own to make two-tone pieces of black and sienna. Popovi's son, Tony Da, established his reputation by decorating work with inlaid turquoise and *heishi* (shell).

Some of these same styles and techniques also flourish at Santa Clara, which is close to San Ildefonso both in distance and in the fame of its pottery. Several decades ago at the pueblo, Lela and Van Gutierrez developed a polychrome form, which their children, Margaret and Luther, refined further. Sarafina and Geronimo Tafoya established a dynasty of potters that produced work in a variety of modes, including the polished, carved ware that is most characteristic of Santa Clara. Their talented heirs include Margaret Tafoya, Camilio Tafoya, Christina Naranjo, Teresita Naranjo, Joseph Lonewolf, and Grace Medicine Flower.

At Hopi, Nampeyo inspired a dramatic resurgence of pottery earlier this century. Fascinated by shards of ancient Hopi work, she created the distinctive orange ware that became the dominant form in her village. Her daughters, granddaughters, and great-granddaughters, who normally use the Nampeyo name with their own in signing work, perpetuated the tradition. In recent decades some Hopi artists ventured into other styles, such as the white clay forms of Joy Navasie (Frogwoman) and Helen Naha (Featherwoman).

At Acoma, Lucy Lewis and Marie Chino helped establish a distinctive white-clay pottery, shaped very thin and decorated with intricate geometric and animal designs or with more conventional polychrome patterns. Chino's daughters—Rose Garcia, Grace Chino, and Carrie Charlie—and four of the Lewis children—Emma Mitchell, Delores Garcia, Mary Histia, and Ann Hansen—refined the style. The polychrome work at Zia, a well-established tradition in the pueblo, resembles some of the Acoma pottery but is made with red clay.

A few villages, most notably Cochiti, specialize in clay figurines instead of pots. In some ways these pieces reflect the curio orientation in Pueblo pottery that was popular before the current renaissance began, but many of them today are exquisite creations, particularly the storyteller figures of Helen Cordero and other talented Cochiti artisans.

The work of these and other potters is the most visible sign today of Pueblo endurance and devotion to cultural heritage. Styles and design patterns may be in flux, as they always have been to some degree, but the substance of the craft has remained essentially unchanged across the centuries. Pueblo artisans still are using basic elements of the original techniques that the Anasazi developed about fifteen hundred years ago, and much of the inspiration for their current designs goes back to that earlier period.

Two of the most powerful nations of the modern world, imperial Spain and the United States, overran the Pueblos during periods of vigorous expansion. They caused some changes in the way of life, but neither managed to complete the spiritual and cultural conquest they intended. Pueblo pottery, religion, social customs, and other traditional practices remain a magnificent demonstration of the strength and vitality of a culture much older than both of the conquering nations.

CHAPTER TWO

Our Spanish Forefathers

O UR BRITISH forefathers came to the New World to escape from the Old. They felt hopeless about their lives in England and wanted to carve a different destiny for themselves.

Our Spanish forefathers felt hopeless about nothing. They came to the New World to reshape it in the image of the Old, on behalf of God, gold, and glory. New Mexico was one of several miscalculations along the way. Santa Fe, or *La Villa Real de la Santa Fe de San Francisco* (the Royal City of the Holy Faith of St. Francis), did become an Old World capital, as the name implies, but the colony yielded little gold or glory and the native population took to God only in limited and frustrating ways.

Some of the first Spanish explorers to reach New Mexico might have guessed this fate in realistic moments, but hope blinded the *conquistadores*. Cabeza de Vaca, shipwrecked on the Texas coast in 1528, wandered the Southwest for eight years. Though his most impressive discovery was Native Americans living in permanent mud homes, growing corn, beans, and squash, that was enough to inspire visions of cities of gold. A second small party, led by Friar Marcos de Niza, failed to find the fabulous cities but reported seeing them from a distant hilltop.

The friar's account stimulated a major expedition, headed by

Francisco Vásquez de Coronado, that included three hundred volunteer soldiers, a band of Christian missionaries, and several hundred Mexican Indian servants. Coronado baptized some Southwestern residents between 1540 and 1542 but returned to Mexico City without glory or gold. His quest had cost about two million dollars in today's currency. Refusing to believe that the investment was futile, the authorities tried the explorer for not looking far enough.

The Early Colonists

The first colonizing expedition left Mexico City in 1598 with 130 families, hundreds of Indian servants and "eight seraphic, apostolic, preaching priests," as they were described. They entered New Mexico with a flagellation rite, a fiesta, and a play. Arriving near the present site of El Paso on Holy Thursday, the colonists observed the day with medieval *penitente* ceremonies that are still practiced to some degree in northern New Mexico. A chronicler among the colonists wrote that "the soldiers, with cruel scourges, beat their backs unmercifully until the camp ran crimson with their blood. The humble Franciscan friars, barefoot and clothed in cruel thorny girdles, devoutly chanted their doleful hymns."

Shortly afterward, the group encountered some friendly Native Americans and celebrated possession of the new land. Following a fiesta, the colonists presented an edifying drama to their new neighbors, showing the local residents joyfully welcoming the first priests and begging for baptism. The play may have been entertaining, but it wasn't much as prophecy.

The colonists settled originally near San Juan Pueblo, just north of the present town of Española, and immediately began to search for riches and souls. Typically, their reports to Mexico City were grander than their real discoveries. Within a few years the Franciscans claimed sixty thousand Native American converts, probably three times the total population of the area. One of the pioneers who traveled the region speculated on the local geography, reckoning that New Mexico was a peninsula extending northward between Newfoundland and China, within sight of the latter at some point yet to be found. The reports ran so contrary to actual experience that the main chronicler of the colony was later tried for writing "beautiful but untrue accounts."

Decimated by starvation, desertion, and Indian revolts, the Spanish abandoned the San Juan settlement in 1610 in favor of a new beginning at Santa Fe. The change brought few significant improvements to their lives, but the colonists gradually began to adjust their expectations and adapt to the environment. They survived a meager existence for several generations before famine and religious passion created a major upheaval.

The Pueblo Revolt

In the 1670s a drought forced both colonists and the local Pueblos into subsisting on hides boiled with roots and herbs, a diet probably related to the epidemic that followed. In the midst of this distress, the Spanish governor decided to obliterate all traces of Pueblo religion. Many of the native residents had accepted Catholicism, but only as a supplement to their traditional beliefs, which they never considered dropping. The governor tried forty-seven Pueblo shamans for sorcery and hanged three. For his own good he should have executed at least four, because one of those released, Popé, was a charismatic and powerful leader.

Popé devised an ingenious plan for a mass insurrection against the Spanish and organized the various pueblos to carry it out simultaneously. On August 10, 1680, they began slaughtering the Spanish, starting with residents of small outlying villages and moving toward Santa Fe. Spanish survivors barricaded themselves in the Palace of the Governors as the Pueblos burned the town around them, and then eventually fled south to El Paso.

The colonists remained there for twelve years, until new

recruits could be mustered for a reconquest. To lead the return, the Viceroy of New Spain chose Don Diego de Vargas, a proven soldier from an illustrious Madrid family. De Vargas's initial expedition to Santa Fe in 1692 encountered no resistance, and he went back to Mexico proclaiming a peaceful victory. When he returned the following year, however, to reestablish the colony, the Pueblos fought back. De Vargas had to take the Palace of the Governors by force, and afterward he executed seventy of the defenders and enslaved four hundred others. The Pueblos continued to resist for three bloody years before the Spanish completed the reconquest.

Adobe Towns

The colonists had to rebuild their settlements almost totally. As before, they used adobe for construction, supplementing their own knowledge of the material with concepts borrowed from the Pueblos. They made adobe bricks with mud and straw, drying them in the sun at the building site. They bonded the blocks together with wet adobe and later plastered them with the same mixture to make walls that were too thick to be pierced by arrows.

The Spanish kept their houses close to the ground, with low ceilings and flat roofs. Log beams, or *vigas,* laid on top of the walls, supported the earthen roof, composed of brush and soil. The home of an *hidalgo,* a gentleman, differed from that of a peasant primarily in the length of the vigas, which determined the size of the house. Everyone had dirt floors, mixed with animal blood to produce a hard clay surface. Most rooms contained a small kiva fireplace in the corner, designed to take upright logs.

The furnishings were simple and crude during the colonial period. Even hidalgos owned little beyond handhewn chests, benches, stools, and a table. The settlers crafted most of their furniture, since New Mexico's isolation precluded the importation of many bulky goods.

The religious art that decorated homes and churches was easier to bring from Spain and Mexico, though much of it was made locally too. *Retablos,* religious paintings on flat boards, were almost always imported until the nineteenth century because drawing skills and paints were rare in the early colony. More people knew woodcarving, which they used to decorate vigas and furniture and to sculpt *bultos,* or wooden statues. Most of the bultos were images of saints, called *santos,* though carvers also made *reredoses,* or altar screens, and *muertes,* the distinctive death carts that are a vivid symbol of the colonists' struggle with life.

Colonial Life

Doctors were scarce in New Mexico. The only "surgeon and dentist" on record in Santa Fe in the eighteenth century seems to have impressed residents more with his tools than his cures. He had "two cases for instruments, one with five razors, and whetstone, and the other one with six lancets trimmed with tortoise shell and silver." During most of the colonial period, residents relied on home remedies, using herbs, other plants, and whiskey distilled in the area.

Los ricos, the rich, kept these medical staples in locked store-rooms, along with hanging meat cuts and strings of dried fruit and chile. Wealth was based on the amount of land and sheep owned, but everyone was a farmer. In the summer the colonists enjoyed fresh corn, chiles, beans, onions, and various fruits, but for most of the year they ate dried produce and cornmeal made into tortillas. The women cooked meals in the fireplace, using heavy kettles, or outside in *hornos,* beehive-shaped adobe ovens. They served the food on pottery, much of it made by the Pueblos.

While working at home, women wore full, short skirts of serge and tight, low-necked blouses that some early American visitors considered indecent. When they left the house, ladies who could afford it wrapped themselves in imported shawls, or, for special occasions, dressed in European finery. They often used red clay for rouge but sometimes switched to a heavy white powder of ground bones for *fandangos,* or dances.

Men generally owned a more extensive and expensive wardrobe than women, because of their exclusive hold on official and ceremonial roles in the colony. Hidalgos needed fancy uniforms, with gold lace if possible, for military formalities. At other times they wore woolen pantaloons, leather jackets, and high boots, well suited for riding. Wool *serapes* and imported flat *sombreros* protected them from the weather.

The residents wove the fabrics for most of their clothes. The usual cloth was *sabanilla,* a woolen plain-weave they made in large quantities for basic garments and bedding. It was sometimes embroidered with floral or geometric designs in the distinctive, long *colcha* stitch.

In the latter colonial period weaving became a refined craft in New Mexico. At the same time that the Navajos were developing their weaving skills, the Spanish independently established a similar tradition, known as the Rio Grande style. Design patterns from the Orient—transmitted through fabrics made in Saltillo, Mexico—heavily influenced both groups. Rio Grande blankets and rugs are not as well known today as their Navajo counterparts, but Spanish artisans did some exceptional work.

Life was austere on the whole, crafted by hand from scarce resources, but it seldom lacked gaiety. Fiestas in celebration of Mardi Gras, Easter, Christmas, saints' days, marriages, and other special occasions were frequent and important. When Mexico won its independence from Spain in 1821, the festivities in the Santa Fe capital lasted five days. On the first morning the residents raised the new flag and then joined in a spontaneous parade. Afterward everyone gathered at the Palace of the Governors. The head of the city council led a cotillion, which opened a grand *baile,* or ball, where celebrants danced to lively guitar and violin versions of the same tunes that were played more solemnly in church. A puritanical American trader who happened to be in town was shocked at the revelry: "All classes abandoned themselves to the most reckless dissipation," including "vice and licentiousness of every description," which went on "night and day" with "no time for sleep."

A generation later, when the U.S. Army seized the territory from Mexico, no one celebrated. Suddenly New Mexico was severed from its historical and cultural roots in the Spanish Empire. The residents gradually adjusted to the new situation, after a few ineffective attempts at insurrection, but for many years afterward army band concerts were more common than fiestas on the Santa Fe plaza.

The Spanish Heritage Today

Fortunately, the Spanish heritage was too entrenched to perish, despite the attempts of some early Americans to destroy it. The Spanish language still flourishes in New Mexico, particularly in the north, and so do Spanish Catholic traditions, from delightful Christmas customs to penitente flagellations at Easter.

The strength of the heritage today is particularly evident in the vitality of colonial crafts. Weaving and woodcarving died out in most of New Mexico in the late nineteenth century, but the local traditions were maintained and refined in small mountain villages between Santa Fe and Taos. The recent work of weavers Teresa Archuleta Sagel, Juanita Jaramillo, Maria Vergara-Wilson, and the Trujillo, Ortega, and Cordova families reflects a commitment to preserve the Rio Grande style.

Vergara-Wilson, among others, has helped to resurrect colcha stitchery, while Eliseo and Paula Rodriquez have inspired new respect for the old art of straw appliqué on wood. Leo Salazar, Horacio Valdez, Anita Romero Jones, Felix López, Eluid Martinez, Ben Ortega, Charles M. Carillo, and several members of the López family in Cordova have all carved santos as reverent and expressive as any made locally in past centuries.

Felipe Archuleta took the woodworking tradition in a new direction, creating whimsical sculptures of various animals. Other carvers, including Alonzo Jimenez, Jimbo Davila, Max Alvarez, and Felipe's son Leroy Archuleta, continue today in the same vein. The coyotes these artisans crafted became so popular that mass-produced imitations now clutter the shelves of almost every shop in Santa Fe and Taos.

As long as its cultural heritage is an inspiration, northern New Mexico will stay heavily Spanish. The colonists didn't find gold, or fully convert many Pueblos, but they did entrench their way of life in an area very remote from home. Four centuries later, the region remains an outpost of the Old World in the New.

CHAPTER THREE

Anglo Traders and Artists

*I*N NEW MEXICO the term *Anglo* covers a broad range of people. Applied to almost anyone who is not Hispanic or Indian, it is a polite way of saying non-native, or outsider, in contrast with the more pejorative *gringo*. Residents have conferred the title, at times at least, on Italians, Jews, African Americans, and even an occasional Briton.

The first Anglos to visit New Mexico were escorted into Santa Fe under military guard, as prisoners, just a few years before the city's 200th anniversary. A small party of U.S. explorers trespassed on the Spanish Empire accidentally in the winter of 1805–1806. Under orders from President Thomas Jefferson to find the sources of western tributaries of the Mississippi River, Lieutenant Zebulon Pike and his men stumbled instead upon the headwaters of the Rio Grande in the Colorado Rockies. A Spanish militia unit arrested the Americans and took them to Santa Fe for questioning, treating them more as curiosities than as captives.

The Santa Fe Trail

Local policy toward Anglo visitors changed considerably in the following two decades. When Mexico won its independence from Spain, the new republic wanted to establish good relations with its neighboring republic to the northeast. In 1821 a Mexican militia unit from Santa Fe encountered a group of Missourians wandering the plains, trading with Indians. The Santa Feans invited the traders to return home with them to sell their wares, opening the Santa Fe Trail.

A parade of Anglos came and went over the trail between Missouri and New Mexico in the next half century. At the peak of its activity, trade along the route employed ten thousand men and grossed millions of dollars annually for both Mexican and American merchants.

The existence of the trail made New Mexico a natural target for the United States in the 1846–48 war with Mexico. President James K. Polk started the conflict mainly to acquire California from Mexico, to realize America's "manifest destiny" of expanding to the Pacific Ocean. The U.S. Army occupied New Mexico on the way west.

The Army vs. the Anthropologists

The army stayed for the rest of the nineteenth century and became an important presence in the area. The soldiers weren't particularly impressed with their billeting. One of them wrote home about his "perfect contempt" for Santa Fe, which another called "the Siberia of America." New Mexico was to them, as a third soldier described it, "a dirty, filthy place built entirely of mud." The army erected a sawmill as soon as it arrived, with the intention of replacing adobe buildings with proper wood structures.

This attitude toward adobe prevailed among Anglo residents until the early twentieth century. There was still a good deal of adobe construction in the territorial period, before New Mexico gained statehood in 1912, but almost everyone who could afford it wanted to use milled lumber and brick for trim at least. Residents modified many historic homes in the territorial style, adding decorative layers of brick along roof lines and Greek Revival doors, windows, and portals. The ideal for most

Anglo residents was an all-brick house with a pitched roof, like those in their original hometowns.

Feelings changed along with Anglo settlement patterns around the time that statehood was granted. With New Mexico firmly incorporated into the United States, and the Navajos and Apaches of the area conquered, the U.S. Army moved out. As the soldiers left, anthropologists and artists moved in.

The anthropologists were attracted initially by the work of Adolph Bandelier, a Swiss scholar of international reputation who lived in Santa Fe in the 1880s. Bandelier's studies of the Pueblos stimulated considerable interest in North American prehistory. In 1907 the Archaeological Institute of America opened a center in Santa Fe, the School of American Research. The early leaders of the school, particularly Edgar Hewett and Sylvanus Morley, replaced the army colonels as the prime molders of Anglo opinion in the territory.

Unlike their predecessors, the anthropologists understood and appreciated the historical character of northern New Mexico and wanted to preserve it. They helped to inspire a revival of the Spanish Pueblo architectural style that still influences much new construction in the area.

Painters and writers of the early Santa Fe and Taos art colonies assisted energetically in the preservation efforts. They began arriving in New Mexico about a decade after the anthropologists, but they soon outnumbered the scholars. By the 1920s the art colonies were a major force in local life, and since then they have remained one of the primary Anglo influences in Santa Fe and Taos.

The Early Santa Fe and Taos Art Colonies

The first Anglo artists in the area arrived in Taos in the late 1890s. Ernest Blumenschein and Bert Phillips were popular and successful artists in the East when they passed through the vil-

lage doing illustrations for a magazine article. They were immediately attracted to the serenity and primitive charm of New
Mexico and soon moved permanently to Taos.

Blumenschein and Phillips, along with several other established artists who followed them west, formed the Taos Society
of Artists in 1912. Mostly educated in Paris, the society members excelled within the representational traditions of their day.
Their literal documentation of New Mexican life became so
popular elsewhere that the Atchison, Topeka & Santa Fe
Railroad commissioned them to do paintings to hang in its
offices and print on calendars, as a form of advertising in the
early days of the tourism industry.

The Santa Fe art colony started to crystallize a few years
later, with Robert Henri and John Sloan leading the way in the
1910s. Major figures of their day, both men continued to live
mainly in New York, though Sloan maintained a summer home
in Santa Fe for more than thirty years.

A number of less established artists moved to the city permanently in the same period. Five of these, all under thirty
years of age and newly arrived in town, banded together for a
show at the Museum of Fine Arts in 1921, calling themselves
Los Cinco Pintores, the five painters. A spirited group, influenced by Cézanne and other postimpressionists, they reacted
against the prestige of the Taos Society and declared that their
purpose was "to take art to the people and not surrender to
commercialism." The work of Jozef Bakos, Fremont Ellis,
Walter Mruk, Willard Nash, and Will Shuster seems fairly traditional today, but that was not the way the artists intended it
or how the public originally received it.

In the 1920s the international avant-garde invaded New
Mexico. Mabel Dodge Luhan, once described as "a reposeful
hurricane," moved her radical salon from New York City to
Taos during the conservative backlash following World War I.
She "willed," as she put it, a global roster of visitors, including
D. H. Lawrence, Max Weber, Paul and Rebecca Strand (who

brought Georgia O'Keeffe with them), John Marin, Marsden Hartley, and Andrew Dasburg. Edmund Wilson described the resident circle as an "extraordinary population of rich people, writers, and artists who pose as Indians, cowboys, prospectors, desperadoes, Mexicans and other nearly extinct species." Two of Luhan's guests—O'Keeffe and Dasburg—stayed in the area and became legendary presences.

During the Great Depression and for the following two decades, the art colonies grew as slowly as the rest of Santa Fe and Taos. A few major artists, including Laura Gilpin, Eliot Porter, and Agnes Martin, moved to New Mexico in this period, but the next large influx of Anglo artists didn't occur until the 1960s, when Paul Sarkisian and Fritz Scholder initiated an immigration that later included Larry Bell, Ken Price, Bruce Nauman, Rick Dillingham, Glenda Goodacre, Judy Chicago, Herb Ritts, and Terry Allen. In 1970 Clinton Adams moved the Tamarind Institute from Los Angeles to Albuquerque, stimulating a significant upsurge in printmaking in New Mexico and consolidating Albuquerque's position as another major center for artists in the state.

The Art Colonies Today

Most of the new arrivals in recent years have been young artists, coming to the area without established reputations. Many of them have made distinctive use of the local environment, cultural and natural, in their work. Luis Jimenez developed sophisticated fiberglass sculptures of cowboy-and-Indian scenes that reflect the popular mythology of the West in glittery plastic. Ken Saville's drawings and constructions place human frailty and darkness in the vibrant context of colorful Southwestern images. Geoffrey Landis presents Indian rugs and other icons in sensuous new ways in his paintings.

Photography has thrived as an art form in the state for many years. Most major American photographers have worked in New Mexico and many moved here, including Eliot Porter,

Beaumont Newhall, Paul Caponigro, Meridel Rubenstein, and Douglas Kent Hall. Fine crafts and sculpture also flourish, the latter centered at the Shidoni Foundry and Gallery in Tesuque.

Although Anglo artists continue to play a pivotal role in the New Mexico scene, the art colonies today are more culturally diverse than in the past. A number of Native American painters, printmakers, and sculptors—including Jaune Quick-to-See Smith, Emmi Whitehorse, the late Allan Houser, and Bob Haozous—have gained national recognition using traditional references and elements of style in work that is contemporary in concept and resonance. Many local Hispanic artists, such as Luis Tapia and Frederico Vigil, move beyond traditional formats but maintain a strong sensitivity for their heritage.

The diversity of people, media, and styles makes the art colonies today less cohesive than before, and less focused in their local influence, but their impact on New Mexico is as pervasive as ever. The adobe-hating soldiers of the U.S. Army might have found another way to California if they had known the future they were opening. Certainly Ernest Blumenschein and Bert Phillips would be startled by what they began. They would understand, no doubt, why the art colonies continue to flourish but would be amused, at best, to learn that New Mexico is as full of galleries and collectors as the fast-paced art centers of the East that they left so far behind in the 1890s.

PART TWO

Santa Fe

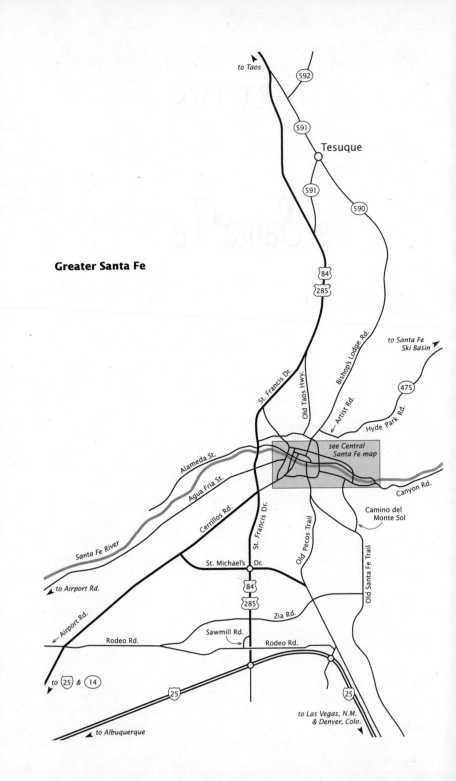

CHAPTER FOUR

A Historic Walking Tour

*T*HE BEST WAY to see the sights of Santa Fe is on foot—exploring the places that interest you, shopping as you go, stopping in museums, absorbing the charm at a relaxed pace. The following self-guided walking tour, which covers the main historic attractions, allows you to do it on your own in your own style.

The full tour takes most of a day at a leisurely pace, but it breaks naturally into shorter segments for briefer strolls. If time or stamina is limited, concentrate first on the area near the central plaza and leave the Canyon Road portion for another day.

The Plaza

A decade before the Pilgrims landed at Plymouth Rock, some fifty Spanish soldiers and their families erected crude mud and timber shelters around the central plaza of Santa Fe. From that bare beginning—for almost four centuries—the plaza has been the center of Santa Fe life and the first destination for most visitors.

The original plaza was larger than it is today, extending east in a rectangular shape to the site of the present cathedral. In the seventeenth century, while the Puritans settled the rest of New England, mounted soldiers used the area as an assembly and drill ground. All major public activities—proclamations, games,

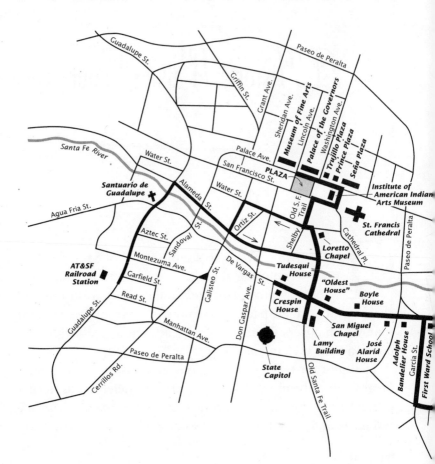

markets, fiestas, even bullfights—occurred there as well. It's where residents celebrated Mexico's independence from Spain in 1821 and where General Kearney proclaimed the annexation of New Mexico by the United States to an unenthusiastic citizenry in 1846. Today the plaza is the site of Indian Market, Spanish Market, and much of Fiesta, annual events that attract hordes of happy traders and rowdy revelers. Even on an average tourist day now, particularly in the summer, the area can exude the aura of a carnival.

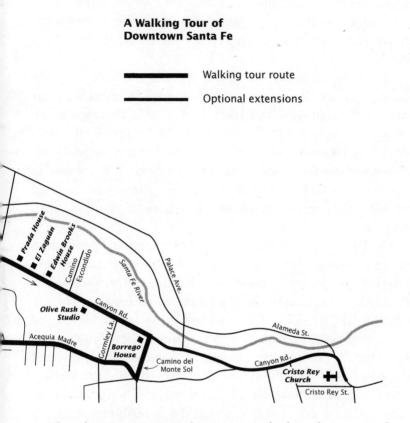

A Walking Tour of Downtown Santa Fe

Walking tour route

Optional extensions

The plaza's most tumultuous period, though, was in the mid-nineteenth century, when it was the western terminus of the **Santa Fe Trail**. As the Yankee traders approached Santa Fe at the end of their arduous journey from Missouri, they charged the town center, shouting and cracking 12-foot whips, scattering dust, dogs, and chickens in all directions. Before slowing down, the long wagon trains, which carried about five thousand pounds of merchandise each, raced in a great spiral about the four sides of the plaza. Crowds gathered quickly, eager for outside news, new provisions, and the chance to make some money from the high-living, road-weary visitors. As the plaza filled with wagons, the traders made their way around the gambling rooms that lined nearby streets, playing monte and dancing fandangos with the "relentlessly coquettish *mujeres* of Santa Fe," as one trader described the ladies.

Facing north from the plaza, toward the Palace of the Governors, try to imagine another raucous moment from the past, the **Pueblo Revolt of 1680.** In August of that year about twenty-five hundred Pueblo Indians looked angrily in the same direction, chanting songs of vengeance day and night, determined to drive the Spanish from the Pueblo land. Barricaded in the palace, which was larger then, were a thousand terrified people and many more starving sheep, mules, horses, goats, and cattle.

The Pueblos had already killed several hundred Spaniards in villages north of Santa Fe and they were now plundering and burning the church at the east end of the plaza. One of the Pueblo leaders, wrapped in red taffeta taken from the church, offered the Spanish a choice of two crosses: red for war or white for a peaceful departure. The Spanish elected to stay and fight, but they didn't have a chance. The Pueblos easily diverted the water supply for the Palace, which was carried in an irrigation ditch, or *acequia,* alongside the plaza. They expelled the colonists for a dozen years, forcing the Spanish Empire into a more serious retreat than the mighty Aztec and Incan warriors ever managed.

The Spanish recaptured the Palace and the plaza in 1693, but this may not be evident in scanning the area today. The Pueblos have come back in force in recent years, bearing pots and bracelets this time instead of torches. Only Indian artisans are allowed to sell work under the portal of the Palace, and they are there almost every day, stoically accepting the stares and questions of curious visitors along with their money.

The Palace of the Governors

In continuous use since 1610, the Palace is the **oldest government building in the United States.** Over a hundred leaders—Spanish, Pueblo, Mexican, and American—have ruled from here. Some of them claimed sovereignty over half of the present-day United States, east to the Mississippi River, west to the Pacific Ocean, and south into the Mexican state of Chihuahua.

The original structure built by the first Spanish governor, Pedro de Peralta, extended much farther north and west than the present Palace. The enclosed central patio was large enough for a ten-acre vegetable garden. There were defense towers on the two corners facing the plaza, but no portal at the time.

When the Indians evicted the Spanish in 1680, they transformed the Palace into a typical Pueblo village. They blocked up the small Spanish windows and doors and entered rooms from the top by ladders. Like the Taos Pueblo, the structure grew upward, probably to three or four stories. One of the towers was converted into a kiva, which the returning Spanish reluctantly used for their own worship for over a decade, until they completed a new parish church.

Almost everything except the roof beams, or vigas, was originally made of dirt. The walls, then as now, were adobe. For the floor, the colonists mixed animal blood with the soil to pack the surface and produce a sheen. It wasn't until the late nineteenth century that tin replaced the dirt roof piled several feet high above the vigas. Before then at least one resident of Santa Fe called it the **"roof garden."** "Most every desert plant grew and flowered and died a natural death in the five feet of earth which held the moisture of ordinary downpours but let the cloudbursts trickle through. The inside was really the only place where we had any need for umbrellas; outside the continuous line of portals protected us." The place has seldom, if ever, looked like a palace.

Probably the best known today of the Palace's many residents was U.S. Territorial Governor Lew Wallace, author of *Ben Hur*, who lived here in the 1880s. Wallace's description of his writing chamber would probably have applied to many rooms at the time. "The walls were grimy, the undressed boards of the floor rested flat upon the ground; the cedar rafters, rain-stained as those in the dining-hall of Cedric the Saxon, and overweighted by tons and tons of mud composing the roof, had the threatening downward curvature of a shipmate's cutlass."

The building has always been expensive to maintain because of its construction and size. Spanish, Mexican, and U.S. governors constantly petitioned their various central governments for money for repairs, but never got as much as they requested. The upkeep costs made the Palace a political football at the turn of the century. The U.S. government granted the building, and its maintenance costs, to the territorial government of New Mexico. The governor protested, saying the territory couldn't afford it. He offered it to the Smithsonian Institution, which rejected it as an unmanageable property. Stuck with the unwanted possession, the legislature decided in 1909 to make the Palace into the **Museum of New Mexico** and appropriated funds for its restoration.

At first the Palace housed all of the museum. Since then separate facilities have been built in Santa Fe for the state's collection of fine art, folk art, and Indian art. See the following chapter, "Memorable Museums," for more information on the various institutions.

The Museum of Fine Arts

Directly west of the Palace, the Museum of Fine Arts has an unusual history among American art museums. Most museums originate as repositories for the lifelong collections of art patrons. When the Museum of Fine Arts opened in 1917, it was the first in the United States—and it has been one of the few since then—that was inspired by local artists to exhibit their current work.

As soon as the legislature established the Museum of New Mexico in the Palace of the Governors, the first director, Dr. Edgar Hewett, began thinking about a separate facility for art. At first he set up a small gallery within the Palace and provided free studios to artists in the back of the building. Predictably, demands for the space grew, and within a few years Hewett managed to convince the legislature to build an art museum across the street.

Robert Henri and John Sloan, established artists from the East who spent considerable time in Santa Fe, advised Hewett on museum operations. They advocated the **"open-door"** policy that the institution took for many years—allowing any local artist to exhibit new work on a first-come, first-served basis. Curators made no effort to build a collection of "Old Masters" from past centuries and distant places, though gradually the museum did begin to acquire a wealth of New Mexico work.

As the local collection increased in value, art patrons of the city became active in the affairs of the museum and the artists lost their ease of access. The quality of exhibitions has been more consistent since the elimination of the open-door policy, but some of the original vitality may have been lost in the process.

Completed in 1917, the museum was an early and influential expression of the modern **Spanish Pueblo architectural style.** Its massive walls, terraces, and recessions reflect the organic lines of Pueblo buildings. The Spanish Franciscan mission churches, particularly the one at Acoma, inspired the St. Francis Auditorium, an entrancing spot for the concerts and other performances held there. Residents and visitors alike hailed the synthesis of traditions represented in the new building, and it became a model for the style that still guides much architectural design in New Mexico.

See Chapter 5 for information on the museum's exhibits and hours.

West of the Plaza

In the nineteenth century **Santa Fe's rowdy gambling district** lay farther west of the plaza along Palace Avenue and San Francisco Street. Buffalo hunters, *vaqueros*, politicians, traders, and soldiers came here to drink the raw whiskey called Taos Lightning and to find love, or a semblance of it, with lavender-powdered *señoritas* in black veils.

The strongest personality among them was the beautiful and shrewd Doña Tules Barcelo, who owned the largest and fanciest of the gambling halls and a bank as well. One puritanical trader, who referred to the *cantinas* as "pandemoniums," called Doña Tules a woman "of very loose habits," and was shocked that she was "openly received in the first circles of society." He imagined with pleasure how socialites in the East would have rejected her, but felt exasperated that she wouldn't have cared. Ruth Laughlin told Doña Tules's story in fictional form in *The Wind Leaves No Shadows* (Caxton Printers, paperback edition, 1978).

Today, the shops that line West Palace Avenue and San Francisco Street still cater to visitors—and probably profit from them more than the old cantinas did—but the current businesses offer different lures. Make a loop through the area if you're interested in shopping, but when you're ready to continue the sightseeing tour, head east from the plaza on Palace Avenue.

East Palace Avenue

As a reward for his military leadership in the Spanish reconquest of Santa Fe in 1693, Captain Arias de Quiros obtained a large land grant directly east of the Palace of the Governors. The captain's domain included all of the area now covered by the long, low portal that runs down the north side of Palace Avenue from the plaza to the cathedral. He cultivated most of the land and lived in a two-room house, nothing of which remains.

The property was divided over time into smaller but still substantial estates. In typical Santa Fe fashion, the homes wrapped around spacious interior courtyards. You can still get a good sense of the old style in several spots along East Palace Avenue.

The first courtyard that opens onto the street is **Trujillo Plaza,** at 109 East Palace. The former residence contains shops now, but during World War II it was an office for the Manhattan Project, which developed the first atomic bomb in nearby Los Alamos. Even the existence of Los Alamos was a carefully guarded secret, so the scientists involved reported for duty and received their mail at Trujillo Plaza.

A few doors down the street, the **Prince Plaza** today serves as the outside waiting area for The Shed restaurant. In the past it was the courtyard of a hacienda owned in the early nineteenth century by Antoine Roubidoux, a French-Canadian trader, and later by L. Bradford Prince, a territorial governor of New Mexico.

Seña Plaza, across the street from the cathedral, exudes Santa Fe charm. Lined with shops today, it was the scene of grand Spanish hospitality in the nineteenth century, hosted by Doña Isabel and Don José Seña. From a small house he inherited on the property, Don José gradually built a hacienda of thirty-three rooms. He and Doña Isabel and their eleven children occupied the south, east, and west sides of the courtyard, quartering their horses, chickens, and servants along the north front. The home was one story tall except on the west side, where outside stairways led up to a large ballroom, a chamber sufficient in size to hold the legislative assembly temporarily when the capitol burned in 1892. Later owners added the second stories on the eastern and northern portions of the building in the 1920s during a dedicated and expert restoration.

St. Francis Cathedral

The cathedral is the most visible legacy of the most influential person in local history, **Archbishop Jean Baptiste Lamy,** whose bronze statue stands in front of the church. It's ironic that a

Frenchman played such a major role in shaping the fortunes of a Spanish colonial town in the American West, and the irony shows in the Romanesque style of the cathedral, so different from the rest of local architecture.

Willa Cather gracefully described Lamy's life in Santa Fe (as Bishop Latour) in *Death Comes for the Archbishop* (Vintage Books, paperback edition, 1990). Arriving in 1851 during a wild frontier period in the village, when the church's authority was disintegrating throughout the Southwest, Lamy energetically restored clerical influence, established schools and a hospital, and gradually instilled a sense of refinement into Santa Fe life. His own notion of refinement, unfortunately, always remained European, not fully sympathetic to local ways.

Lamy wanted a cathedral in Santa Fe that expressed God's glory with the same magnificence as the churches in his native Auvergne. The parish church, or *parroquia,* which served as his cathedral for many years, was a simple adobe structure built in the early eighteenth century. The bishop and his French architects built the new cathedral around the old parroquia, making it much wider and half again as long, but retaining and using the original church until the new one was completed.

In 1869, with high ceremony, workers laid an elaborately engraved cornerstone, which was promptly stolen. Construction proceeded anyway and continued until 1886, the year after Lamy's retirement. The early French plans called for steeples rising 160 feet from the two towers, but they were abandoned along the way.

The most interesting part of St. Francis Cathedral is the remaining portion of the old parroquia, the **Chapel of Our Lady of the Rosary.** Builders removed the choir loft and part of the walls when they constructed the new church, making the chapel smaller than before, but it has been in continuous use since 1718.

The chapel is dedicated to the **oldest madonna in North America,** a small, sixteenth-century wooden statue carved in

Mexico and brought to Santa Fe around 1625. First known as Our Lady of the Assumption, she was renamed La Conquistadora (Our Lady of the Conquest) after she accompanied the Spanish in exile from 1680 to 1693 and returned with them as a protector during the reconquest from the Pueblos. Colonists built the chapel in her honor on the site of the original parish church, which the Indians destroyed in 1680, and she has remained the community's most important symbol of Spanish unity and religious devotion ever since. After years of pressure from the Pueblos, the Catholic Church recently gave La Conquistadora an additional name, Nuestra Señora de la Paz (Our Lady of Peace), to emphasize the ultimate result of the reconquest.

The cathedral is open to visitors daily from early morning to late afternoon. There is no admission charge, but contributions are welcome. Directly across the street, the **Institute of American Indian Arts Museum** (see Chapter 5), in addition to enthralling exhibits, offers sanctuary from the busy streets in several restful sitting areas.

Loretto Chapel

Two short blocks from the cathedral, at the corner of Water Street and Old Santa Fe Trail, one of Archbishop Lamy's French architects designed another church. The Sisters of Loretto commissioned the **Chapel of Our Lady of Light** in the 1870s to serve the girls' school they operated on the present site of the Inn at Loretto. Modeled after St. Chapelle in Paris, it remains a Gothic gem of the frontier period.

The architect didn't live to see his work completed because the bishop's nephew, John Lamy, shot and killed him, suspecting the Frenchman of adultery with his wife. That caused a serious glitch in the construction. The builders couldn't figure out how the architect planned to erect a stairway to the choir loft, since there didn't seem to be room for it. They put in a loft but finished the job without providing any means of reaching it.

Distressed, the nuns prayed for the help of St. Joseph, a carpenter by trade. Before long a carpenter appeared and constructed a circular **"miraculous staircase"** without using nails or any visible means of support. Local legend attributes the work to St. Joseph because the artisan disappeared, without pay or even thanks, as soon as he completed his masterpiece. You can see the staircase and the rest of the chapel from early morning to late afternoon daily for a small admission fee.

The walking tour continues south along Old Santa Fe Trail to the San Miguel Chapel, a short stroll away. If you want to explore all of downtown Santa Fe, though, you may wish to take a mile-long detour to the sights and shops of Guadalupe Street. Head west on Water, go left on Galisteo to Alameda, and then right to Guadalupe.

Guadalupe Street Detour

At the corner of Guadalupe and Alameda, you'll see the Santuario de Nuestra Señora de Guadalupe to your left across the Santa Fe River. Built in the last few years of the eighteenth century, the **Chapel of Our Lady of Guadalupe** was designed and constructed in the style typical of New Mexican church architecture of that period. The walls, floor, and roof were adobe, and the shape was cruciform. The three-tiered tower contained sand-cast copper bells.

Subsequent renovations in the nineteenth and twentieth centuries altered many features, but an extensive preservation effort in recent decades has revived much of the chapel's original feel. You can see the attention to detail in the restored altar wall, colored in the old style by adding ox blood to the plaster.

The oldest surviving shrine to the Virgin of Guadalupe in the United States, the Santuario is open to visitors Monday through Friday all year, and on Saturday during the summer, from 9:00 to 4:00. The church charges no admission, but donations are appreciated and needed for maintenance.

A couple of blocks south of the Santuario on Guadalupe is the **Atchison, Topeka & Santa Fe Railroad** depot. A lively complex of shops and restaurants sits between the two landmarks, along with a pair of historical curiosities.

At the corner of Guadalupe and Garfield, across from the depot, the University Plaza started off as a college in the 1880s. Protestant evangelists founded the school to convert "heathen" New Mexicans in the recently conquered Catholic territory. The missionaries intended their "University of New Mexico" to be a fountainhead of "moral education," but they found life in Santa Fe so disagreeable and the residents so unheeding that they soon abandoned the project.

The other historical curiosity of the area is the railroad itself. Despite its name, and the fact that it paralleled and replaced the Santa Fe Trail, the Atchison, Topeka & Santa Fe Railroad never made it to Santa Fe. The city was one of the few in America unwilling to pay for rail service. Archbishop Lamy argued passionately for the value of the railroad, but other civic leaders weren't interested in building better connections to the rest of the country. All the bishop could obtain was a spur from the route at a junction south of the city that is still named Lamy. The main line went to Albuquerque instead, stimulating its growth from a provincial village into New Mexico's most populous city. Several days a week, the **Santa Fe Southern** (505-989-8600) offers leisurely train rides to Lamy on the original spur tracks.

Until recently the Guadalupe area remained an appendage of the railroad depot, occupied largely by freight warehouses. A slow but sustained renovation began in the 1970s, first on Guadalupe Street itself and later on the side streets. The neighborhood has gotten almost as fashionable and crowded as the plaza and Canyon Road now, but it retains an offbeat spirit that appeals to residents and visitors alike.

To continue the regular walking tour, return to the Santuario

and go right on Alameda. Follow the Santa Fe River back to Old
Santa Fe Trail, turning south to reach the San Miguel Chapel.

San Miguel Chapel

In the colonial era, particularly in the seventeenth century, the
Santa Fe River served as the dividing line between social classes
in the city. Spanish soldiers and priests lived north of the river,
on the plaza side, and their Indian servants from Mexico lived
on the south side. The Indians named their area Analco, meaning "the other side of the water."

The most important structure in the **Barrio de Analco** is the
San Miguel Chapel, founded around 1610 to serve as a mission
church for Native Americans. The Pueblos gutted the church
and razed all of the nearby homes during the 1680 Revolt. The
walls of the original chapel are still intact but no longer visible.
When the Spanish rebuilt San Miguel in 1710, they altered the
shape of the structure and put up new outer walls alongside the
old ones.

Worrying more about Indian raids in 1710 than they had in
1610, the Spanish restored the chapel as a fortress. In addition
to thickening the walls, they placed the windows high on the
building and added adobe battlements to the roof. The roof
line changed again the next century with the addition of a
triple-tiered tower, which was replaced by the current square
tower in the 1870s.

The most prominent feature of the interior is the fine reredos, or altar screen. Artisans crafted it in 1798 to display the
small **gilded statue of St. Michael,** the patron of the chapel, and
the attached paintings. Priests took the seventeenth-century
statue in procession throughout the frontier colony in 1709 to
raise money, goods, and services for the church's restoration.

The chapel is open to visitors daily from midmorning to late
afternoon, except on Sundays, when it's closed in the morning.
Donations are appreciated, but there is no admission charge.

Lamy Building

The Christian Brothers, who maintain the San Miguel Chapel, once operated a school in the adjoining two-story building that faces Old Santa Fe Trail. The Brothers sold the property in 1965 to the state of New Mexico, which named it the Lamy Building and filled it with state offices, including a tourism center that offers visitor information and public restrooms.

At the time of its construction in 1878, this was the largest and highest adobe structure in Santa Fe. Originally it had a third story, destroyed by fire in the 1920s, that served as the school dormitory. The surviving floors of the building housed administrative offices and classrooms.

The Christian Brothers founded **St. Michael's College** in different quarters in 1859, on instructions from Bishop Lamy, as a school for boys, providing formal secondary and college education for the first time in the area. In 1947 the Brothers separated the high school and college levels, establishing the College of Santa Fe and St. Michael's High School, both now located in other areas of town.

Historic Homes of East De Vargas

Santa Feans rebuilt the Barrio de Analco neighborhood in the early eighteenth century. It was no longer strictly a district for servants, but class associations lingered for more than a hundred years. Some of the lovely homes on East De Vargas today originally belonged to laborers and low-ranking soldiers.

Two of the historic houses are west of the San Miguel Chapel, on the short block between Old Santa Fe Trail and Don Gaspar. Both remain private residences, open to the public only on special occasions, but you can get a good sense of their style from the street.

The **Gregorio Crespín House** at 132 East De Vargas occupies land that General De Vargas granted to Juan de León Brito in the late seventeenth century as a reward for service in the

Spanish reconquest of Santa Fe. He or a subsequent owner built the house sometime between 1720 and 1750, according to tree-ring specimens taken from the vigas. A deed from 1747 shows Gregorio Crespín selling the property for 50 pesos.

The home grew larger over the years and certainly more valuable. In the mid-nineteenth century it contained five rooms, all opening onto the portal by the garden. Several decades later the owner at the time added the territorial trim.

At 129–135 East De Vargas, the **Roque Tudesqui House** probably dates from the mid-eighteenth century, though there is no record of its construction. A successful Italian trader in the early days of the Santa Fe Trail, Tudesqui bought the home around 1839, a couple of years before his marriage to a prominent local señorita.

The other historic homes on De Vargas are east of the San Miguel Chapel, on the way to Canyon Road. The first place you pass, and the only one regularly open to the public, is the **"Oldest House"** at 215 East De Vargas. The name derives from a long-standing belief that Pueblo Indians laid the foundations for the structure in the thirteenth century, although the vigas in the current ceiling, according to tree-ring specimens, date back to only about 1750. Whatever the original building date, and the accuracy of the claim to being "the oldest house in the United States," the western portion is a good example of ancient adobe construction. Most Santa Fe residents lived in similar rooms in the early centuries, part Indian and part Spanish in architecture, with low, log ceilings, dirt floors, thick adobe walls, and a corner fireplace for heating and cooking.

The **Boyle House** at 327 East De Vargas is probably as old as most of the structure of the "oldest house." It existed for certain by the 1760s, and the four-foot-thick walls suggest the possibility of an earlier origin.

José Alaríd built the home named for him at 338 East De Vargas, on the corner of Paseo de Peralta, in the late years of Mexican rule in Santa Fe. He sold the house in 1854, and it changed hands a number of times after that, eventually becoming a part of the large real estate office that occupies the property today.

One former owner, Anita Chapman, served as territorial librarian. Her immediate successors in the office were also women, which caused a legal controversy in the early twentieth century. Ultimately the state supreme court had to decide whether a woman could serve in a public position in New Mexico. In a split decision, the court ruled that the office of librarian did not require "judgment in any respect," and so the duties were "not incompatible with the ability of a woman to perform."

Across Paseo de Peralta from the Alarid home, at 352 East De Vargas, is the **Adolph Bandelier House,** which the Swiss scholar rented during his ten-year stay in Santa Fe in the 1880s. Bandelier was the first outsider to understand the historical and anthropological significance of the Santa Fe area and to write about it for other outsiders. His research on the Pueblos, which involved living in Indian villages for weeks at a time and traveling thousands of miles on foot and horseback, resulted in a novel called *The Delight Makers* (Harcourt Brace Jovanovich, paperback edition, 1971). He wrote scientific papers as well, but had the good sense to realize that his findings were only tentative and best expressed as fiction. The novel is ponderous but definitely worth reading for imaginative insights about the early Pueblos.Later owners of the house may be better known locally than Bandelier. Santa Fe merchant Henry Kaune, whose wife was Bandelier's niece, bought it in 1919. The Kaunes established a popular local grocery in Santa Fe, still thriving today.

Just beyond the Bandelier House, East De Vargas dead-ends into Canyon Road, one of the most romantic and picturesque streets in the United States and certainly the oldest one still in use.

Canyon Road

The Pueblo Indians established Canyon Road as a trail at least a century before any Europeans arrived to stay in the Americas.

The footpath, which ran the same course as the current paved street, followed the Santa Fe River over the Sangre de Cristo Mountains to the Pecos Pueblo. The Spanish conquistadores maintained the route, calling it *el camino de cañón*.

By the early eighteenth century the Spanish started building homes and cultivating fields along Canyon Road. Sections of some of the current buildings date from this period, when the style of the street's architecture was established in a way that hasn't changed substantially since. The old houses that line the narrow, winding street come almost flush with the pavement, giving a pedestrian at times the feeling of being channeled through an adobe tunnel.

The frequently plain facades along the street present a deceptive impression about the interiors. Residents built the homes around a central patio, or *placita*. As families grew and children started their own families, they added new rooms and separate structures around the placita, producing rambling compounds that are only partially visible from the outside. Since the patio was the center of family and social life, landscaping was reserved for that area, and the finest architectural details face inward around it, blocked from the dust and noise of the street by the front wall.

Early this century Canyon Road became the center of the **Santa Fe art colony.** Not as many artists live and work there today as in the past—rents are high—but the neighborhood has retained its artistic character. City zoning designates it as a "residential arts and crafts zone," limiting its use to homes, studios, art galleries, crafts shops, restaurants, and related neighborhood services. It's an ideal place for exploring both the residential character of the old city and the work of Southwestern artists.

First Ward School Building (400 Canyon Road)

This 1906 building illustrates some of the mishaps of modernization in Santa Fe. At the time of construction, it seemed a symbol of enlightenment in two important respects. First, the architect used kilned bricks rather than adobe blocks. The bricks were standardized and regular in form, unlike the adobes, and much easier to maintain, which seemed at the time to give them destiny's edge. Also, the city erected the building as a public school, which municipal leaders expected to displace the existing church schools established by Archbishop Lamy. Both expectations proved wrong. Some of Lamy's schools are still thriving and brick is even less common today in Santa Fe than at the turn of the century.

The Board of Education sold the building in 1928. At various times since then it has been a theater for foreign films, a zoo for indigenous birds and animals, and an art gallery.

Juan José Prada House (519 Canyon Road)

Early maps of Santa Fe indicate that this house existed before the Boston Tea Party, though written records go back only to the years right after the Civil War. In the 1860s, when Juan José Prada lived here, a central corridor divided the residence into two sections. Prada sold the western portion in 1869 and his widow deeded the eastern half to her daughter and son-in-law in 1882. Both deeds stipulated that the front door of the corridor, facing the street, be left open for access to a dance hall in the rear of the house.

The dance hall was gone when Mrs. Charles Dietrich purchased the property a half-century ago and joined the two sections. One of the pioneers of historic preservation in Santa Fe, Mrs. Dietrich lived in the house for many years and was instrumental in saving other old Canyon Road homes from destruction. The building remains a private residence.

Behind the house is one of the few surviving examples of the New Mexican equivalent of frontier log cabins. From the earliest Spanish days, inhabitants used *jacal* construction for some purposes, particularly for outbuildings. The small barn on the Prada property is typical, with squared-off cedar logs set upright in the ground, the cracks filled with adobe. Jacal buildings could be as solid and well insulated as most log cabins, but they were seldom used as residences because of the superior protection provided by thick adobe walls.

El Zaguán (545 Canyon Road)

When James Johnson bought this rambling old hacienda in 1849, it consisted of two or three rooms, built at an uncertain earlier date with four-foot-thick walls. A prominent merchant in the days of the Santa Fe Trail, Johnson operated a general store on the northeast corner of the plaza, bringing in his merchandise by wagon train from Missouri. Behind the house, he built large corrals for the oxen and horses used on the long trek.

Johnson enlarged the house considerably and converted it to territorial style, noticeable from the street by the brick coping on the roof. The new rooms, with walls only three feet thick, included a private chapel, a library that contained the largest collection of books in New Mexico at the time, and a chocolate room, where chocolate was ground and served each afternoon. At one point there were twenty-four rooms, plus quarters for the servants across the street. As the house grew, so did its *zaguán*, the covered passageway visible from the street that has given the place its name.

Adolph Bandelier, the pioneering anthropologist, designed the garden west of the house in the 1880s. The two horse chestnut trees, which have become city landmarks, were already there at the time, but Bandelier brought in the peony bushes from China that still flourish over one hundred years later.

Among the buildings that Mrs. Charles Dietrich saved from destruction in the 1920s and 1930s, El Zaguán is now owned by the **Historic Santa Fe Foundation.** Inside, the house has been converted into rental apartments of various sizes, but the exterior remains unchanged.

Edwin Brooks House (553 Canyon Road)

Only marginally visible from the street, this venerable adobe played a significant role in the history of the Santa Fe art colony. Painter William Penhallow Henderson and his wife, poet Alice Corbin, remodeled a small, old home on the property after they moved to the city from Chicago in 1916. Among the changes, they added a second story, creating a distinctive two-level living room and balcony that features huge, hand-adzed wood beams and lintels.

Later, the well-known painter Fremont Ellis bought the house and worked in its studio for many years until his death in 1985. His family still owns the home and remains active in Santa Fe cultural life.

Olive Rush Studio (630 Canyon Road)

A member of the Society of Friends (the Quakers), Olive Rush had already established her reputation as an artist when she moved to Santa Fe in 1920 and bought this home, becoming one of the first women to join the budding art colony. Before then, the old adobe had been in the Seña and Rodríguez families for generations. The original owners may have built the house in the first half of the nineteenth century, judging by the thickness of the walls, but records from those days are not very informative. There were no surveys and deeds were seldom filed. Families held the same property for generations and knew its boundaries by birthright.

Rush preserved most of the home in its original state, even retaining the adobe plaster of the facade instead of covering it with stucco. The Society of Friends, who now use it as a meeting house, has maintained it with the same care.

Borrego House (724 Canyon Road)

This is one of the few houses on Canyon Road whose history can be traced with Spanish deeds. A smaller version of the residence existed in 1753, when it was sold as part of a farm. The farm, like others nearby, extended south from the street a few hundred yards to the *acequia madre,* the source of irrigation water.

The Borrego family owned the home for seventy-five years during the nineteenth century. They added the large front room, for political and social entertaining, and the territorial-style portal along the street. They also left some incredible deed tangles. The original purchaser, Rafael Borrego, willed half of the property to his widow and half to his children. From then until 1939, various parts of the house were owned by different people, sometimes not of the same family. By the time Rafael's widow died in 1872, the Borregos were deeding individual rooms, a fairly common practice in Santa Fe before the twentieth century.

Mrs. Charles Dietrich purchased all of the rooms between 1928 and 1939 and restored the house beautifully. The property changed ownership several times after that, but it has served as a restaurant for many years now.

Camino del Monte Sol

The street just beyond the Borrego House, Camino del Monte Sol, is almost as famous for its artists as Canyon Road. Los Cinco Pintores (the five painters), along with several other painters and writers, built homes on the camino early this century. Before then, the city called the undeveloped street Telephone Road, but the artists found the designation offensive and renamed it after a nearby mountain.

One block south, Camino del Monte Sol intersects with Acequia Madre, a pleasant street to follow back toward the center of town. There is, however, another important sight several blocks farther up Canyon Road. The Cristo Rey Church may be too much of an uphill hike for some people, but others will find the extra effort well rewarded.

Cristo Rey Church

The church houses the most famous piece of Spanish colonial art in New Mexico, an ornately carved stone altar screen commissioned in 1760. Originally made for the military chapel, La Castrense, which once stood on the plaza, the reredos became a model for many later handhewn wooden altar screens in New Mexico.

The church was built in 1940 to commemorate the four hundredth anniversary of Coronado's expedition into New Mexico. Renowned architect John Gaw Meem designed it in classical Spanish mission style. He used nearly two hundred thousand adobe bricks in the construction, all made from the soil on the site, the traditional practice. Parishioners, working under professional supervision, contributed much of the labor.

Meem scaled the church, one of the largest adobe structures in existence, to fit the great reredos. After La Castrense was demolished, Bishop Lamy concealed the altar screen behind a wall in the cathedral. The French prelate disliked local religious art, particularly in his Romanesque church. Meem gave the work a much more proper home.

Cristo Rey is usually open to visitors from the early morning to the early evening free of charge. After a look around, go back down Canyon Road to Acequia Madre.

Acequia Madre

The only remaining acequia, or irrigation ditch, in Santa Fe, the "mother ditch" flows directly along the street that bears its name and is still used to water gardens and trees near its path. Before Santa Fe knew the technology of deep wells and running water, the acequias played a critical role in agriculture. They carried melting snow from the mountains into the fields and orchards of the village during the growing season, when rainfall was undependable. Even today, the acequias remain a cherished and practical part of life along Acequia Madre and north of Santa Fe in rural areas and small towns.

The Pueblos used ditch irrigation at least a thousand years ago, but the Spanish introduced the elaborate irrigation code that still prevails today. Land ownership along an acequia provides rights to shares of water from the ditch, with larger fields getting larger proportions of the water. Generally water rights are transferred along with land, but owners can lose their rights by not contributing adequately to the maintenance of the system. The annual cleaning of the ditches, supervised by the *mayordomo de la acequia,* often remains an important community activity. Everyone with water rights works together to clear the main ditch of winter debris from its source down to the last homestead.

At Garcia Street, where the acequia disappears temporarily, go right to return to Canyon Road. A short jog on Paseo de Peralta leads you to Alameda, where you can follow the Santa Fe River to Old Santa Fe Trail and then back to the plaza area.

CHAPTER FIVE

Memorable Museums

EVEN PEOPLE who avoid museums in other cities should make an exception in Santa Fe. Both the Palace of the Governors and the Museum of Fine Arts would be worth touring even if they were empty. The Museum of International Folk Art, the best institution of its kind in the world, is full of joy, and the several superb collections of Southwestern Indian art are full of elemental energy. For studious sightseeing or just visual delight, Santa Fe's museums should not be missed.

Many of them are conveniently grouped close together, as indicated on the map. The Palace of the Governors, the Museum of Fine Arts, and the Institute of American Indian Arts Museum are within two blocks of each other in the center of town, on or near the plaza. The Museum of International Folk Art, the Museum of Indian Arts and Culture, and the Wheelwright Museum of the American Indian sit side by side on Camino Lejo, a short street just off Old Santa Fe Trail, about two miles south of the plaza. The Center for Contemporary Arts and the Santa Fe Children's Museum occupy adjacent plots on and close to Old Pecos Trail, a little south of its intersection with Old Santa Fe Trail. El Rancho de las Golondrinas, the School of American Research, and the Randall

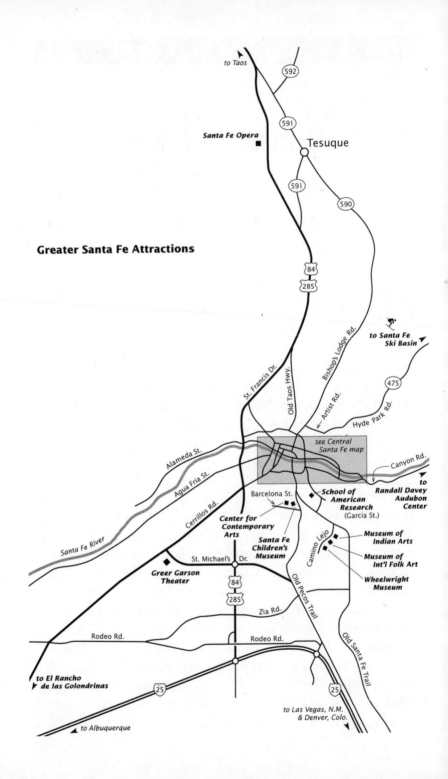

Greater Santa Fe Attractions

to Taos

592

591

Santa Fe Opera ■

Tesuque

591

590

84
285

to Santa Fe
Ski Basin

475

St. Francis Dr.

Old Taos Hwy.

Bishop's Lodge Rd.

Artist Rd.

Hyde Park Rd.

*see Central
Santa Fe map*

Alameda St.

Canyon Rd.

to
Randall Davey
Audubon
Center

Agua Fria St.

Barcelona St.

♦ **School of
American
Research**
(Garcia St.)

Cerrillos Rd.

**Center for
Contemporary
Arts**

Santa Fe River

**Santa Fe
Children's
Museum**

Camino Lejo

♦ **Museum of
Indian Arts**

♦ **Museum of
Int'l Folk Art**

**Wheelwright
Museum**

♦ St. Michael's Dr.

**Greer Garson
Theater**

84
285

Old Pecos Trail

Zia Rd.

Rodeo Rd.

Rodeo Rd.

Old Santa Fe Trail

to El Rancho
de las Golondrinas

25

25

to Las Vegas, N.M.
& Denver, Colo.

to Albuquerque

Davey Audubon Center are more isolated, but each enjoys a wonderfully singular setting.

The Palace of the Governors, the Museum of Fine Arts, the Museum of International Folk Art, and the Museum of Indian Arts and Culture are all state institutions, required by law to charge admission. The fee for each is $4 for adults, but you can get a three-day pass for $5 that allows you to come and go at all four places, a much better value. Children under 16 are free. The state museums are open daily, except major holidays and Mondays in the winter, from 10:00 to 5:00. Admission policies and hours for the other museums are detailed in the descriptions below.

Museum of International Folk Art

The most fascinating of the state institutions, the Museum of International Folk Art gives appropriate recognition to Spanish crafts in New Mexico, but it also exhibits European decorative arts, Latin American work, and toys, jewelry, and costumes from all ends of the earth. There's nothing quite like it anywhere else.

Florence Dibell Bartlett established the museum in 1953 to house her personal folk arts collection. The acquisition in the early 1980s of the Girard collection—over 106,000 pieces gathered around the world by Alexander and Susan Girard—firmly solidified the museum's international leadership in its field. Mr. Girard designed a long-standing exhibition of some of the work that will astonish and amuse children and adults alike. Everyone leaves smiling.

The 1989 opening of the Hispanic Heritage Wing considerably expanded the facilities, allowing the museum to showcase more regional art and to present a regular schedule of demonstrations, workshops, and performances. With the collection's depth in traditional Hispanic art, the shows in the new wing are usually outstanding.

Along with the following two institutions, the museum is

part of the cultural cluster on Camino Lejo, just off Old Santa
Fe Trail, and, like the others, it's open from 10:00 to 5:00 most
days. Call 505-827-6350 for exhibition or other information.

Museum of Indian Arts and Culture

The newest state museum, opened in 1986, exhibits work for-
merly housed with the older Laboratory of Anthropology, right
next door. The legislature established the laboratory in 1931 to
preserve and protect the Indian heritage of New Mexico.
Before land can be developed in the state, the lab has to certify
through archaeological research that the site does not have historical significance. The law also entrusted the institution with
the care of Indian art and artifacts belonging to the state.

The Museum of Indian Arts and Culture now presents this
bountiful collection to the public and provides interpretive
exhibitions on the prehistory and ethnology of Southwestern
Indians. Rotating shows draw from more than fifty thousand
pieces of basketry, pottery, jewelry, textiles, and clothing—
much of it very old, rare, and priceless. As a counterpoint to the
archaeological exhibits, artists offer live demonstrations of traditional techniques and Native American concessionaires prepare and sell local Indian food.

The museum is on Camino Lejo, adjacent to the Museum of
International Folk Art. For details on exhibits and activities,
call 505-827-6344.

Wheelwright Museum of the American Indian

Mary Cabot Wheelwright, a wealthy New England scholar,
established this private museum in 1937 in collaboration with
a Navajo shaman, Hosteen Klah, to help preserve disappearing
aspects of Navajo religion and ceremony. Although the two
founders did not speak each other's language, they worked
together for many years documenting spiritual aspects of
Navajo life. Hosteen Klah himself wove tapestries that illus-

trate the sacred sand paintings used in healing rites, still one of the treasures in the collection. Architects even designed the building in the shape of a traditional hogan, with its door facing east toward the rising sun and its ceiling composed of interlocking "whirling" logs.

When the Navajos took up their own preservation efforts, the museum returned much of the original collection to them and broadened its scope. Exhibits today feature American Indian arts and artifacts from any period or place, including paintings, weavings, silverwork, and more. For family fun in the summer, catch the Southwestern tales of storyteller Joe Hayes, usually presented outdoors on the grounds on weekend evenings.

The museum shop downstairs, built to resemble an old Navajo trading post, is almost as large and interesting as the exhibition area. Browse through the display cases, even if you can't afford to buy any of the jewelry or pottery, to get a sense of the superior craftsmanship of today's finest Southwestern work.

The Wheelwright (505-982-4636) is on Camino Lejo, behind the Museum of International Folk Art. It's open Monday through Saturday 10:00 to 5:00 and Sunday 1:00 to 5:00. Donations are requested.

Palace of the Governors

Described architecturally in the walking tour in Chapter 4, the historic Palace of the Governors is an ideal spot for its exhibitions on New Mexico history. A series of displays chronicle four centuries of the state's past, from the Spanish colonial era through the American frontier period up to modern times. The artifacts in the collection range from old stagecoaches and printing presses to rare religious art.

The Palace also houses an extensive historical library, with manuscripts dating from the seventeenth century, and a shop specializing in books on the Southwest. One of the museum's main annual events is the popular Mountain Man Rendezvous and Buffalo Roast, usually scheduled for the second week of August. The period costumes, trade fair, and entertainment make it a special evening even if your appetite isn't fixed on buffalo.

Directly on the plaza, the Palace of the Governors (505-827-6474) is part of the Museum of New Mexico, open most days from 10:00 to 5:00.

Museum of Fine Arts

Another historical building described in the walking tour in Chapter 4, the Museum of Fine Arts features twentieth-century paintings, prints, sculpture, and photography, mostly from New Mexico. Not all of the exhibits are regional, but many have a direct connection to the state. Some of the shows come from the museum's eight-thousand-piece collection, which was recently enhanced with the acquisition of several important Georgia O'Keeffe paintings that the artist kept for her own enjoyment until her death. Ongoing exhibits range from paintings done by leaders of the early Santa Fe and Taos art colonies to dynamic new work by contemporary area artists. The museum shares the same hours and admission policies as the Palace of the Governors, which is directly next door. Call 505-827-4455 for additional information.

Institute of American Indian Arts Museum

Santa Fe's Institute of American Indian Arts has trained many prominent Native American artists, including Dan Namingha, Doug Hyde, Barry Coffin, and Earl Biss. The faculty has been equally notable, ranging from sculptor Allan Houser to jewelry artist Charles Loloma. With this kind of talent in residence, the institute accumulated a wonderfully diverse collection of modern Indian work, some of which is on permanent display in this new museum, opened in 1992.

Special changing exhibits often focus on the origins of contemporary Native American art and they always demonstrate the quality and diversity of work across the country. Outdoors, behind the main gallery, the Allan Houser Art Park features sculpture by the namesake master and other artists and also serves as a performance space.

The museum occupies the renovated old Federal Building downtown, across from St. Francis Cathedral at 108 Cathedral Place. It's open from 10:00 to 5:00 daily except Sunday, when it opens at noon, and on Monday in the winter, when it's closed. Admission is $4 for adults and $2 for students and seniors. Children under 16 are free. Call 505-988-6281 for additional information.

Center for Contemporary Arts

In the last two decades the Center for Contemporary Arts has established a national reputation as an exhibition and performance space for living artists, particularly people working outside the commercial mainstream. The ambitious schedule of activities features gallery shows, an "Explorations in Music" series, theater workshops, creative dance events, readings by local poets, an extensive cultural program for teenagers, and more.

The Cinematheque film series operated by the private, nonprofit organization is one of the best in the United States. Almost nightly, the center presents carefully selected films that include classics of the American and foreign cinema, ethnographic documentaries, video art, and new independent work.

The gallery is open Monday through Friday 10:00 to 5:00 and Saturday 12:00 to 4:00, but many events are scheduled in the evening. Call 505-982-1338 for details. The center is at 291 East Barcelona, near the intersection with Old Pecos Trail. Some activities are free and the others are always a value.

Santa Fe Children's Museum

The Children's Museum features hands-on, participatory exhibits in the arts, humanities, and sciences. One of the few attractions in town oriented to kids under 12, it offers opportunities to create, scamper, and learn, all in a lively, fun environment. Youngsters might make their own cartoon movies, paint their faces, explore the Earthworks horticultural project, even check out the living habits of giant cockroaches. The atmosphere of discovery is exciting and the program of workshops, demonstrations, and performances delights both children and parents.

At 1050 Old Pecos Trail, around the corner from the Center for Contemporary Arts, the museum is open from 10:00 to 5:00 Thursday through Saturday and noon to 5:00 on Sunday all year. During the summer, the museum opens on Wednesdays as well. Admission is $1.50 for kids under 12 and $2.50 for anyone older. Call 505-989-8359 for additional information.

El Rancho de las Golondrinas

A living museum of Spanish colonial life, the "Ranch of the Swallows" offers a compelling, authentic look at New Mexico history. From 1710 until late in the nineteenth century, this was the last stop before Santa Fe on the arduous Camino Real (Royal Road) from Mexico City. A short drive by car from the plaza today, this sprawling farmstead was a full day's journey in the early years by horseback or carriage.

Up to fifty colonists once lived and worked at El Rancho de las Golondrinas. Now carefully restored, the ranching village reflects their lifestyle, chores, and passions, fostering appreciation and respect for the Spanish colonial heritage.

The sights include reconstructed houses from the eighteenth and nineteenth centuries, farm buildings, blacksmithing and wheelwrighting facilities, several water mills, and a winery. The importance of religion in daily life can be seen in the *oratorio,* or private chapel, and the *morada,* a special sanctuary for members of the powerful penitente brotherhood.

The ranch is open for self-guided tours Wednesdays through Sundays in June, July, and August from 10:00 to 4:00. The best times to visit are during the spring and fall festivals, usually held on the first weekends of June and October, when local Spanish artists demonstrate colonial crafts and perform traditional folk music and dances. On festival weekends there isn't a more fascinating place in the area.

El Rancho de las Golondrinas is in the village of La Cienega, a few miles south of the Santa Fe city limits just off I-25. The usual $3.50 general admission charge for adults (less for children and seniors) goes up a little on festival weekends. Call 505-471-2261 for additional information.

School of American Research

The School of American Research has been an important force in Santa Fe life for most of the twentieth century. The Archaeological Institute of America established it as a research center in 1907 to further the study of American prehistory. Anthropologists working at the school contributed considerably to early local and national interest in the Southwestern heritage, encouraging preservation efforts and the growth of tourism.

A major force in the development of the Museum of New Mexico, the organization was housed for many years in the Palace of the Governors. In 1972 it moved to its present headquarters in a lovely residential compound at 660 East Garcia Street.

The center's outstanding collection of Southwestern Indian art can be seen only on special tours that cost $15, normally scheduled on Friday at 2:00. Call 505-982-3584 for a reservation.

Randall Davey Audubon Center

No single place can represent the totality of the Santa Fe heritage, but the Randall Davey house and educational center comes close. Once a Spanish land grant, later the site of the U.S. Army's sawmill, then the home and studio of one of the early leaders of the local art colony, the expansive estate offers a little of everything. You can tour the historic home, which was originally the mill, see Randall Davey's art, and learn about the flora and fauna of northern New Mexico on nature trails that wind through the Audubon Center's wilderness area. The staff organizes and presents a series of natural history workshops, bird walks, and other activities.

The Randall Davey Audubon Center (505-983-4609) is at the end of Upper Canyon Road. It's open daily from 9:00 to 5:00, except on weekends during the winter, for a small donation. House tours, which cost extra, are offered only in the summer, usually on Monday afternoon.

CHAPTER SIX

Festivals, Fiestas, and Other Good Times

SANTA FE abounds with arts festivals, fairs, and celebrations, particularly in the summer. From the opening of the opera in July through Indian Market in late August, a flurry of gallery openings, special shows, concerts, and other performances dominate social and economic life.

Even during the slower months of the year, when fewer people visit, the range of activities and entertainment remains vibrantly diverse. Compared to big cities, Santa Fe may be quiet and quaintly secluded, but there are always things to do. Our review of the cultural and entertainment calendar starts with the major summer arts events, which brought fame to the city originally, and continues with a roundup of other special but lesser-known activities. See the Santa Fe map in Chapter 5 for the primary venues.

Santa Fe Opera

When John Crosby founded the Santa Fe Opera in 1957, opera in the United States was dominated by European talent and repetitive stagings of standard repertory. Crosby was convinced that opera could be more exciting, innovative, and American. He planned carefully for several years to create an outdoor summer festival that would feature and cultivate American musical talent. He chose Santa Fe as a location because most larger cities "have a great deal of rain, lots of mosquitos and lots of airplanes overhead."

The original opera house was acoustically solid but not very grand, built at a cost of $115,000 to provide seating on wooden benches. It burned during the eleventh season and was replaced with a magnificent open-air theater that sits in a large natural bowl in the Tesuque hills, peering out onto the resplendent evening skies. Even people who prefer other kinds of music attend the opera for its setting.

The productions are lavish and adventuresome, emphasizing new and neglected works. The annual season customarily includes some standard repertory, but the old warhorses are usually less exciting for the performers and the audience than the seldom-seen compositions. The Santa Fe Opera, despite its relative youth among major American companies, holds the national record for premieres, averaging one a summer.

The season opens in late June or early July and runs until the end of August. In July, performances are usually on Wednesdays, Fridays, and Saturdays; in August, they are almost daily. Admission is a bargain compared to opera prices in most cities, but it is not cheap. For people on a tight budget, standing-room tickets can be an incredible value, about the same cost as a movie. For ticket information and orders, call 505-986-5900 or 505-986-5959.

Santa Fe Chamber Music Festival

You may know about the Chamber Music Festival just from the stunning posters donated for many years by Georgia O'Keeffe, one of the festival's most devoted fans during her lifetime. The music always lives up to the promise of the posters—spiritually powerful, immediate, and complex. Even though the festival is fifteen years younger than the Santa Fe Opera, it approaches nearly the same level of national and international recognition.

As in the case of the opera, the setting for performances is delightful, in the St. Francis Auditorium of the Museum of Fine Arts, an intimate hall modeled after a Spanish mission chapel. A roster of stellar artists from around the world fills the chamber almost daily during the seven-week season for concerts, discussions, and public rehearsals.

The music ranges broadly from classic to innovative, including in recent years a Marilyn Horne recital, string quartet performances, jazz concerts, and even a dinner dance with the Glenn Miller Orchestra. Each year the festival features a composer-in-residence who creates a commissioned piece, directs rehearsals of the work, and explains aspects of its composition in a special lecture.

The festival season opens in early July and closes near the end of August. Concerts are held most evenings, and other events are scheduled daily. Call 505-983-2075 for the specifics.

Santa Fe Desert Chorale

The Desert Chorale is a youngster compared to the Santa Fe Opera and Chamber Music Festival, but its aspirations are equally lofty. Lawrence Bandfield directs professional singers from throughout the country in an ambitious program of choral music from the Renaissance to the avant-garde. In one recent season, six varied programs presented such selections as Johannes Brahms's fervent *Zigeunerlieder,* African American spirituals, and the Southwest premiere of R. Murray Schafer's delightful *Felix's Girls.* The July and August concerts are staged primarily at the Santuario de Guadalupe, though the chorale sometimes moves to other venues, including Albuquerque. Call 505-988-7505 for the current repertory and reservations.

María Benítez Teatro Flamenco

The premier flamenco dancer in America, María Benítez grew up in Taos and maintains a home in Santa Fe. Most of the year she and her troupe are on tour, but they return to Santa Fe each summer for a season of energetic, passionate, and popular performances. Benítez leaves no one bored or distracted.

She performs in the María Benítez Club at the Radisson Picacho Hotel, at 750 North St. Francis, near the northern end of town on the road to Taos. Call the box office at 505-982-1237 for times and tickets, or call her Institute for Spanish Arts (505-983-8477) for additional information on the dance company and its summer workshops.

Santa Fe Stages

New in 1995, Santa Fe Stages presents an international professional theater festival during June and July at the Greer Garson Theater Center on the campus of the College of Santa Fe, on St. Michael's Drive near Cerrillos Road.

In the initial season, Montreal's Les deux mondes collaborated with Teatro dell'Angolo of Turin, Italy, on a production of *Promised Land*. Britain's RJC Dance Theater mixed reggae, rock, and jazz dance styles in a series of performances, and María Benítez choreographed an electrifying version of *La Tragédie de Carmen*, starring mezzo-soprano Suzanna Guzman. Other works included Leslie Harrel Dillen's *Mabel*, an evening with Taos legend Mabel Dodge Luhan, and an innovative interpretation of Hamlet, featuring Obie Award–winner Ray Dooley.

With that kind of brilliant beginning, Santa Fe Stages seems destined to shine in the years ahead. Call 505-982-6683 for schedule and ticket information.

SITE Santa Fe

Also new in 1995, SITE Santa Fe presents major international art exhibits every other summer. Inspired by the grand and global biennials in cities such as Venice, the organizers hope to produce shows of monumental caliber.

While the aspirations are worldly, the themes relate to the local setting, seeking a unity and relevance lacking in similar biennials. The first event was called "Longing and Belonging: From the Faraway Nearby," a title taken partially from Georgia O'Keeffe, who signed her correspondence "faraway nearby." Artists from a dozen countries, including New Mexicans Bruce Nauman and Meridel Rubenstein, addressed issues of identity in an age when roots become blurred by an increasingly international culture. It was a remarkable debut, breathtaking in scope but grounded in Santa Fe spirit.

For information on the next exhibits in 1997 and 1999, call 505-989-1199.

Gallery Openings

The opening of a new show in a gallery can be as much of a performance as anything produced by the opera. The artist is center stage, obligingly or not playing a complex variety of roles as interpreter of the work, loyal servant of the gallery, and friend of patrons. The fun starts for observers when other performers from the gallery and the crowd compete for the same roles and the spotlight. Never the best time to see an artist's new work, openings are nonetheless lively events and among the best entertainment values in town.

Although they occur during the entire year, openings are far more concentrated in the summer than at any other time. Check for listings in the Friday "Pasatiempo" section of the *New Mexican,* the local newspaper, or call favorite galleries. Admission is always free and so are any libations offered.

Indian Market

Held on the third weekend of August, Indian Market is Santa Fe's busiest time. Hundreds of the best Indian artists in the country, chosen carefully each year to maintain high standards of quality, display and sell their finest work on the plaza. The assembled trove of traditional and contemporary art attracts a swarm of collectors, dealers, and the curious. The professionals among them show up on the plaza before sunrise on Saturday to beat each other to the best of the pottery, jewelry, weaving, and other work. The most frenzied round of buying is over before breakfast, but the selection remains excellent and the crowds huge for the rest of the weekend. Prices, as high as the quality, can shock the uninitiated.

The sponsor of the event is the Southwestern Association for Indian Affairs (505-983-5220). The organization was formed in the early 1920s to defeat the Bursum Bill, legislation that would have taken land and water rights from the Pueblos, but today it focuses on the preservation and encouragement of Southwestern Indian art.

Spanish Market

Spanish Market is not as popular or well known as Indian Market, but it's the best occasion in the United States to see and buy traditional Spanish colonial crafts and their contemporary offshoots. The Spanish Colonial Arts Society sponsors the annual fair, held on the last full weekend of July, to recognize artistic achievement in local crafts. Juries of experts give awards in the areas of woodcarving, ironwork, weaving, colcha stitchery, jewelry, furniture, and straw inlay. The work is often stunning and always an impressive display of the persistence of the Santa Fe heritage.

Few of the pieces you'll see are routinely available in Santa Fe shops or galleries. This is the place to buy them, at prices quite reasonable for the artistry involved. Traditional crafts are displayed around the sides of the plaza and the contemporary work is along Lincoln Avenue. Contact the Spanish Colonial Arts Society (505-983-4038) for more information.

Santa Fe Area Farmer's Market

Nothing in town is more fun or flavorful than the Farmer's Market, where the agricultural and culinary arts get the spotlight. In operation from May through October on Tuesday, Saturday, and Sunday, it's a must for a true taste of Santa Fe, attracting a diverse crowd of growers and buyers who represent the full array of local lifestyles.

Farmers and gardeners from all over northern New Mexico offer vegetables, fruits, flowers, baked goods, fresh salsas, pestos, and other treats. If it grows in the area or can be made by a creative home business, you'll find it on sale at a fair price.

On Tuesday and Saturday morning the market opens at 7:00, and reaches its peak between then and 9:00, though it doesn't shut down completely until noon. On Sunday the hours are 10:00 to 3:00. For years the market has used the parking lot of the Sanbusco Center, on Montezuma one block west of Guadalupe, but the organizers are looking for a larger space and may move in the near future. Call 505-983-4098 to verify the location or get other information.

Other Summer Events

On Tuesday and Thursday from June through August, the Summerscene program (505-438-8834) offers free music on the plaza at noon and again later at 6:00. Half the workers downtown bring a picnic to the lunchtime concert, and scores of parents bring their kids to the evening performance. The music runs the gamut from folk to light opera, from salsa to bluegrass.

A commercial production company stages concerts with big-name popular musicians on some summer nights at the Paolo Soleri outdoor amphitheater on the campus of the Santa Fe Indian School, near downtown on Cerrillos Road. In the past, the stars have included Santana, the late Frank Zappa, Lyle

Lovett, and Bob Dylan. Call 505-256-1777 for the current schedule and information on tickets, which sell out fast.

A semiprofessional company, the Southwest Repertory Theater (505-982-1336) presents three Broadway plays each summer, usually a musical, a comedy, and a drama. The talented troupe is based at the James A. Little Theater on the campus of the New Mexico School for the Deaf, at the corner of St. Francis Drive and Cerrillos Road. Prices vary for each production.

For good, free theater in July and August, head to St. John's College, just off Old Santa Fe Trail and Camino del Monte Sol, for Shakespeare in Santa Fe. A professional cast stages one of the Bard's plays annually, performing outdoors in a courtyard near the college library on weekend evenings. Call 505-982-2910 for details.

Fiesta de Santa Fe

Fiesta falls at the end of the crowded summer season, the weekend after Labor Day. Though the city continues to attract a lot of visitors through Christmas, the event coincides with an important turning point in the annual tourism cycle, the return of the city to its residents. For nine months or so after Fiesta each year, locals will be able to find a parking space downtown, obtain dinner reservations, sit peacefully on the plaza, and otherwise enjoy their hometown. Santa Fe becomes itself again during Fiesta, and in the process the residents release a bit of pent-up tension and creative craziness.

This wasn't Fiesta's original purpose, but it's not altogether inconsistent with the founding intent. City leaders started the event in 1712 to celebrate the Spanish reconquest of Santa Fe from the Pueblos in 1692–93. Many of the activities still focus on the seventeenth-century struggles, but others are more contemporary in origin and character.

The first major activity, the burning of Zozobra on Friday evening, is one of the twentieth-century embellishments. A forty-foot marionette representing Old Man Gloom, Zozobra stands taller than almost any building in town. Will Shuster, one of the founders of the local art colony, created the almost mythic being in the 1920s, burning a smaller version at an annual party in his backyard, to dispel gloom from the city in preparation for the rest of Fiesta. Long ago the event was moved to a city park and now much of the town participates. While Zozobra flails his arms and groans miserably, the assembled citizenry torches the giant effigy in a fireworks ceremony more dramatic than any Fourth-of-July celebration.

Free of gloom for the next year, the crowd walks to the plaza, about a mile away, celebrating en masse. Music, merriment, eating, and parading continue on the plaza for the next two days.

On Saturday morning, for the children's pet parade, almost every child in the city shows up in costume with a real or an imaginary animal friend. In the afternoon specially selected and carefully rehearsed residents, on horseback in seventeenth-century dress, reenact Don Diego de Vargas's triumphant entry into the city in 1692. Being chosen to play the Don's role is almost a greater honor locally than being elected mayor. A grand ball in the evening ends the day's festivities, just as it did a couple of hundred years ago.

On Sunday afternoon most of the town gathers again for the Hysterical/Historical Parade, which is more of the former than the latter. Various neighborhood and civic groups compete to mount the most imaginative float, many of which feature caustic commentary about local and national political issues. Fiesta concludes solemnly on Sunday night with mass in the cathedral and a candlelight procession from there to the Cross of the Martyrs, a hilltop memorial to the twenty-three Franciscan priests killed in the 1680 Pueblo Revolt.

Santa Fe Wine & Chile Fiesta

During the last weekend of September, a newer fiesta celebrates different traditions, particularly the area's long love for chiles.

Santa Fe chefs and restaurateurs started the four-day event in 1990 in collaboration with California and New Mexico wineries. It's grown quickly in prestige and participation, attracting both residents and visitors to an annual series of master classes with respected guest chefs, wine seminars and tastings, special meals and cooking demonstrations at local restaurants, and much more.

Over the years featured activities have included a Champagne and Dirty Boots Western Dance, agricultural tours, and a horseback ride to a cowboy campfire breakfast. The "Big Event" of every fiesta comes on Saturday afternoon, when dozens of restaurants and wineries serve samples of their specialties, offering a gluttonous plethora of goodies. Call 505-988-7124 to whet your appetite.

Skiing and Other Mountain Recreation

The Taos Ski Valley (see Chapter 13) is better known nationally, but the Santa Fe Ski Area offers a similar experience of sunny, high-altitude schussing between Thanksgiving and Easter. The vertical drop from the 12,000-foot summit isn't as great as in Taos, and most of the trails aren't as daunting, but on the whole the skiing rivals most in the Rockies. The slopes attract less attention than elsewhere partially because there's no lodging at the base. You have to stay at the bottom of the mountain in Santa Fe, scarcely a hardship, and make the thirty-minute drive to the Ski Area daily.

Seven chair lifts usually keep the upbound lines flowing quickly and the thirty-eight trails provide plenty of variety in the ways to get down. With an even 40-percent split between intermediate and expert runs, all experienced skiers have ample terrain to master. Beginners get less desirable tracks in their 20-percent share, but they can upgrade skills in relatively affordable classes at the ski school. For additional information call 505-982-4429 in the winter, or in the summer 505-983-9155, a number that also serves as the hotline on snow conditions during the season.

Cross-country skiing flourishes nearby, on trails that lead into the Santa Fe National Forest off the road to the Ski Area. The closest popular route starts at the Black Canyon Campground, about nine miles from downtown, but many people go a little higher up the mountain to the Borrega, Aspen Vista, or Windsor Trails.

In the summer the same arteries attract day hikers, while backpackers are more likely to head to one of the wilderness areas in the Santa Fe National Forest, particularly the enormous 223,000-acre Pecos Wilderness or the Dome Wilderness near Bandelier National Monument (see Chapter 23). Contact the local Forest Service office (1220 St. Francis Drive, 505-988-6940) for maps and details about all the activities.

For information on other outdoor recreation in northern New Mexico, see Chapter 13. Note that Santa Fe has as many river-rafting companies as Taos, all listed in the yellow pages, but they run the same upper stretches of the Rio Grande.

Celebrating Christmas

Aglow with local traditions, Santa Fe at Christmas truly earns its nickname of "the city different." Residents outline homes and businesses with *farolitos,* customarily made with a candle anchored in sand inside a small paper bag. Many businesses have gone to electric farolitos, with light bulbs and plastic bags, but few people resort to such convenience at home.

The soft, warm lighting provided by the farolitos is often supplemented by roaring *luminarias,* bonfires made from carefully stacked logs. The luminarias represent the fires of Bethlehem shepherds and are traditionally lighted on Christmas Eve, when the favorite local activity is walking through the most brightly decorated neighborhoods, particularly along Canyon Road and Acequia Madre.

Luminarias also blaze on other nights preceding Christmas outside homes participating in the Las Posadas pageant. Based loosely on a sixteenth-century Spanish miracle play, Las Posadas is a reenactment of Mary and Joseph's quest for shelter. Every parish church seems to have a slightly different version of the ritual, but they all start with a mass, followed by a procession to the home of a parishioner who is serving as host for the evening. There the parishioners playing Mary and Joseph entreat for shelter. The host refuses repeatedly before inviting everyone in for food and Christmas carols. Simple but powerful, the pageant is performed in Spanish by most of the local parishes for nine nights starting on December 16. One of the more elaborate versions is staged on the plaza by the Museum of New Mexico a few nights before Christmas. The museum's production includes shepherds, livestock, and even Lucifer.

Occasionally a local group also presents Los Pastores, another Spanish miracle play that was popular in Santa Fe in past centuries. Melodic folk tunes, rhyming verses, and antiquated Spanish words characterize the drama, which focuses on the shepherds who made the journey to Bethlehem. In New Mexican folk versions, the shepherds offer local gifts in the adoration scene—dishes of tamales, *milagros* (little charms), herbs, and woolen fleeces.

The Serene Arts Season

After the Santa Fe Opera and Chamber Music Festival wrap up in August, and their musicians scatter to the ends of the globe, local performing artists and companies have the stage to themselves through the next spring. They don't enjoy the resources and international stature of the summer institutions, but they often brim with talent and commitment. It's a season for culture without the crowds, when the relaxed local atmosphere may be more conducive to appreciation.

Two symphony orchestras perform from September through May, filling many evenings with luscious music. The Santa Fe

Pro Musica (505-988-4640) offers both orchestral and chamber ensemble concerts, the latter usually in the lovely Loretto Chapel. The Santa Fe Symphony (505-983-3530) features an ambitious series of classical and contemporary concerts under the direction of Stewart Robertson. Most of the performances are at the Sweeney Center downtown, at Marcy Street and Grant.

Smaller musical groups with regularly scheduled events include two chamber ensembles, the Oncydium Chamber Baroque (505-988-0703) and Serenata of Santa Fe (505-989-7988 or 505-983-5240), and two choruses, the Sangre de Cristo Chorale (505-662-9717) and the Santa Fe Women's Ensemble (505-982-4075).

Theater troupes tend to form and dissolve almost monthly, reflecting the changing circumstances of people who have to support themselves in other jobs. The oldest survivor is the Santa Fe Community Theater (505-982-4262), which operates out of a fraying facility in a historic neighborhood at 142 East De Vargas. It stages the annual Fiesta Melodrama each September, lampooning the political and the pompous. For information on other current companies and their performances, contact the Santa Fe Theater Alliance (505-984-8464), a federation of groups, or the Railyard Performance Center (505-982-8309), the site for many innovative and experimental productions.

The sponsor of Spanish Market, the Spanish Colonial Arts Society (505-983-4038), started the lesser-known Winter Market in 1989, scheduled for the first full weekend in December. All artists and craftspeople juried into the summer show can participate in the winter event, though fewer take the opportunity. A great spot for Christmas shopping, the show is held at La Fonda Hotel on the plaza.

Most literary activities in Santa Fe happen in the "off season." Writers were an important part of the original art colony and many live in the area today, including John Nichols, Scott Momaday, Tony Hillerman, and Elizabeth Tallent. Readings and workshops are presented on an occasional basis at the College of Santa Fe, the main public library, and a number of bookstores. Recursos de Santa Fe (505-982-9301), which offers a fascinating range of educational programs, sponsors a literary center and an annual writer's conference in August that attracts a number of respected authors.

Year-Round Entertainment

A variety of talented local musicians perform around the city on a regular basis. Classical guitarists Ruben Romero and Antonio Mendoza awe any audience. Pianists John Gooch, Doug Montgomery, Charles Tichenor, and Rebecca Ryan play with gusto and grace. Father Frank Pretto and David Salazar both lure big local crowds for their Latin music, and so do Bill and Bonnie Hearne for tunes from the American country folk tradition. Friday's "Pasatiempo" section of the *New Mexican* lists performance dates and places for these and other area musicians, and covers additional nightlife options as well.

If you're more interested in film than music, Santa Fe offers almost two dozen screens. Most show mainstream movies, but a few theaters specialize in imaginative, out-of-the-mainstream selections. The nonprofit Center for Contemporary Arts (505-982-1338), described in Chapter 5, hosts the delightful Cinematheque series. Commercial theaters with an eye toward excellence include the Jean Cocteau (418 Montezuma near Guadalupe, downtown, 505-988-2711) and Grand Illusion (St. Michael's Village, on St. Michael's Drive, 505-471-8935). For live dinner theater, head to the Old Santa Fe Music Hall (100 North Guadalupe, downtown, 800-409-3311 or 505-983-3311), which features a family-friendly show about the city.

People who like to lay down a bet get their kicks at the Downs at Santa Fe racetrack, just south of the city limits off I-25, or at one of the new Pueblo-owned casinos in the area. The thoroughbreds and quarter horses at the Downs (505-471-3311) run from June through Labor Day, mainly on weekend days. A half-dozen miles north of town on U.S. 84/285, the Camel Rock Casino (505-984-8414) is the closest of the Indian gaming halls. It offers blackjack, poker (including hold'em tournaments), video slot machines, craps, and the local favorite, bingo.

For a quieter and more relaxing time, try a soak under the stars. Ten Thousand Waves (505-988-1047 or 505-982-9304) is a Japanese-style bathhouse in the mountains, about three and a half miles from the plaza up the road to the Santa Fe Ski Area. Patrons don kimonos and sandals in sexually segregated dressing areas before going to their assigned tubs, all outside. Book on a night with a full moon for the ultimate experience.

CHAPTER SEVEN

Best Resorts, Inns, and B&Bs

OR LODGING in Santa Fe, smaller is usually better. The large hotels and motels are more likely to provide a swimming pool and television set, and they usually offer more services for business travelers, but once you are in your room in a typical large establishment you might as well be in Omaha. With only a few important exceptions, the large hotels and motels lack local character.

For the full Santa Fe experience, visitors should try to reserve well in advance at one of the many resorts, inns, or B&Bs that convey a sure sense of place. Those recommended below differ substantially in amenities, rates, and styles, but they all offer some degree of special character and most provide good value in their price range.

If you plan your trip too late to find room at the inn, contact the Accommodations Hotline at 800-338-6877 or Santa Fe Central Reservations at 800-982-7669. These reservation services can also help with short-term condominium and vacation-home rentals, but for that type of lodging you may find more options at Frontier Property Management (800-746-8222) and The Management Group (800-283-2211). Downtown condominiums with stylish accommodations include Otra Vez en Santa Fe (505-988-2244) and Zona Rosa (800-955-4455).

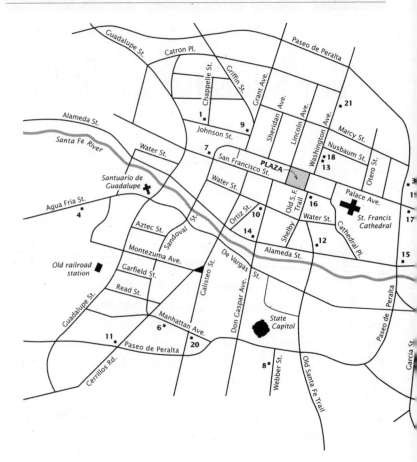

We quote exact rates in the following descriptions, rather than using vague categories like "moderate" and "expensive," because many of the best places in town offer substantial variety in room styles and prices. Rates do change and fluctuate on a regular basis, but the figures we quote are accurate at press time for the summer season and they tend to remain consistent over time as a basis of comparison among different places. Prices generally drop from November through March except during holiday periods. Be sure to ask about package discounts, shoulder-season values, and other special deals.

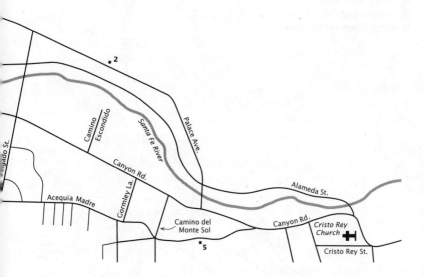

Central Santa Fe Accommodations

1. Adobe Abode
2. Alexander's Inn
3. Dancing Ground of the Sun
4. Dos Casas Viejas
5. Dunshee's
6. El Paradero
7. Eldorado Hotel
8. Four Kachinas Inn
9. Grant Corner Inn
10. Hotel St. Francis
11. Hotel Santa Fe

12. Inn at Loretto
13. Inn of the Anasazi
14. Inn of the Governors
15. Inn on the Alameda
16. La Fonda Hotel
17. La Posada
18. Plaza Real
19. Preston House
20. Pueblo Bonito
21. Territorial Inn

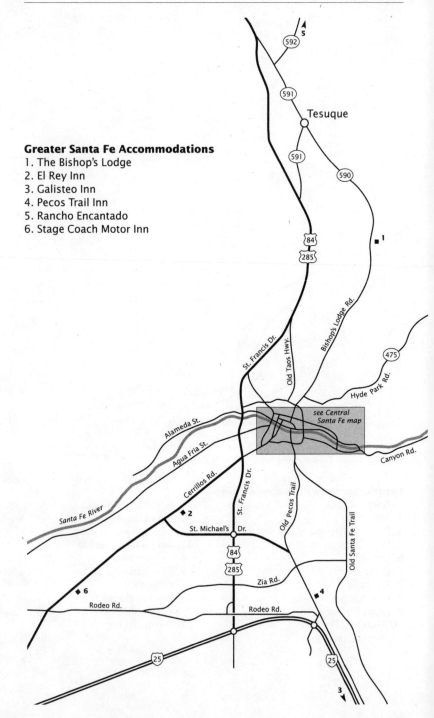

Greater Santa Fe Accommodations
1. The Bishop's Lodge
2. El Rey Inn
3. Galisteo Inn
4. Pecos Trail Inn
5. Rancho Encantado
6. Stage Coach Motor Inn

BEST RESORT HOTELS

The Bishop's Lodge.
Rates in July and
August, at the peak of
the season, range from
$195 to $355 for
accommodations only.
The MAP plan
increases the cost by
about $75 for a
couple, plus another
$50 for a child. The
rates drop during
other months, to a low
of $95 to $249 from
January through
March.
P.O. Box 2367, Santa
Fe 87504.
505-983-6377,
fax 505-989-8739.
Major credit cards.

In Willa Cather's *Death Comes for the Archbishop,* the prelate commences his retirement in a poignant scene. He and a longtime companion ride north from the city on horseback, up the big hill that separates Santa Fe from the Tesuque Valley. At the top of the hill they part, the companion returning to town and the bishop continuing on to his private estate in the valley. This beautiful inn, about three miles from the plaza, was his destination.

At the time, Archbishop Lamy had only a small adobe house and a chapel on the land. A later owner, Joseph Pulitzer of publishing fame, built two large summer homes on the property for his daughters and their families. When Denver mining magnate Jim Thorpe purchased the place in 1918, he left the chapel as it was when the bishop died and converted the homes into two of the resort's luxurious lodges. Still in his family, the hotel retains its gracious, antique aura despite modernization of the facilities and a limited degree of expansion.

The rooms vary considerably, but each offers Southwestern ranch-style charm. Some of our favorites are among the least expensive quarters, the standard rooms in the original Pulitzer lodges, full of vintage character. Ask for number 118 or a similar chamber with a terrace and large bath. If you upgrade to a deluxe room, you get a fireplace and a more private patio or deck. The new superior deluxe rooms and suites provide an extra measure of contemporary luxury, but all the accommodations come with air conditioning, TVs, and morning newspapers.

The Lodge has its own stables and over a thousand acres of riding trails, plus four tennis courts, a trap- and skeet-shooting range, and a fitness center. The heated outdoor swimming pool, near the center of the grounds, is supplemented by an indoor Jacuzzi and saunas.

In the summer families can take advantage of a full children's program. Kids from four to twelve are picked up early in the morning for a day of supervised play, and are entertained again in the evening. The program is one of the features of special MAP (Modified American Plan) rates in June, July, and August, which also include breakfast and a choice of lunch or dinner.

The resort's cooking has improved considerably in recent years, with the kitchen developing true finesse with contemporary regional and continental dishes. Santa Feans flock to the bountiful buffets at breakfast and lunch, and come increasingly to the more elegant but still casual à la carte dinners. In the warmer months you have the option of dining on the restaurant terrace, overlooking the lovely grounds, or inside in one of the handsome, art-filled dining rooms.

Rancho Encantado.
Summer rates in the main lodge start at $190 and go up to $260 for a casita. The condominiums range from $160 for a locked-off bedroom (without kitchen) to $415 for six people in a two-bedroom villa. Route 4, Box 57C, Santa Fe 87501. 800-722-9339, 505-982-3537, fax 505-983-8269. Major credit cards.

The "Enchanted Ranch" is about eight miles north of Santa Fe, in the same valley that houses The Bishop's Lodge and the small village of Tesuque. The resort spreads out across piñon-dotted hills that afford a grand view of the Jemez Mountains and the sunset. The enchanted setting has enticed such guests as Princess Grace and Prince Rainier of Monaco, Nelson Rockefeller, Maria Callas, John Wayne, and Robert Redford.

The 22 rooms and suites in the intimate inn rank among the most attractive accommodations in the Santa Fe area. The least expensive quarters in the Main Lodge, built in 1932, convey the flavor of the old Southwest in an elegantly simple way. The cottage rooms nearby come with fireplaces, and the Casa Piñon and *casita* suites also add a parlor and wet bar or refrigerator. Most of the chambers feature terraces, viga ceilings, handpainted tiles, New Mexico art, and other regional *rancho* accents.

The contemporary one- and two-bedroom

condominiums built across the road in recent years share much of the charm and give guests the bonus of a full kitchen and living room. The Betty Egan House, the four-bedroom home of the resort's late founder, now functions as a B&B, an inn within the inn.

The management emphasizes a relaxed environment at Rancho Encantado but also provides all the outdoor activities anyone could desire, including escorted trail rides into the Sangre de Cristo Mountains, hiking paths, a hilltop swimming pool and hot tub (covered in winter), tennis courts, and more. The restaurant's food quality has varied over the years but the wonderful views are a constant, from either the front patio or the inside dining room.

BEST INNS, HOTELS, AND MOTELS

El Rey Inn.
Rates vary during the year but are always low for the atmosphere and service. In midsummer a double is $64 to $125.
1862 Cerrillos Road, P.O. Box 4759, Santa Fe 87502-4759.
505-982-1931.
Major credit cards.

El Rey may be the best motel in the West, perhaps the country. Bucking the trend toward chain-inspired homogenization, it exudes individual personality, local character, and value—a delightful package for a traveler anywhere.

The 86 rooms differ substantially in decor, but each evokes the Southwestern heritage in tasteful and compelling ways. Many come with adobe fireplaces, rough-hewn vigas, and tile murals, and some offer kitchen facilities to supplement the complimentary continental breakfast. Even the smallest, least expensive quarters enjoy a lovely garden setting accented with fountains and tiled walkways. The new deluxe rooms in the Spanish Colonial Courtyard wing, at the top of the rate scale, feature the work of regional artisans and influences from fine French inns. Some of them overlook the heated swimming pool and adjacent hot tub cabaña.

Eldorado Hotel.
Regular doubles cost
$239 at the peak of
the season. For butler
service, rates start at
$339.
309 West San
Francisco, Santa Fe
87501.
800-955-4455,
505-988-4455,
fax 505-982-0713.
Major credit cards.

If you need butler service in Santa Fe, and don't care about the cost, this is the place to get it. Only the fifth-floor rooms offer the amenity, along with fireplaces and terraces, but everything else reflects a similar sense of big-city style.

Many residents hate the hotel building, an imposing presence downtown that's out of scale for Santa Fe. The architects made an effort to harmonize with the local environment, but Eldorado's bulk and boxiness undermine the intent. The management makes its amends with good service, elegant dining at The Old House, and a commendable level of community involvement.

Galisteo Inn.
Rates range from $60
to $175 for the gem
called Cottonwood.
HC 75, Box 4, Galisteo
87540.
505-466-4000.
MC, V.

The premier country hideaway near Santa Fe, the Galisteo Inn occupies a 240-year-old hacienda set on eight serene acres. In the tiny, arty village of Galisteo, 23 miles southeast of Santa Fe, the retreat provides a relaxing combination of bucolic beauty and spacious comfort.

The carefully restored adobe home features handhewn vigas, kiva fireplaces, and old plank floors. The twelve guest rooms vary in amenities, though each is decorated in an authentic New Mexico style. The most expensive quarters contain a private bath, king bed, and a sitting area, while the least expensive have twin beds and a shared bath. Some face a pasture where horses graze, and others overlook the 50-foot heated pool, which is open from May to October. A sauna, outdoor hot tub, and mountain bikes are included in the rates, along with a continental breakfast, while massages and horseback riding can be arranged for an extra charge.

The fixed-price dinners served Wednesday through Sunday evenings are usually innovative, enticing, and reasonably priced. You start with a soup or salad, perhaps a cauliflower, onion, and chipotle chowder or romaine leaves with a lemon anchovy vinaigrette. The entrée might be mesquite-smoked lamb chops, Southwest chicken mushui, or chile-seared salmon. You wrap up the evening with dessert, maybe the pear cornmeal bread pudding with goat milk caramel.

Hotel St. Francis.
High-season rates range from $80 to $180 for a double room and $225 to $350 for suites. 210 Don Gaspar, Santa Fe 87501. 800-529-5700, 505-983-5700, fax 505-989-7690. Major credit cards.

The St. Francis is the modern reincarnation of the old De Vargas Hotel, originally built in the 1880s. When the first hotel burned in a spectacular fire, the present structure replaced it in 1924. It was a grand place for the next couple of decades, the primary gathering spot for state politicians, but it had faded substantially by 1986, when a group of investors restored its simple but romantic elegance.

Each of the 82 rooms is different, though most come with brass and iron beds, fluffy comforters, and period appointments. Bathroom fixtures include porcelain pedestal sinks and the original style of hexagonal tile. The least expensive "petite" and "standard" rooms are quite small.

A good choice for business meetings among the recommended hotels, the St. Francis offers a convenient downtown location, several conference rooms, and a handsome, light-filled restaurant. Locals and visitors alike enjoy the afternoon tea, served in the classy lobby and outside on the hotel veranda.

Hotel Santa Fe.
Junior suites run $169 in high season and regular rooms cost $129. Master suites are also available. 1501 Paseo de Peralta at Cerrillos Road, Santa Fe 87501. 800-825-9876, 505-982-1200, fax 505-984-2211. Major credit cards.

One of the city's newest inns, the Hotel Santa Fe distinguishes itself with reasonably priced junior suites, its most popular category of lodging. "Junior" in this case makes an ideal arrangement for families, incorporating a sitting room with a sofa bed separate from the actual bedroom, microwave oven, and an honor bar. All the quarters come with the usual comforts and Santa Fe decor, and some have a balcony, a feature you should request in advance if desired.

The 131-room hotel keeps costs down by dispensing with a regular restaurant and room service. A small deli provides simple but hearty breakfasts, which guests enjoy at tables in the spacious lobby, where you can also sip cocktails in the evening around a majestic fireplace. The hotel sits at a busy intersection on the fringes of downtown, but you seldom notice the traffic on the other side of the wall from your room or even from the pool and Jacuzzi.

The tribal government of the Picuris Pueblo owns and manages the Hotel Santa Fe in partnership with a group of local entrepreneurs. Many of the employees are Picuris natives, and they try to treat you as they would if they were welcoming you to their home.

Inn at Loretto.
Rates start at $165 for a double room and go up to $325 for a suite. 211 Old Santa Fe Trail, Santa Fe 87501. 800-727-5531, 505-988-5531, fax 505-984-7988. Major credit cards.

Built on the site of the old Loretto Academy, established by Archbishop Lamy in the 1850s, this Best Western hotel still maintains the lovely Loretto Chapel that served the former school. When the inn was completed in 1975 it became an instant city landmark, the only large building constructed in recent years that effectively conceals its size through Spanish Pueblo recesses and terraces.

The 137 rooms boast the expected Best Western amenities as well as contemporary Southwestern design touches. The covered terrace adjacent to the swimming pool and restaurant is popular with locals for lunch and late-afternoon margaritas.

Inn of the Anasazi.
The least expensive quarters cost $235 during the summer, but you really need to step up to the $265 rooms for the full experience. Junior executive suites are $395.
113 Washington Avenue, Santa Fe 87501.
800-688-8100, 505-988-3030.
Major credit cards.

Robert Zimmer, one of the visionaries who shaped the prestigious Rosewood hotels group, opened the Inn of the Anasazi in 1991 to immense fanfare. The inn hasn't lived up to the publicity in all ways, but it's certainly the most inspired and aspiring hotel downtown.

Though only steps from the plaza, the Anasazi shutters its guests from the bustle and noise behind massive wooden doors, enveloping you in a tranquil Southwestern milieu. The designers sought to pay tribute to the ancient Anasazi culture, wanting guests to feel like they were entering a prehistoric ruin elegantly updated for the twenty-first century. Carefully selected art graces the handplastered walls, beautiful rugs cover pine floors, and potted cacti cast the spell of the desert into all corners.

The 51 guest rooms and 8 suites are smaller than you expect for the price, but they come with a gaslit fireplace, a four-poster bed, and traditional viga-and-latilla ceilings. The restaurant, described in Chapter 8, features contemporary regional cuisine that's as well crafted and pricey as the rooms.

Inn of the Governors.
Summer rates range from $149 to $259.
234 Don Gaspar, Santa Fe 87501.
800-234-4534, 505-982-4333, fax 505-989-9149.
Major credit cards.

Once a simple downtown motel, the Inn of the Governors has grown immensely in charm in recent years. The combination of good location, Southwestern charisma, and unpretentious hospitality make it a perfect match for many people.

The choicest of the moderate-size standard rooms, the least expensive quarters, are the ground-floor chambers on the west side of the property, which enjoy small semiprivate patios. Many of the larger superior, deluxe, and mini-suite rooms come with kiva fireplaces, and those in the Governor's Wing have balconies.

The Mañana Restaurant serves hearty breakfasts, often its best meal. In the warm months, eat on the outdoor terrace adjacent to the heated swimming pool. Later in the day stop by the Mañana Bar, a popular watering hole known for its live piano music.

Inn on the Alameda.
Prices in season for a double room range from $170 to $215. Suites start at $260. 303 East Alameda, Santa Fe 87501. 800-289-2122, 505-984-2121, fax 505-986-8325. Major credit cards.

Small enough to feel intimate, large enough to have a 24-hour switchboard, and new enough to have a Jacuzzi and fitness center, the Inn on the Alameda is a good choice for anyone from a harried executive to a romantic couple.

Owners Joe and Kathy Schepps keep the staff on their toes, providing some of the best service in the city. Location adds to the allure, giving guests equally easy walking access to both Canyon Road and the plaza, a few blocks away.

The rooms combine handcrafted Santa Fe decor and standard luxury amenities, including all of the usual conveniences. Many of the deluxe chambers and suites come with kiva fireplaces and private patios or balconies. The rates include a bountiful continental breakfast, which can be enjoyed in the handsome lobby library, the Agoyo lounge, or your own room.

La Fonda Hotel.
The summer rates start at $155 for a single and $170 for a double. Several expensive suites are also available. 100 East San Francisco, Santa Fe 87501. 800-523-5002, 505-982-5511. Major credit cards.

An inn called La Fonda was well established on this site, adjacent to the plaza, before the opening of the Santa Fe Trail. At the time of the American occupation in 1846, the inn became the U.S. Hotel, where guests paid one dollar a day for room and board but sometimes had to sleep on and under the billiard tables in the lobby when the town was crowded.

The present building dates from 1920, though it has been enlarged several times since then. A group of local investors planned and designed the hotel to reflect the historical traditions of the city in architecture and furnishings. The owners fell short of money, however, and sold the property to the Fred Harvey Company, one of the earliest large-scale promoters of Western tourism. For several decades, until Santa Fe was readily accessible to individual motorists, La Fonda was the grand station for tours of the Pueblo country. The staff served elegant dinners in the evening to affluent guests, while Indians danced in the lobby. Locally owned again, the atmosphere is now more reflective of the town's informality than of grand touring.

The rooms are thoroughly New Mexican in decor, with Spanish Colonial furniture, beamed ceilings, and, in some cases, adobe fireplaces. The lobby, virtually a Santa Fe monument, opens into the festive La Plazuela restaurant and La Fiesta lounge, which offers nightly entertainment. The rooftop Bell Terrace has grand views over the town, but unlike the swimming pool, it's not heated for year-round enjoyment.

La Posada.
La Posada has a wide range of rate categories, around two dozen at last count. If you're looking for character, avoid the least expensive rooms, though they are reasonably priced for the location at $115 in the high season. Doubles go up to $295 and suites range from $195 to $397.
330 East Palace, Santa Fe 87501.
800-727-5276,
505-986-0000,
fax 505-982-6850.
Major credit cards.

Spread over six landscaped acres near the plaza, La Posada is closer in style and appearance to the Tesuque resorts than any of the other downtown hotels. Although each of the 119 rooms is different, and some are fairly conventional, many are romantically Southwestern. The best quarters feature kiva fireplaces, viga ceilings, handpainted tiles, and other traditional accents. Unfortunately the charm in the accommodations and setting doesn't always extend to staff service, which seems to us a little lackadaisical at times.

The center of the complex is the Staab House, a Victorian mansion built in 1882, where the restaurant and lounge are located. The dining room serves a hearty breakfast, with both New Mexican and American specialties, and offers an enticing salad-bar lunch with a daily special. The elegant Victorian lounge, with overstuffed chairs, crystal chandeliers, and leather barstools, makes an intimate spot for drinks and conversation.

Pecos Trail Inn.
Regular rooms run
between $79 and $90
in the summer,
depending on the
bedding and the
kitchenette option. A
couple of apartments
with living rooms and
full kitchens cost
$150.
2239 Old Pecos Trail,
Santa Fe 87505.
505-982-1943.
MC, V.

The only motel on Old Pecos Trail, the most
scenic entrance to Santa Fe, the 16-room inn
offers some of the best value in the city. Secluded
from the bustle on five piñon-dotted acres, but
just a short drive from everything, it blends
serenity with New Mexico spice.

New owners spruced up the 1950s structure
in recent years, from the swimming pool to
Peppers Restaurant & Cantina. The renovated
rooms are spacious if not altogether special, decorated with handcrafted furnishings and local
posters. Many come with a kitchenette, though
you may want to forego cooking in favor of the
complimentary continental breakfast and the
spirited lunches, happy hours, and dinners at
Peppers.

Plaza Real.
In peak periods double
rooms are $159, junior
suites go for $199,
and deluxe suites cost
$249.
125 Washington,
Santa Fe 87501.
800-279-7325,
505-988-4900.
Major credit cards.

A new hotel in the old, time-honored territorial
style, the Plaza Real sits in the center of downtown, just steps from the plaza. The location
alone gives it an edge over most places, but the
ultimate appeal is sincere service, crafty design,
and competitive prices.

The 56 rooms and suites are arranged around
an attractive courtyard, which they usually overlook from a small balcony. The regular rooms
blend regional flavor smartly with contemporary comfort, while the suites add amenities,
extra sitting space, and, in some cases, inviting
fireplaces. A complimentary continental breakfast features fresh-squeezed orange juice.

**Stage Coach Motor
Inn.** In high season
the Cawleys charge
just $49 to $55 for a
double room. Family
units and a suite with
a kitchen and fireplace
go for $70 to $80.
3360 Cerrillos Road,
Santa Fe 87505.
505-471-0707. MC, V.

Built originally as a bordello decades ago, the
Stage Coach is a semiprecious relic, for its old-
fashioned budget rates as well as its vintage
Pueblo-style facade. Barbara and Bernard
Cawley, the personable proprietors, maintain
their 14 rooms carefully and groom the garden
with homey devotion. Don't expect anything
more than simplicity or anything less than a
sunny spirit.

BEST B&BS

Adobe Abode.
Rates for two people range from $100 to $155.
202 Chapelle, Santa Fe 87501.
505-983-3133.
MC, V.

The adobe in this case is a 1907 house just four blocks from the plaza. Pat Harbour moved in after coming to the city from St. Louis in the late 1980s and renovated the property over several years. With careful attention to all the details, she gradually made the old abode into a grand B&B.

Two of the three guest rooms in the main house draw their design inspiration from Britain. Bloomsbury, the least expensive quarters, features a four-poster queen bed, and English Garden is accented with floral prints on the fabrics, including the spread on the brass double bed. Both have oversized showers covered with colorful handmade tiles. The Provence Suite comes with a full living room and separate bedroom, all aglow with the sunny mood of southern France.

The Courtyard Compound behind the main house also contains three rooms. Casita de Corazon, or "little house of the heart," has a small patio and twin beds. Cactus offers a larger terrace, a queen bed, a kiva fireplace, and a motif that takes its cues from Oaxaca, Mexico. Bronco is a rip-roaring cowboy chamber, saddled up with Western decor, that provides the same core amenities as Cactus.

The comforts common to all the rooms include private baths, individual phone lines, TVs, and fluffy robes. Guests also get a full breakfast, with an emphasis on hearty, creative dishes such as sausage-spinach scramble with fiesta baked tomatoes and blue corn waffles with banana-pecan syrup.

Alexander's Inn.

The two rooms with a shared bath are $85 each in the summer and the Cottage costs $150. The other rooms range in-between in price.
529 East Palace, Santa Fe 87501.
505-986-1431.
MC, V.

Hostess Carolyn Delecluse named her B&B after her son, though he's much younger than her house, built in 1903 in a quiet residential neighborhood within walking distance of the plaza and Canyon Road. She renovated the home tastefully to blend modern comfort with historic charm.

At the top of the rate scale, the detached Casita and Cottage accommodations provide the highest measure of Southwestern ambience. Both suites, they feature a kiva fireplace in the living room, and upstairs, a king or queen bed. Five other rooms, more country-American in decor, are in the two-story main house, a brick pitched-roof bungalow brimming with sunshine. The Lilac Room, the former master bedroom, comes with a four-poster bed, a fireplace, and stained-glass windows. Two smaller rooms share a bath, but the rest have their own, along with TVs, phones, robes, and fresh flowers.

Carolyn serves an ample breakfast of home-made bread or muffins, granola, fresh fruit, juice, and coffee, available in the room or on a garden veranda. For the active, she offers mountain bikes and guest privileges at a local club with fitness and recreation facilities.

Dancing Ground of the Sun.

Summer rates range from $130 to $160.
711 Paseo de Peralta, Santa Fe 87501.
800-645-5673,
505-986-9797.
MC, V.

An easy walk from the plaza on the fringes of downtown, Dancing Ground of the Sun specializes in spacious privacy. Each of the suites in the artfully renovated four-plex comes with a private bath, a well-equipped kitchen, and a dining area for enjoying the continental-plus breakfast on your own.

The facade of the small complex doesn't dazzle, but the interiors do, offering a blend of handcrafted quality, Southwestern spirit, and modern comfort in the form of TVs, phones, and even washers and dryers in a couple of cases. All the quarters feature queen or king beds, most enjoy fireplaces, and except for one studio, they provide a living room separate from the bedroom. Owner Connie Wristen's decor themes pay tribute to traditional Native American ceremonies, honoring harvest abundance in the Corn Dancer suite and the merriment of the sacred prankster in the Clown Dancer chamber.

Dos Casas Viejas.
Rates run from $145 for a deluxe room to $195 for a suite.
610 Agua Fria,
Santa Fe 87501.
505-983-1636.
MC, V.

Santa Fe's most delightful lodging surprise is hidden behind a gate along residential Agua Fria Street, a ten-minute walk from the plaza. An intimate inn with a half-dozen stunning rooms, Dos Casas Viejas is a B&B that rivals any resort in the area in hideaway elegance.

The creation of Jois and Irving Belfield, the walled compound encompasses two adjacent adobe homes restored to their original 1860s character. The architecture and antique furnishings evoke the past, but the amenities are state-of-the-art. Along with a kiva fireplace, old vigas, a Mexican tiled bath, and a private patio, you get a phone, TV, oil paintings, and an ambience of relaxed sophistication.

The hosts deliver a first-class continental breakfast to your chamber or serve it at individual tables on a handsome dining terrace. If you still don't feel sufficiently pampered, indulge in the most uncommon luxury of all for a B&B, the heated forty-foot lap pool.

Dunshee's.
Two people pay $110 in the B&B suite and $120 in the Casita. Additional guests pay $15 each.
986 Acequia Madre,
Santa Fe 87501.
505-982-0988.
MC, V.

Artist Susan Dunshee, a longtime Santa Fean, offers gracious hospitality in a quiet, historic residential neighborhood. A quick walk from Canyon Road and a mile from the plaza, the two-house adobe compound surrounds you with authentic local flavor.

The romantic suite in the main house features two kiva fireplaces, one in the spacious living room and the other in the separate bedroom. Vigas support the ceiling and Mexican tiles cover the floors and private bath. Antiques and folk art sit comfortably alongside a TV, phone, queen bed, microwave, and refrigerator. Guests have their own entrance plus a flower-filled patio, where Susan serves her delightful breakfasts in warm weather.

Dunshee's Casita, the only other accommodation, is a two-bedroom, one-bath guesthouse. A bargain for a family or two couples traveling together, it comes with a full kitchen stocked with the fixings for a continental breakfast. Skylights bring in the sun through the vigas in the ceiling, and a kiva fireplace provides warmth on winter evenings. The stereo system, TV, phone, iron, library, and lovely linens make you feel right at home.

El Paradero.
Summer rates go as low as $70 for a double with a shared bath, and as high as $130 for a suite. 220 West Manhattan, Santa Fe 87501. 505-988-1177. No credit cards, but personal checks accepted.

Though the original building was a Spanish farmhouse, constructed on the rural outskirts of the town in the early nineteenth century, this carefully remodeled fourteen-room inn is close to the center of the city today, about a ten-minute walk from the plaza near Guadalupe Street. The owners added a few modern touches, such as phones, during the renovation, but El Paradero has retained the simple, eccentric character of an old adobe home.

Even the small economy rooms with shared baths are colorful, cheerful, and full of light. Some of the moderately priced rooms have fireplaces, and the most expensive quarters upstairs feature fine furnishings and usually a balcony with a mountain view. Among the latter, number 12 is a gem. Two suites in a detached Victorian home offer a kitchenette and a living room with a fireplace. The ample and tasty breakfast includes seasonal fruit, homebaked goods, homemade jams, fresh-ground coffee, and special daily entrées.

Four Kachinas Inn.
High-season rates are
$98 to $115.
512 Webber Street,
Santa Fe 87501.
800-397-2564,
505-982-2550.
MC, V.

Instead of starting with a historic home, Andrew Beckerman and John Daw built their B&B from scratch in 1992, allowing them to tailor the property to their purpose. You won't know the Victorian-style main house is new by looking at it, but you'll notice the difference in modern comforts such as TVs, phones, tub-showers in the private baths, and even wheelchair accessibility in one room.

Southwestern in style, the quarters get their names and inspiration from different Hopi kachinas. At least one image of the supernatural beings graces each room, along with local wood furniture, Saltillo tile floors, and other hand-crafted accents. Three ground-floor rooms enjoy private garden patio entrances, and another upstairs offers mountain views. John delivers a homemade continental breakfast to your chamber, but if you wish you can eat outside in the intimate courtyard or in the guest lounge. Near the state capitol, the Four Kachinas Inn is a ten-minute walk from both the plaza and Canyon Road.

Grant Corner Inn.
Summer rates start at
$85 for a small single
and go up to $140 for
a deluxe double. Two
additional rooms are
available five blocks
away at the Grant
Corner Inn Hacienda, a
Southwestern-style
condominium, for
$115 and $120.
122 Grant Avenue,
Santa Fe 87501.
505-983-6678.
MC, V.

In a turn-of-the-century home tucked enticingly behind a weeping willow tree, the Grant Corner Inn brings Old World flavor to downtown Santa Fe. Just two blocks from the plaza, the hospitable Walter family offers 11 rooms of varying sizes and rates, each furnished with lovely antiques. Venerable armoires, quilts, and four-poster beds mix felicitously with such modern conveniences as TVs, phones, and ceiling fans. Most of the rooms enjoy private baths and a couple come with porches.

The complimentary breakfast is one of the best morning meals in Santa Fe, attracting a lot of paying patrons on the weekend. The selections range from banana waffles to New Mexican soufflé and always include fresh fruit, fresh-squeezed juice, and homemade rolls and jellies. Later in the day guests gather again in front of the fireplace in the dining room or outside on the veranda for complimentary wine.

Preston House.
The smallest and least expensive room, with a shared bath, is $75 in the summer, and the largest suite goes for $160.
106 Faithway Street, Santa Fe 87501.
505-982-3465.
Major credit cards.

George Preston, the law partner of a notorious land speculator, built the B&B's main house in 1886. The only surviving example of Queen Anne architecture in the city, the structure reflects popular Anglo tastes of the late nineteenth century, when adobe was considered dirty. Several decades later, when adobe was back in fashion, new owners covered the brick facade with stucco to blend better with the rest of the local architecture.

Artist Signe Bergman, originally from California, converted the home and adjoining residences into the 15-room inn, which is just a few blocks from the plaza. Six chambers in the original house and two in garden cottages reflect the property's Victorian heritage, flaunting floral wallpaper, lace, period antiques, and stained glass. The other rooms, more Southwestern in character, occupy an adobe compound directly across diminutive Faithway Street.

A pair of rooms in the main house share a bath, but the others enjoy private facilities. Some come with a fireplace, private entrance, and sitting parlor, and most have a TV and phone. All guests get an elaborate continental breakfast and full afternoon tea, plus a decanter of sherry and robes in the room.

Pueblo Bonito.
The cost is $95 to $140.
138 West Manhattan at Galisteo, Santa Fe 87501.
505-984-8001.
MC, V.

A ten-minute walk from the plaza, Pueblo Bonito is serenely secluded from the nearby bustle behind massive adobe walls. Converted from a small apartment complex that was originally a turn-of-the-century estate, the inn offers a variety of comfortably rustic casitas with kiva fireplaces, private baths, queen beds, TVs, and handmade regional furnishings. Several suites come with a kitchen and a living room furnished with a sofa bed.

Herb and Amy Behm serve a continental breakfast buffet with fresh fruit, fresh-squeezed juice, cereal, and homemade breads in the sunny dining room or on a pleasant central terrace, where guests also sip afternoon tea later in the day.

Territorial Inn.
Rates start at $90 year-round and go up to $150.
215 Washington Avenue, Santa Fe 87501.
505-989-7737.
MC, V.

Tree-lined Washington Avenue, which runs a few short blocks from the plaza to the edge of the downtown district, was once a street of grand homes. Today the only residence left among the restaurants and shops houses the Territorial Inn, the attractive creation of owner-manager Lela McFerrin.

Most of the ten guest rooms in the hundred-year-old, two-story structure are up a wonderful winding stairway. Varying from large to cozy, and elegant to quaint, the quarters reflect the Victorian ancestry in decor. All come with a TV and phone, eight have private baths, and two enjoy fireplaces, like the shared living room. The complimentary continental breakfast is delivered to your door, if you wish, or served in a tranquil garden with a gazebo-enclosed hot tub.

CHAPTER EIGHT

Special Restaurants and Local Hangouts

SANTA FEANS love to eat out. Even before the tourism boom of recent decades, the city supported a wealth of restaurants. Now there are hundreds of establishments in town offering food and drink, and both the quality standards and variety are better than ever.

It's difficult to make discriminating, honest recommendations among so many local favorites, but that's the only way to provide real help to a visitor. The normal listing of popular suspects is as useful as a straw at a wine bar. Without apology, our choices represent personal judgments developed over twenty years of eating out in Santa Fe, and they reflect, we hope, the experience gained in writing numerous cookbooks and travel guides on a broad range of subjects. The main criterion in the selections is exceptional cooking, but we also pay careful attention to good value, sympathetic service, and amiable atmosphere. Whatever your budget and tastes, you should find plenty of places that please among the recommendations.

Be sure to sample the local New Mexican cooking, a piquant expression of Santa Fe's living heritage. The city's long isolation from the rest of Hispanic America produced a distinctive cuisine, simple in ingredients but wonderfully spicy. The native food differs notably from any of the regional styles of Mexico, from Tex-

Mex cooking, and from the elegant fare called "Contemporary Southwestern," which is also renowned in town.

The dominant ingredient of New Mexican food is the chile, sometimes called a pepper but actually more closely related to the tomato plant than to the shrub that produces black pepper. Native to tropical America, chile has been grown in the state for at least four hundred years. Cooks make young, freshly harvested pods into a green sauce, or allow the same chiles to mature and dehydrate to form the basis for a red sauce.

The sauces may end up in virtually anything, from eggs to tuna salad, but they take center stage in many of the most popular local dishes. In *carne adovada* the red chile is cooked into the pork, not added later, and the same is true of New Mexican burritos, red and green enchiladas, *calabacitas* (a squash specialty), and stuffed *sopaipillas* (puffy fried bread). Chiles appear in other forms in *rellenos* (whole and oozing cheese) and *posole* (flecked in the hominy-like brew). Both red and green chile can be hot or mild, depending on the pods used, but neither will be bland.

If you want to learn how to prepare the local dishes at home, try the Santa Fe School of Cooking (116 West San Francisco in the Plaza Mercado, 505-983-4511). The school also has a shop for regional food products, which can be found as well at the Chile Shop (109 East Water, 505-983-6080) and the Coyote Cafe General Store (132 West Water, 505-982-2454). The most useful cookbooks are Huntley Dent's *The Feast of Santa Fe* (Simon & Schuster, 1985) and our own *Rancho de Chimayó Cookbook: The Traditional Cooking of New Mexico* (Harvard Common Press, 1991).

Even the best New Mexican cooking in Santa Fe is reasonably priced. It's difficult to spend more than $15 a person on a full meal, including drinks, dessert, and a tip, and easy to be satisfied for $8 or less. Other types of restaurants, except the bakeries, delis, and fast-food establishments, tend to be more expensive.

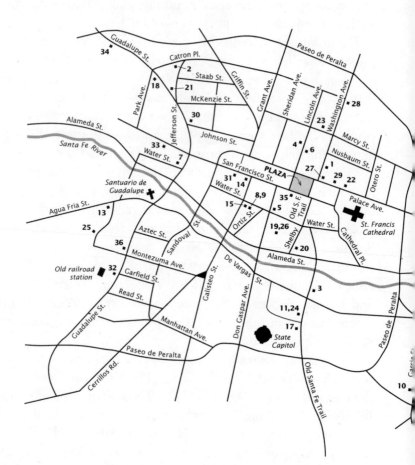

The price categories used in the restaurant descriptions are based on the cost of an entrée alone and are relative only to New Mexico. With just a few exceptions, the most expensive meals in town would be moderately priced by New York or international standards. "Expensive" in our reviews means that entrées cost over $18. Under $8 is "inexpensive," and in-between is "moderate." In the listings, standard abbreviations are used for credit cards.

Central Santa Fe Restaurants

1. The Anasazi Restaurant
2. Bagelmania
3. Bistro 315
4. Cafe Escalera
5. Cafe Pasqual's
6. Carlos' Gospel Cafe
7. Corn Dance Cafe
8. Coyote Cafe
9. Coyote Cantina
10. Downtown Subscription
11. Dragon Room Bar
12. El Farol
13. Encore Provence
14. Evangelo's
15. Galisteo News
16. Geronimo
17. Guadalupe Cafe
18. Il Primo Pizza
19. India Palace
20. Julian's
21. La Bell's
22. La Casa Seña Cantina
23. La Traviata
24. Pink Adobe
25. Pranzo Italian Grill
26. Real Burger
27. Roque's Carnitas
28. Santacafé
29. The Shed
30. Shohko Cafe
31. Tia Sophia's
32. Tomasita's Cafe
33. Vanessie of Santa Fe
34. Whistling Moon
35. F. W. Woolworth
36. Zia Diner

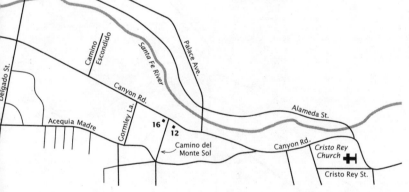

The recommendations are organized by types of cuisine, according to the dominant style of cooking in the restaurant. Some of the places blend in other influences as well, as we note, and many of them offer a selection of local dishes among the varied choices. Dress, along with service, is casual almost everywhere.

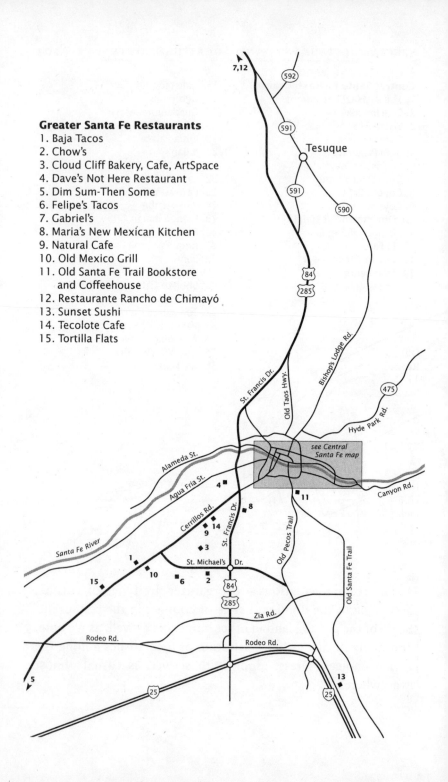

Greater Santa Fe Restaurants
1. Baja Tacos
2. Chow's
3. Cloud Cliff Bakery, Cafe, ArtSpace
4. Dave's Not Here Restaurant
5. Dim Sum-Then Some
6. Felipe's Tacos
7. Gabriel's
8. Maria's New Mexican Kitchen
9. Natural Cafe
10. Old Mexico Grill
11. Old Santa Fe Trail Bookstore and Coffeehouse
12. Restaurante Rancho de Chimayó
13. Sunset Sushi
14. Tecolote Cafe
15. Tortilla Flats

AMERICAN

Carlos' Gospel Cafe.
125 Lincoln, downtown in the central plaza of the First Interstate Bank building.
505-983-1841.
Closed Sunday.
Lunch only.
No reservations or credit cards.
Inexpensive.

A local favorite for a number of years, this free-spirited lunch cafe offers sandwiches, soups, and salads to the tune of its namesake songs. Carlos is justly famed for his Hangover Stew, a potent potato, corn, and green chile chowder with Monterey Jack cheese. If the vegetarian route won't do, try one of the stalwart sandwiches, which range in attitude from a Miles Standish (turkey breast with cranberries, cream cheese, and mayonnaise) to a Gertrude Stein (Swiss cheese, avocado, sprouts, and such) to a Jack Dempsey (roast beef, of course). Just leave room for the "Say Amen Desserts," baked fresh daily.

Dave's Not Here Restaurant.
1115 Hickox, a few blocks south of the intersection of Paseo de Peralta and St. Francis.
505-983-7060.
Closed Sunday.
Lunch and dinner.
No reservations or credit cards.
Inexpensive.

Dave sold this neighborhood cafe many years ago, but he left his designer hamburgers behind. Served with a choice of green chile, fried onions, guacamole, or almost anything you could want, the mountainous burgers abound with homey savor. So do the honest-to-goodness French fries, made from tasty real potatoes. The New Mexican side of the menu also excels, particularly the chiles rellenos, and the homemade desserts will satisfy anyone's sweet tooth. That's a lot of reasons to search the side streets for this unpretentious spot, where the checks are as small and friendly as the restaurant.

Natural Cafe.
1494 Cerrillos Road.
505-983-1411.
Closed Sunday and Saturday lunch.
Lunch and dinner.
Reservations advised for dinner.
Inexpensive to moderate.
MC, V.

Many Santa Fe restaurants offer vegetarian options these days, but the Natural Cafe led the way and still attracts the biggest crowd of non-carnivores in the city. Though chef-owner Lynn Walters serves fresh fish and free-range chicken, she made her name on dishes such as black bean soup, brown rice and steamed vegetables, grilled polenta with red chile sauce, and tempeh curry. Lynn's desserts are simply sumptuous, as you can learn on your own from her cookbook, *Cooking at the Natural Cafe in Santa Fe* (The Crossing Press, 1992).

Pink Adobe.
406 Old Santa Fe Trail, downtown.
505-983-7712.
Open daily for lunch and dinner.
Reservations necessary. Moderate for lunch, expensive for dinner.
Major credit cards.

The Pink, as locals call it, is such a famous local institution that it's often difficult to get in. For almost fifty years Rosalea Murphy's restaurant has offered the most intimate, cozy atmosphere of any spot in Santa Fe, plus a menu that's nicely balanced between New Mexico and New Orleans cooking. At lunch try the Gypsy Stew, the Creole Salad Bowl, the fried catfish, or one of the rotating daily specials. On the evening menu, the chicken enchiladas, the chile-smothered Steak Dunigan, and the apple pie with hard sauce are culinary masterpieces.

Tecolote Cafe.
1203 Cerrillos Road.
505-988-1362.
Closed Monday.
Breakfast and lunch.
No reservations and usually a waiting line in the morning.
Inexpensive. MC, V.

Despite its inauspicious appearance and location, Tecolote serves the best breakfast in town and, according to several national food writers, one of the best breakfasts in the country. Among the many treats, the kitchen makes the ultimate rendition of the Santa Fe omelet, a local specialty loaded with green chile and cheese. Other regional favorites include *huevos rancheros* (fried eggs on a corn tortilla covered with chile) and a breakfast burrito (scrambled eggs in a homemade flour tortilla topped with chile). Tecolote allows you to put together an excellent breakfast without chile, but that would be perverse behavior here.

Although lunch isn't quite up to the standards of the breakfast, it's still an outstanding value. The selection ranges from hearty soups to burgers, but is mainly New Mexican in tone. You won't do much better than the carne adovado burrito, brimming with red chile savor.

Vanessie of Santa Fe.
434 West San
Francisco.
505-982-9966.
Open daily. Dinner
only. Reservations
advised.
Moderate to
expensive.
Major credit cards.

You won't find a better all-around chop house in the Southwest. Vanessie keeps the menu selective, ensuring that the kitchen works only with the choicest ingredients. The result is superlative steaks and luscious lamb chops, along with solid versions of roasted chicken, grilled fish, and broiled lobster. The portions are Gargantuan, but that's no excuse to pass up the perfectly fried onion loaf or perhaps the cheesecake; one order of either will satisfy an entire table. The piano lounge, recommended below under "Bars," provides a congenial interlude before or after getting sumptuously stuffed.

Zia Diner.
326 South Guadalupe.
505-988-7008.
Open daily for lunch
and dinner.
No reservations.
Inexpensive to
moderate.
Major credit cards.

A diner with a difference, Zia's pays tribute to the diner tradition in both design and dishes but does it with attitude. The meat loaf comes with mashed potatoes, as you would hope and expect, but green chile and piñon nuts add sparkle to the taste. The eclectic menu hops from bountiful burgers to hummus with pita. If the chicken-fried steak sounds too weighty, go for one of the great dinner salads, especially the cobb or Caesar. It's hearty, unpretentious food, both tasty and well priced.

ASIAN

Chow's.
720 St. Michael's, in a
southside shopping
center.
505-471-7120.
Closed Sunday.
Lunch and dinner.
Reservations advised
for dinner. Inexpensive
at lunch, moderate at
dinner.
Major credit cards.

Average Chinese restaurants thrive in Santa Fe for some reason. Chow's is not great by San Francisco or New York standards, but it's exceptional for the town. The kitchen applies a light, bright touch to contemporary dishes, presenting snappy versions of firecracker dumplings, hot and sour green beans, ranch spring rolls, and eggplant in black bean sauce. Not everything succeeds, but you'll find plenty to praise, including the eager service.

Dim Sum–Then Some.
N.M. 14 at County Road 45, across from the Lone Butte General Store.
505-474-4111.
Lunch and dinner on Saturday, brunch on Sunday.
Reservations advised.
Moderate. MC, V.

Born in China but raised in the United States, Mimi Ho and Nai Smith opened their weekend dim sum restaurant more as a passion and a pastime than as an ordinary business. That's why the sisters ended up in such an unlikely location, in a former ranch house a dozen miles south of Santa Fe. On Saturday and Sunday they prepare a changing variety of dumplings and other small dishes, brought out of the kitchen on trays in the traditional fashion for your selection. The choices might include *bao* dumplings with bok choy, shrimp *su mai,* sesame noodles, soy-soaked cucumber salad, and vegetable egg rolls. Some of the tidbits are superb and all are intriguing.

India Palace.
227 Don Gaspar at Water, downtown.
505-986-5859.
Open daily for lunch and dinner.
Inexpensive at lunch, moderate at dinner.
Reservations advised for dinner.
Major credit cards.

Instantly popular with residents when it opened several years ago, the India Palace entices patrons with a blend of London culinary finesse and attentive service. The parking lot location fades from memory as soon as you step inside the cozy East Indian domain, filled with music and the savory smells coming from the tandoori oven. Start with one or two of the heavenly breads, particularly the onion *kulcha* and the spinach *paratha*. The lamb curries are always dependable, and so is the *sag paneer*, perhaps the best of the vegetarian choices. For a broad sampling from the menu, come at lunch for the brimming, bargain-priced buffet, also served at an equally good sister restaurant, the India House at 2501 Cerrillos (505-471-2651).

Shohko Cafe.
321 Johnson Street, downtown at the corner of Guadalupe. 505-983-7288. Closed Sunday in the winter. Lunch and dinner. Reservations advised except for the sushi bar, where they are not accepted. Moderate to expensive. Major credit cards.

Shohko Fukuda led Santa Fe into the world of international dining in the 1970s, when she challenged local tastes with her first small Japanese cafe. Now well established in a larger, full-scale restaurant that beautifully blends Oriental and Southwestern decor, Shohko continues to shine. Some Santa Feans like to crowd into the long, lively sushi bar, where the quality ranges from excellent to satisfactory depending on the fish available. Others prefer table seating and ordering from the menu, which features traditional Japanese dishes, some Chinese specialties, and Shohko's singular nod to New Mexican flavors, her green-chile tempura.

Sunset Sushi.
Old Las Vegas Highway, which runs east from Old Pecos Trail parallel to I-25. 505-982-6705. Closed Sunday. Lunch and dinner. No reservations. Moderate. Major credit cards.

A part of the appeal here is the place, a tiny sushi counter smack in the middle of the Sunset General Store, one of the brashest and most enterprising businesses in Santa Fe. From Seoul, South Korea, via California, former accountant Allen Jung took over a conventional convenience store on the edge of town and transformed it into an amazing emporium, offering everything from velvet paintings to Chinese take-out, Asian spices to doughnuts, dog food to fine wines. In the midst of the madness, the self-described "working-crazy guy" sells excellent sushi. Try the lunch combo, which on our last visit included miso soup and delectable morsels of octopus, mackerel, tuna, and shrimp.

BAKERIES, COFFEEHOUSES, AND DELIS

Bagelmania.
420 Catron, off Guadalupe near downtown. 505-982-8900. Open daily. Breakfast and lunch. No reservations. Inexpensive. MC, V.

The deli slogan asks the question, "If a seagull flies over the sea, what flies over the bay?" The bakers in residence provide the answer, offering some of the best bagels in the Southwest, along with bialys, muffins, pies, and more. The other cooks in the kitchen produce oozing omelets, mountainous meat sandwiches, and smoky fish platters. Almost anything you can get in a New

York deli, in fact, you can get here, from lox to pastrami. Even the mood is Manhattan—except much sunnier.

Cloud Cliff Bakery, Cafe, ArtSpace.
1805 Second Street.
505-983-6254.
Open daily. Breakfast and lunch weekdays, brunch on weekends. No reservations. Inexpensive. Major credit cards.

Not only an "ArtSpace" itself, displaying good local work, Cloud Cliff serves as the neighborhood center for Santa Fe's new SoHo, the "Crossing" art district. Away from the high rents downtown and on Canyon Road, a low-tech industrial area on Second Street, between Cerrillos Road and St. Francis Drive, has become a haven for artists' studios and adventuresome galleries. Cloud Cliff provides communal and culinary succor for the neighborhood. At breakfast the chile-and-cheese home fries, omelets, and other treats come with a basket of breads from the bakery, which occupies half the building. The lunch specials roam the creative countryside of down-home cooking, pairing a turkey meat loaf with mashed potatoes or a spinach burrito with black beans and rice. It's all tasty, if not quite as transcendental as the milieu.

Downtown Subscription.
376 Garcia, one block off Canyon Road.
505-983-3085.
Open daily. Breakfast and lunch. No reservations or credit cards. Inexpensive.

It's not exactly downtown, but it's definitely a place that locals subscribe to. Santa Feans come to the combination newsstand and coffee bar to get away from tourists, to talk about current events, to eavesdrop on one another, even to have an espresso, cappuccino, or quiche. Magazine racks line the walls, offering information and ideas to inspire any kind of conversation.

Galisteo News.
201 Galisteo.
505-984-1316.
Open daily. Breakfast and lunch.
No reservations or credit cards. Inexpensive.

On a busy downtown corner, Galisteo News is the spot to stop and stare at Santa Fe. Grab a table outside, pick up a latte inside, and laze away part of the day watching the people go by. The menu is limited and nothing's memorable, but the sights take up the slack.

Old Santa Fe Trail Bookstore and Coffeehouse.
613 Old Santa Fe Trail.
505-988-8878.
Open daily. Breakfast, lunch and dinner on Monday through Saturday; brunch Sunday.
No reservations.
Inexpensive.
Major credit cards.

The literati gather here for good coffee and cafe cuisine, served in a felicitous bookstore setting. The selections are simple though often scrumptious. Try the New Mexican specialties for local flavor, or take a break from the B.L.T. rut with a P.B.T., a portobello, basil, and tomato sandwich. If you time your visit with one of the poetry readings or performances, you can share your meal with the muses.

BARS

Coyote Cantina.
132 West Water, downtown.
505-983-1615.
Open daily from April to October. Lunch and dinner.
No reservations.
Food inexpensive to moderate.
Major credit cards.

In the warmer months of the year, the open-air rooftop bar of the Coyote Cafe offers festive sanctuary from the busy streets below. Sample specialty drinks such as "la ultima" margarita, made with Tesoro tequila, or the Brazilian Daiquiri, a blend of rums flavored with fresh pineapple and Mexican vanilla beans. The talented kitchen produces on its promise of "fiery and fun food," turning out fish tacos, Cuban sandwiches, vegetarian tamales, seafood pastas, and turkey *mole*, among other delights.

Dragon Room Bar.
406 Old Santa Fe Trail, downtown.
505-983-7712.
Major credit cards.

A few years ago, an international edition of *Newsweek* rated the Dragon Room as one of the world's best bars, joining New York's "21" Club as the only two U.S. establishments on the list. It feels sometimes like the whole world is here, jostling for a table, the complimentary popcorn, and the wayward hope of a drink. Come early or late for better odds on any or all. A part of the popular Pink Adobe restaurant, the bar sometimes slows down after dinner, when you might want to try the French Chocolate Coffee—cognac, Godiva chocolate liqueur, crème de cacao, coffee, and whipped cream.

El Farol.
808 Canyon Road.
505-983-9912.
Open daily. Lunch and
dinner.
Reservations advised
for dinner. Food
moderate to
expensive.
Major credit cards.

Long a Canyon Road hangout for artists and assorted bohemians, El Farol exudes local funk, the quality now called "Santa Fe Style" in its more refined versions. Go for a drink and the almost nightly music, if you can squeeze into the jam-packed bar, but be a little wary about the food. A meal off the Spanish tapas menu can get costly, relative to the quality, though all of the appetizer dishes seem reasonably priced on their own. When you're truly hungry, go directly to the paella.

Evangelo's.
200 West San
Francisco, downtown.
505-982-9014.
Open daily.

A colorful local dive until the tourism boom of the 1980s, this downtown bar got dressed up a bit—but not too much—and became a rendezvous for rock-and-rollers, yuppies, beer lovers, and other street folk. It's still the place in town if you want to *drink,* and now you can also carouse with the crowd.

**La Casa Seña
Cantina.** 125 East
Palace, downtown in
Seña Plaza.
505-988-9232.
Open daily. Dinner
only. No reservations.
Bar food inexpensive
to moderate.
Major credit cards.

Music may soothe the savage in beasts, but cabaret rouses the ardor in the audiences at this upscale cantina. The servers are also singers, and they belt out Broadway show tunes as they work. The joyful mood spills over to the patrons, encouraging them to order more chicken wings, nachos, quesadillas, and other items from the bar menu.

Vanessie of Santa Fe.
434 West San
Francisco.
505-982-9966.
Open daily. Dinner
only. Bar food
inexpensive to
moderate.
Major credit cards.

Located in the previously recommended restaurant of the same name, this is the most popular piano bar in town. From the early evening until late, Doug Montgomery, Charles Tichenor, or another keyboard master plays with cosmopolitan pizzazz. If you don't need a full dinner, you can satisfy yourself easily from the bar menu, which allows you to combine light dining with some prodigious entertainment.

CONTEMPORARY SOUTHWESTERN

The Anasazi Restaurant.
113 Washington, downtown in the Inn of the Anasazi.
505-988-3030.
Open daily. Breakfast, lunch, and dinner.
Reservations advised, especially for dinner.
Moderate for breakfast and lunch, expensive for dinner.
Major credit cards.

Far more than a hotel dining room, the restaurant at the Inn of the Anasazi aspires to be the best in the city. It's too new to know whether the kitchen can reach that lofty goal, or even sustain the ambition, but the staff is certainly earnest in its efforts.

The Anasazi once described its cooking as "innovative interpretations of Southwestern cuisine honoring foods of the Earth from the American Indian, foods of the soul from Northern New Mexico and foods of substance from the American cowboy." All that plus French techniques, Italian pestos, a trace of Thai, and fusion dishes such as tortilla soup with pot stickers. Earnest and eager too.

The founding chef, Peter Zimmer, left shortly before our press deadline, but his style is likely to last. At lunch, the menu might offer swordfish crusted with red and blue corn tortillas with a tropical BBQ sauce, a grilled buffalo burger, and buttermilk-and-pecan-fried chicken salad. In the evening look for heavier entrées such as a dry-rubbed beef tenderloin with white-cheddar mashed potatoes as well as a few meatless dishes, maybe a vegetable and rice relleno with a tamarind orange pesto, salsa, and Ibarra chocolate. The cooking won numerous awards during Zimmer's tenure and should continue to in the future.

Cafe Pasqual's.
121 Don Gaspar, downtown.
505-983-9340.
Open daily. Breakfast, lunch, and dinner.
Reservations at dinner only. Moderate for breakfast and lunch, expensive for dinner.
Major credit cards.

Talented chef-owner Katherine Kagel has roamed the globe for culinary influences during her many years at Pasqual's, but seems to be settling comfortably now into a style that's primarily Southwestern and Mexican. She still makes dinner dishes with Asian flavors, such as Sauteed Shrimp with Lemongrass-Coconut Sauce, and a Tuscan Insalata de Panzanella, though the thrust of the menu these days is on regional fare. In the evening you might find Pan-Roasted Chimayó Chile-Rubbed Salmon Filet, Yucatecan Pollo Pibil, or Squash and Red Onion Enchilada.

The kitchen usually performs well at dinner, but the small, festive restaurant really shines in the natural light of the daytime. Our favorite meal is breakfast, so good that it almost always attracts a waiting line. Try the breakfast quesadillas, filled with scrambled eggs, guacamole, and Monterey Jack cheese, or the unusual corned beef hash, made with bite-size pieces of brisket on top of home fries. Other good options include chorizo burritos, whole wheat pancakes, and huevos rancheros. In combo with the colorful tile walls and local murals, the breakfast will brighten any day.

Coyote Cafe.
132 West Water, downtown.
505-983-1615.
Open daily.
Reservations necessary, sometimes well in advance.
Moderate for lunch, expensive for dinner.
Major credit cards.

Famous among food followers and fashionable in all circles, the Coyote Cafe put nouvelle Southwestern cuisine on the national map. Chef-owner Mark Miller and executive chef Mark Kiffin set out to dazzle with both their dishes and decor and they seldom fail.

Also a major cookbook author and the mastermind behind newer restaurants in Austin, Las Vegas, and Washington, D.C., Miller developed his personal style using historical ingredients of the region in a range of contemporary preparations. The kitchen carries out the approach skillfully in fare such as *huitlacoche* tamales, red chile onion rings, corn cakes with chipotle shrimp, and cowboy steaks.

The staff—much more genial and efficient than in the early years—serves three courses of selections at dinner in an animated dining room accented with colorful folk art, cowhide chairs, and other insignia of Southwest chic. You can eat lighter but still lively at lunch, offered daily during the summer and on weekends the rest of the year, or in the previously reviewed Coyote Cantina.

Geronimo.
724 Canyon Road.
505-982-1500.
Open daily. Lunch and
dinner.
Reservations advised.
Moderate for lunch,
expensive for dinner.
Major credit cards.

Located in the historic Borrego House on Canyon Road, described in Chapter 4, Geronimo brings the lofty realm of creative cuisine back down to earth. While the Anasazi, Coyote, and Santacafé like to inspire awe, trumpeting you to your table and through a meal, Geronimo matches their culinary results with quiet dignity and relaxed service. You leave feeling that the staff was honored to have you for dinner rather than expecting it to be the other way around.

Chef Gina Ziluca's lunch and dinner menus shift with the seasons. In the winter, the crispy rellenos appetizer might ooze goat cheese, and in the spring, a roasted chicken *mole*. When they're offered, start with the littleneck clams baked with bacon, garlic, chipotle chile, and vermouth. Evening entrées could include a pan-fried chicken breast, braised with roasted peppers and extra virgin olive oil, or trout that's lightly smoked and then grilled. One night we had a superlative steak, perhaps the best of our lives, served with a bourbon cream sauce and rosemary-flavored roasted potatoes. Don't necessarily expect such a sublime meal, but when Ziluca is cooking you should always be ready for the possibility.

Santacafé.
231 Washington,
downtown.
505-984-1788.
Open daily.
Lunch and dinner.
Reservations
necessary. Lunch
moderate, dinner
expensive. MC, V.

Despite sometimes pretentious service and a long-standing difficulty in keeping an executive chef, the award-winning Santacafé enthralls almost everyone. We think the fame is a little overblown, but the kitchen does tackle challenging and tantalizing dishes with considerable success.

Located in the 200-year-old Padre Gallegos House, the restaurant seats you in sleekly simple interior rooms or, during the summer rush, in a lovely courtyard. The menu changes with the seasons but always balances flavors from the

Southwest and Asia. When it's offered, opt for the signature appetizer, smoked pheasant spring rolls with a chile dipping sauce. Main course selections at lunch might include cilantro-chicken ravioli and flash-fried calamari. At dinner, look for options such as a crispy duck breast with hoisin sauce or a grilled filet mignon with green-chile mashed potatoes, a dish once featured on the cover of *Bon Appétit*.

FAST FOOD

Baja Tacos.
2621 Cerrillos Road.
505-471-8762.
Open daily. Breakfast, lunch, and dinner.
Inexpensive.
No credit cards.

Everybody's favorite local taco stand sits in the middle of Santa Fe's main commercial drag, Cerrillos Road. The New Mexican and Mexican menu ranges broadly, but the tacos themselves are a good place to start. Vegetarians get a choice of bean or tofu versions, while meateaters may favor the well-seasoned ground-beef filling. The hustling kitchen staff prepares all the food fresh while you watch.

Il Primo Pizza.
234 North Guadalupe, near downtown.
505-988-2007.
Open daily. Lunch on weekdays, dinner nightly. No reservations or credit cards.
Inexpensive to moderate.

Also known sometimes as El Primo in this Spanish-speaking town, Il Primo makes the best traditional-style pizza in Santa Fe. Go local and try green chile as one of the toppings, all full of flavor. You can eat the pizza hot on the spot, but most people take it out or have it delivered.

La Bell's.
301 Jefferson, off North Guadalupe, near downtown.
505-986-8223.
Closed Sunday.
Breakfast and lunch.
No reservations or credit cards.
Inexpensive.

One of the best cooks in Santa Fe, Bell Mondragón gave up her popular Maria Ysabel Restaurant a few years ago because of the long hours. Now she serves some of the same food in a simpler manner at a former Taco Bell. Her carne adovada and *chicharrones* are as good as ever, and new treats such as Frito pies and breakfast burritos reach similar levels of perfection.

Real Burger.
227 Don Gaspar, downtown.
505-988-3717.
Closed Sunday.
Breakfast and lunch.
No reservations or credit cards.
Inexpensive.

The burgers may be better at Bert's Burger Bowl (235 North Guadalupe) and the hot dogs certainly are superior at Chicago Dog Express (600 Cerrillos Road), but when you're hungry for either in the center of downtown, Real Burger is real satisfying. Other specialties include fajitas, enchiladas, and a meaty bowl of green chile. If you can't get a table inside the cramped, parking-lot cafe, take your meal out to the patio.

Roque's Carnitas.
Corner of Palace and Washington, downtown. No phone, regular hours, reservations, or credit cards. Inexpensive.

Simply not to be missed. The food at this small street stand is so good that Jane and Michael Stern raved about it for pages in *Gourmet*. All you can get, and all you want, are the world-class *carnitas*, grilled bite-size pieces of marinated beef or chicken served in a brimming flour tortilla with grilled green chiles and onions. Roque Garcia and his partner Mona Cavalli set up their stand at lunchtime most days except Sunday from April to October, *mas o menos*. Eat your treat on the plaza, just across the street.

F. W. Woolworth.
58 East San Francisco, downtown.
505-982-1062.
Open daily. Frito pies offered for lunch. No reservations or credit

About the only truly local business left on the plaza, the Woolworth department store makes a mean Frito pie. Have a seat at the old-fashioned lunch counter for a nostalgia trip, or just grab your snack from the street-front take-out window, built for quick service when the pies became so popular years ago.

FRENCH

Bistro 315.
315 Old Santa Fe Trail, downtown.
505-986-9190.
Open daily for lunch and dinner.
Reservations advised.
Moderate.
Major credit cards.

Tiny as a Rocky Mountain tick, this new cafe gets crowded quick. The draw is classic bistro cooking, featuring simple, timeless dishes that thrive on perfect execution in the kitchen. The menu changes daily, but you can count on main courses such as flawless roasted chicken and authentic steak *frites*. The appetizers might include caviar and scallion blinis, gazpacho, and an artichoke-and-arugula salad. We once feasted at lunch on an oxtail soup, so heady and stocky that we skipped dinner for fear of diluting the lingering taste.

Encore Provence.
548 Agua Fria, just outside downtown.
505-983-7470.
Closed Sunday. Dinner only.
Reservations necessary.
Major credit cards.

After years of mediocre French restaurants, Santa Fe finally got a true Gallic star in 1992. Chef-owner Patrick Benrezkellah combines the flavors of his native country and sterling ingredients with skills honed under Michelin-honored chef Guy Savoy. The result is the most consistent of the city's top restaurants, always excellent, though less touted than its few peers.

Sample at least one of the fish preparations, Benrezkellah's favorites, but don't overlook the sweetbreads, served with a reduction sauce that sends you home in bliss. While you can eat richly at Encore Provence, the emphasis is on light sauces, herb seasonings, and olive oil rather than butter. The setting matches the food in finesse, providing romantic intimacy in several small rooms of a converted home near downtown. Expensive and worth it.

ITALIAN

Julian's.
221 Shelby, downtown.
505-988-2355.
Open daily. Lunch in the summer, dinner year-round.
Reservations advised for dinner. Moderate to expensive.
Major credit cards.

Housed in the former Periscope, Santa Fe's first sophisticated restaurant, Julian's captures your attention first with atmosphere. The dining room sparkles with élan, combining casual Southwestern charm with an edge of cosmopolitan art-deco verve.

The refined regional Italian cooking usually sustains the bright mood. At lunch, look for light dishes, perhaps minestrone, a selection of salads, and a range of pastas. The seasonal dinner menu bumps up the heft and elegance. You might find Rotellini di Melanzana (baked eggplant stuffed with several cheeses), Petto di Pollo in Agro Dolci (boneless chicken breast sautéed with raisins, shallots, and capers in a sweet-and-sour sauce), or Costoletta di Vitello alla Piedmontese (grilled veal chop with a demiglace sauce).

Pranzo Italian Grill.
540 Montezuma at
Sanbusco Center.
505-984-2645.
Open daily for lunch
and dinner.
Reservations advised.
Moderate.
Major credit cards.

A sister of Albuquerque's polished Scalo restaurant, Pranzo brings good Italian cooking out of the affected realm it sometimes inhabits in Santa Fe. In an animated environment accented with contemporary art, mellow jazz, and an open grill, the popular cafe serves affordable food with plenty of panache. The lunch menu emphasizes creative pizzas, salads, and soups—try the *ribollita,* a great sausage soup. Many of the same items reappear at dinner, along with a larger selection of pastas and entrées. We often opt for the spinach and ricotta ravioli in a sage cream sauce or the grilled New Mexico lamb chops.

In warm weather, request a table on the second-floor terrace, which overlooks downtown and the Sangre de Cristo Mountains. If you can't get a table anywhere, you can find similar pizzas in the more casual Il Vicino on West San Francisco, under the same ownership.

MEDITERRANEAN

Cafe Escalera.
130 Lincoln, second
floor, downtown.
505-989-8188.
Closed Sunday and for
lunch on Saturday.
Lunch and dinner.
Reservations
necessary. Lunch
moderate, dinner
expensive. MC, V.

Opened in the late summer of 1991, Cafe
Escalera quickly jumped to the forefront of
Santa Fe restaurants and it continues to win
raves, even from Julia Child on a recent visit.
Chef David Tanis displays a rare mastery of elemental cooking, using superlative ingredients in
straightforward, subtle dishes that allow the
ingredients to shine.

The kitchen gets its inspiration from around
the world, but Mediterranean influences dominate the changing menu, which might offer
options such as French lentil salad and new fin-
gerling potatoes bathed in olive oil, chicken
saltimbocca, or fresh tuna scented with Moroc-
can spices. You aren't likely to fault any of the
preparations, always careful and usually compelling. The sleek dining room and attached bar
can be noisy when they are full—frequently the
case.

Whistling Moon.
402 North Guadalupe,
near downtown.
505-983-3093.
Open daily for
breakfast, lunch, and
dinner.
No reservations or
credit cards.
Inexpensive.

There's not a better value for this kind of cooking in the whole Southwest. Tracy Ritter, one of
the former executive chefs at Santacafé, and her
partner Gabriel Hakman created the ultimate
back-to-basics Mediterranean bistro, heavy on
the flavor and light on the tab.

The menu ranges through the entire region,
from Spain to Turkey, from Morocco to Egypt.
For breakfast, try the Tunisian eggs baked with
sausage, peppers, and eggplant, or one of the
paninis from Italy, also served at lunch and dinner. In the evening, you have a choice of a dozen
tapas and *mezze* for starters or light meals, plus
larger servings of salads, pita sandwiches, pizzas, calzones, and pastas. It's all authentic and
luscious as well.

MEXICAN

Felipe's Tacos.
1711 Llano Street, just off St. Michael's in St. Michael's Village.
505-473-9397.
Closed Sunday. Lunch and early dinners until 7:00 P.M.
No reservations or credit cards.
Inexpensive.

True to the border traditions of northern Mexico, Felipe Martínez offers simple but zestful food that you flavor to your own taste at a salsa bar. The soft tacos, made with fresh corn tortillas, brim with grilled marinated chicken or steak. The melt-in-your-mouth quesadillas and bulging burritos feature the same charbroiled meats, or for a vegetarian meal, just cheese, guacamole, and beans. The only deviation from the authentic in the small shopping-center cafe is an emphasis on healthy preparations, using skinless chicken, lean beef, and no lard.

Gabriel's.
U.S. 84/285, north of Santa Fe.
505-455-7000.
Open daily for lunch and dinner.
Reservations advised.
Moderate.
Major credit cards.

Reward yourself for the short drive to Gabriel's, a dozen miles north of town, with a magnificent margarita and an order of the guacamole, made at the table in a stone *metate* with your choice of seasonings. Follow that with the crispy and spicy pork carnitas, the overflowing fish tacos, or the sesame-coated chicken *mole*. If your main course doesn't come with the wonderful *charra*-style beans, get some on the side. The kitchen usually excels with these hearty Mexican dishes, though the menu offers other options as well, from New Mexican favorites to fajitas-style grilled vegetables.

Old Mexico Grill.
2434 Cerrillos Road, in College Plaza South.
505-473-0338.
Open daily. Lunch Monday through Friday, dinner nightly.
No reservations.
Moderate.
Major credit cards.

As popular among locals as any place in town, the Old Mexico Grill greets you with fiesta exuberance that belies its shopping-center setting. The restaurant is faithful enough to Mexican traditions to use the term *arracheras* instead of "fajitas" but contemporary enough to do a vegetarian version as well as the beef original.

The open grill produces many of the best items on the menu, from the *carne asada* to the salmon fillets. If you're looking for a little more complexity, try the paella Mexicana or the mole poblano. All the cooking is as snappy and spirited as the mood.

NATIVE AMERICAN

Corn Dance Cafe.
409 West Water,
downtown.
505-986-1662.
Closed Tuesday in the
winter. Lunch and
dinner. Reservations
advised for dinner.
Moderate to
expensive.
Major credit cards.

Loretta Barrett Oden, the Potawatomi Indian
proprietress, pays tribute to Native American
tastes in an innovative way at her cheerful cafe.
Using ingredients indigenous to the continent—
chiles, beans, corn, squash, venison, wild turkey,
and more—she creates contemporary dishes
that dance on the tongue.

Start with the Kick Ass Buffalo Chile or one
of the Little Big Pies, flatbread topped with a
melange of meat or vegetables. The changing
entrées might include Great Plains Fire Broiled
Trout with Wild Rice Johnnycakes, Houma
Barbeque Shrimp, and Sautéed Pueblo Rabbit.
Whatever you order, you can count on an adventuresome meal.

NEW MEXICAN

Guadalupe Cafe.
422 Old Santa Fe Trail,
downtown.
505-982-9762.
Closed Monday.
Breakfast, lunch, and
dinner.
No reservations.
Inexpensive to
moderate. MC, V.

A local favorite for many years, the Guadalupe
Cafe serves burgers, salads, and other American
standards, but the kitchen's forte is regional
cooking. Tradition shines in dishes such as the
blue corn cheese enchiladas with red chile and
beans, while creativity often comes to the fore in
daily specials based on New Mexican ingredients. Breakfast is always outstanding, and so is
the Adobe Pie served later in the day at lunch
and dinner. You leave any meal full and satisfied, with scarcely a wince from your wallet.

**Maria's New Mexican
Kitchen.**
555 West Cordova,
near St. Francis Drive.
505-983-7929.
Open daily for lunch
and dinner.
Reservations advised.
Inexpensive to
moderate.
Major credit cards.

A Santa Fe institution since the 1950s, Maria's
can't be beat for tequilas and tamales, a compelling combo for us. Toast owner Al Lucero in
the bar before dinner with one of his fifty
mighty margaritas, and then salute the kitchen
over a plate of the distinctive cheese and piñon
tamales. If you need meat, go for the sizzling
fajitas or the tender carne adovada, served with
freshly made tortillas. The mariachi music in the
summer adds a festive note to any dinner.

Restaurante Rancho de Chimayó.
N.M. 503, Chimayó.
505-984-2100 from
Santa Fe or 505-351-
4444.
Closed Monday in the
winter. Lunch and
dinner.
Reservations
necessary.
Moderate.
Major credit cards.

For the quintessential New Mexico dining experience, head to the village of Chimayó, about 25 miles north of Santa Fe. The drive is stunning, particularly at sunset, when the color of the sky is likely to match the red chile *ristras* (strings) hanging from the roof of the old adobe hacienda that houses the Restaurante Rancho de Chimayó.

Our favorite among the traditional dishes is the carne adovada, a heady blend of pork and red chile, which can be ordered as an entrée separately, on a spicy combination plate, or chopped in a burrito. Milder choices include the chicken flautas, the best around, and the sopaipilla relleno, a large sopaipilla stuffed with meat, beans, and chile and topped with more chile and cheese. Leave room for the flan, one of creamiest versions of the dessert in the world.

The Shed.
113 1/2 East Palace,
downtown.
505-982-9030.
Closed Sunday. Lunch
Monday through
Saturday, dinner
Thursday through
Saturday. Reservations
advised for dinner.
Inexpensive to
moderate.
No credit cards.

A venerable local institution, The Shed gets packed quickly at lunch. The line starts forming by 11:30 on most days, but the wait is usually short and pleasant in the courtyard of the restaurant's rambling downtown hacienda.

Start with one of the daily soup specials, listed on a blackboard in each of the charming dining rooms, and finish with a dessert from the same roster. On the regular menu, don't look further for a main course than the blue corn enchiladas with red chile, a classic rendition of the traditional dish. Order them with beans and *posole*, a plate that reaches a peak of perfection.

Tia Sophia's.
210 West San
Francisco, downtown.
505-983-9880.
Open daily for
breakfast and lunch.
No reservations.
Inexpensive.
Major credit cards.

Don't leave town without savoring a breakfast burrito at Tia Sophia's. The kitchen wraps a large flour tortilla around a heavenly mixture of hash browns and bacon, topping it all with chile and cheese. If you blanch at the bacon, you can get beans instead without losing much of the flavor. The daily specials also excel, both at breakfast and lunch. The menu bears a warning that the downtown cafe isn't responsible for "too hot chile," a sure sign that nothing will be bland.

Tomasita's Cafe.
500 South Guadalupe, downtown in the old railyard.
505-983-5721.
Closed Sunday.
No reservations.
Inexpensive to moderate. MC, V.

An anomaly in the restaurant world, Tomasita's is a mass-production food factory with a reliable and first-rate product. Many years ago, when it was a small neighborhood operation, the owners decided to limit their menu to a few New Mexican dishes. Specialization led to a perfection still maintained in much larger, more trendy surroundings.

Try the chiles rellenos, the daily special, or a combination plate. Everything satisfies, in quantity as well as quality, and the service is fast and friendly once you are seated. The waiting line gets long in the thick of the lunch and dinner rush, but the bustling bar keeps you happy in the interim.

Tortilla Flats.
3139 Cerrillos Road.
505-471-8685.
Open daily for breakfast, lunch, and dinner.
No reservations.
Inexpensive to moderate. MC, V.

The *New York Times* once touted Tortilla Flats as the top New Mexican restaurant in Santa Fe and it's been full ever since. The draw is a modestly innovative interpretation of local dishes, offering twists that go beyond the traditional without getting flashy. Burritos come stuffed with beef brisket instead of the usual pork, black beans replace pintos, and quesadillas feature carrots and broccoli along with the cheese. The flavors are refreshing, though not as superior as the big-city novices said.

CHAPTER NINE

Distinctive Galleries and Shops

NEW MEXICO artists and artisans are producing more fine work today than at any other time in the area's long history. Browsing through their creations at Santa Fe galleries and shops is both delightful and enlightening, as important in absorbing the city's heritage as walks along old, adobe-lined streets.

The abundance and quality of current work has stimulated a major gallery boom. In the past two decades the number of shops offering original art and handcrafted products has leaped from a handful to well over a hundred. Today there are considerably more galleries per capita in Santa Fe than in New York City.

The downside to the shopping situation is the recent explosion of schlock souvenir stores and nationally franchised boutiques, the kinds of tourist businesses that often drown the special, distinctive character of popular destinations all across the globe. These shops have sprouted throughout downtown, making something of a theme park out of Santa Fe from the perspective of many long-term residents.

Savvy shoppers and browsers can find plenty of wonderful Southwestern products to buy or just admire, but you have to be choosy about where you look. The following is a selective list of places that carry high-quality handmade or artist-designed work. Most of them represent local artists and artisans, but some, as noted, feature work from elsewhere. Shops come and go, of course, and also change personalities, so a diligent prober will always discover new delights and erstwhile disappointments.

People who are unfamiliar with the unique cultural heritage of the area should consult Chapters 1 through 3, or other appropriate sources, before shopping. The earlier chapters provide a basic orientation to the region's Indian, Spanish, and Anglo artistic traditions and mention some of the prominent artists in each.

Galleries and shops are generally open from 10:00 to 5:00 or 6:00. Many close on Sunday and some also close on Monday during the winter.

Indian Art and Crafts

Joshua Baer & Company. 116 1/2 East Palace, downtown (505-988-8944). Classic American Indian art.

Case Trading Post. 704 Camino Lejo, in the Wheelwright Museum of the American Indian (505-982-4636). Wide range of current work, plus some historical pieces.

Channing Gallery. 53 Old Santa Fe Trail (upstairs), on the plaza (505-988-1078). Broad selection of fine art and ethnographic material.

Cristof's. 106 West San Francisco, downtown (505-988-9881). Navajo rugs, sand paintings, jewelry.

Andrea Fisher Fine Pottery. 211 West San Francisco, downtown (505-986-1234). Strong selection of Pueblo pottery, including pieces from Maria Martínez and other masters.

Kania-Ferrin Gallery. 662 Canyon Road (505-982-8767). Antique Indian art.

Morning Star Gallery. 513 Canyon Road (505-982-8187). Mainly historical pieces. Plains tribes especially well represented.

Robert F. Nichols. 419 Canyon Road (505-982-2145). Pueblo pottery.

Packard's Indian Trading Company. 61 Old Santa Fe Trail, on the plaza (505-983-9241). Wide range of current work. Excellent quality relative to price.

Palace of the Governor's Museum Shop, on the plaza (505-982-3016). Small selection of Pueblo pottery and jewelry.

James Reid. 114 East Palace, downtown (505-988-1147). Navajo jewelry and concha belts.

Textile Arts. 1571 Upper Canyon Road (505-983-9780). Museum-quality textiles selected by Mary Hunt Kahlenberg. Call for an appointment.

Hispanic Art and Crafts

Artesanos Imports. 222 Galisteo, downtown (505-983-5563), and 1414 Maclovia, off Cerrillos Road (471-8020). Mexican furnishings and crafts.

Centinela Traditional Arts. Box 4, Centinela Ranch, on N.M. 76, Chimayó (505-351-2180). Top-quality Rio Grande weavings, from Lisa and Irvin Trujillo and others.

Claiborne Gallery. 558 Canyon Road (505-982-8019). Spanish Colonial furnishings and religious art.

Eclectica. 112 West San Francisco in the Plaza Mercado (505-988-3326). As the name says, an eclectic collection of items, mainly from Mexico.

Foreign Traders. 202 Galisteo, downtown (505-983-6441). Excellent selection of imported folk art and Mexican furnishings.

Jackalope. 2820 Cerrillos Road (505-471-8539). Extensive market for Mexican imports, mainly inexpensive items.

Davis Mather Folk Art Gallery. 141 Lincoln, downtown (505-983-1660). Mexican and New Mexican folk art.

Montez Gallery. 125 East Palace in Seña Plaza, downtown (505-982-1828). High-quality New Mexican folk art and

Spanish Colonial collectibles in two different Seña Plaza locations.

Ortega's Galeria (505-351-2288) and **Weaving Shop** (505-351-4215). N.M. 76, Chimayó. The largest selection of Rio Grande weavings from the area plus other local crafts and folk art.

que tenga Bueno Mano. P.O. Box 762 (505-982-2912). Stunning collection of Latin American folk art and jewelry, assembled by Patricia LaFarge. By appointment only.

Contemporary and Traditional Fine Art

A.O.I. Gallery. 634 Canyon Road (505-982-3456). Contemporary paintings and fine photography by local and international artists.

Bellas Artes. 653 Canyon Road (505-983-2745). Contemporary and venerable art in a variety of styles.

Betts Gallery. 123 Grant, downtown (505-988-4499). Passionate and playful work by a broad range of artists.

Laura Carpenter Fine Art. 309 Read, off Guadalupe (505-986-9090). Sophisticated art in several media, much of it by nationally recognized artists.

Cline Fine Art Gallery. 526 Canyon Road (505-982-5328). A diverse collection featuring representational paintings.

Copeland Rutherford Fine Art. 403 Canyon Road (505-983-1588). Vibrant variety of work by good but often under-recognized area artists.

Linda Durham Contemporary Art. Galisteo (505-466-6600). Primarily abstract painting and photography by nationally known New Mexican artists; an excellent track record for supporting adventuresome new work. By appointment only in the village of Galisteo, about twenty miles south of Santa Fe.

Glenn Green Galleries. 50 East San Francisco, downtown (505-988-4168). Exclusive representative for the late Allan Houser.

Hand Graphics. 418 Montezuma, off Guadalupe (505-988-1241). The town's premier print gallery and atelier.

Horwitch LewAllen Gallery. 129 West Palace, downtown (505-988-8997). A merger of two of the top galleries in town, the new operation represents a broad range of talented Southwestern artists. Lots of delightful imagery.

Charlotte Jackson Fine Art. 123 East Marcy, downtown (505-989-8688). Striking abstract work.

Edith Lambert Gallery. 707 Canyon Road (505-984-2783). Fascinating selection of solid work, much of it with a Southwestern flavor.

Allene Lapides Gallery. 217 Johnson, downtown (505-984-0191). Primarily abstract painting and sculpture by well-established artists. Always exciting.

Nedra Matteucci's Fenn Galleries. 1075 Paseo de Peralta (505-982-4631). Paintings by the Founders of the Taos and Santa Fe art colonies and other artists working in similar styles.

Nedra Matteucci Fine Art. 555 Canyon Road (505-983-2731). Representational work by established and emerging artists.

Ernesto Mayans. 601 Canyon Road (505-983-8068). Painting, prints, and photography.

The Munson Gallery. 225 Canyon Road (505-983-1657). Work in a variety of media, mainly by contemporary realists from the Southwest.

Leslie Muth Gallery. 225 East De Vargas, downtown (505-989-4620). Provocative pieces by outsider and intuitive artists.

Niman Fine Art. 125 Lincoln, downtown (505-988-5091). Represents Dan Namingha.

Owings-Dewey Fine Art. 74 East San Francisco (upstairs), on the plaza (505-982-6244). Primarily paintings by nationally known nineteenth- and twentieth-century American artists.

Gerald Peters Gallery. 439 Camino del Monte Sol, between Canyon Road and Old Santa Fe Trail (505-988-8961). Paintings by the Founders of the Taos and Santa Fe art colonies and contemporary representational work.

Peyton Wright. 131 Nusbaum, downtown (505-989-9888). Primarily abstract painting and photography.

David Rettig Fine Arts. 901 West San Mateo, in the new "Crossing" art district where San Mateo and Second Street meet (505-983-4640). Diverse collection of impressive work by area artists.

Santa Fe Contemporary Art. 901 West San Mateo, in the new "Crossing" art district where San Mateo and Second Street meet (505-988-5678). An artist-owned gallery representing three dozen of the best emerging artists in the area.

Laurel Seth Gallery. 1121 Paseo de Peralta, downtown (505-988-7349). Contemporary Southwestern representational painting.

Shidoni Galleries and Foundry. Bishop's Lodge Road, Tesuque (505-988-8001). One of the best galleries in the country for large-scale sculpture, plus contemporary pieces in other media by emerging artists.

Andrew Smith Gallery. 203 West San Francisco, downtown (505-984-1234). The finest photography gallery in the city, featuring classic and contemporary work.

Turner Carroll Gallery. 725 Canyon Road (505-986-9800). Contemporary American and international art.

Wyeth Hurd Gallery. 301 East Palace, downtown (505-989-8380). Paintings from four generations of a talented and prolific family.

Riva Yares Gallery. 123 Grant, downtown (505-984-0330). Dynamic paintings and sculpture, primarily nonrepresentational.

Zaplin-Lambert Gallery. 651 Canyon Road (505-982-6100). Paintings and prints from the nineteenth and twentieth centuries.

Contemporary Fine Crafts

DeBella. 100 East Palace, downtown (505-984-0692). Beautifully crafted jewelry, primarily gold and gemstones.

Fairchild & Co. 110 West San Francisco, downtown (505-984-1419). Custom and designer jewelry from regional and national artists.

Golden Bough. 211 Old Santa Fe Trail, in the Inn at Loretto, downtown (505-982-3443). Distinctive jewelry, many pieces with gemstones.

Gusterman Silversmiths. 126 East Palace, downtown (505-982-8972). Good, reasonably priced silver jewelry.

Jett. 110 Old Santa Fe Trail, downtown (505-988-1414). Creative designs in jewelry.

Kent Galleries: The Contemporary Craftsman. 130 Lincoln, downtown (505-988-1001). Wide range and large selection of fine regional crafts, plus paintings.

Ross Lewallen Jewelry. 105 East Palace, downtown (505-983-2657). A leading jeweler in the city for many years. Excellent value.

Lightside Gallery. 225 Canyon Road (505-982-5501). Broad selection of crafts with some contemporary paintings.

Mariposa Santa Fe. 225 Canyon Road (505-982-3032). Local branch of a top Albuquerque crafts gallery.

Nambe Mills. 112 West San Francisco, downtown (505-988-3574), and 924 Paseo de Peralta (505-988-5528). Distinctive metal cooking and serving ware made from original designs in Santa Fe.

Okun Gallery. 301 North Guadalupe at Catron, near downtown (505-989-4300). High-quality crafts from recognized artists.

Ornament. 209 West San Francisco, downtown (505-983-9399). Traditional and contemporary jewelry designs.

Quilts Ltd. 652 Canyon Road (505-988-5888). Collectors'-quality quilts in traditional and Southwestern styles.

Running Ridge Gallery. 640 Canyon Road (505-988-2515). Delightful array of fine crafts, many of them sculptural, plus contemporary paintings.

Tesuque Glassworks. Bishop's Lodge Road, next to Shidoni,

Tesuque (505-988-2165). Beautiful glassware direct from the studio of Charles Miner and associates.

Home Furnishings and Architectural Crafts

Architectural Antiques. 1117 Canyon Road (505-983-7607). Spanish Colonial doors, fixtures, and other architectural detail.

Artesanos Imports. 222 Galisteo, downtown (505-983-5563). Mexican ceramic tiles and sinks plus other traditional items for the home.

The Clay Angel. 125 Lincoln, downtown (505-988-4800). Tableware and more with Southwestern flair.

Collaboration. 544 South Guadalupe (505-984-3045). Wonderful Southwestern furnishings by Ernest Thompson and Peter Gould.

Counterpoint Tile. 1519 Paseo de Peralta (505-982-1247). Creative tile designs, many by area artists.

Dell Woodworks. 1326 Rufina Circle, off Cerrillos Road (505-471-3005). Refined custom furniture in a regional style.

Foreign Traders. 202 Galisteo, downtown (505-983-6441). Excellent selection of fine Mexican furnishings.

Volker de la Harpe Carved Doors and Furniture. 707 Canyon Road (505-983-4074). Contemporary and traditional designs made on-site.

La Mesa of Santa Fe. 225 Canyon Road (505-984-1688). Handcrafted items for the table and home.

Santa Fe Interiors. 214 Old Santa Fe Trail (505-988-2227). Handsome Mexican rugs.

Simply Santa Fe. 72 East San Francisco, on the plaza (505-988-3100). Diverse array of regional antiques among other furnishings.

Southwest Spanish Craftsmen. 328 South Guadalupe (505-982-1767). Custom designs and reproductions of Spanish Colonial and provincial furniture.

Taos Furniture. 1807 Second Street, in the new "Crossing" art district where San Mateo and Second Street meet (505-988-1229). Handcrafted local furniture.

Distinctive Clothes and Accessories

Char. 104 Old Santa Fe Trail, downtown (505-988-5969). Primarily suede and leather fashions for women.

Montecristi Custom Hat Works. 118 Galisteo, downtown (505-983-9598). Handmade hats in Western and other styles.

Origins. 135 West San Francisco, downtown (505-988-2323). Delightful collection of unusual women's clothes and accessories.

Overland Sheepskin Company. 217 Galisteo, downtown (505-983-4727). Great coats, slippers, and more from Taos.

Salamander Leathers. 78 East San Francisco, on the plaza (505-982-9782). Stylish contemporary and Western designs for men and women.

Santa Fe Weaving Gallery. 124$^1/_2$ Galisteo, downtown (505-982-1737). Locally made women's clothing.

Simply Santa Fe. 72 East San Francisco, on the plaza (505-988-3100). Eclectic selection of clothing for women, much of it Southwestern or Native American in inspiration.

Jane Smith. 122 West San Francisco, downtown (505-988-4775). Chic Southwestern wear for men and women.

Susan K's Artwear. 229 Johnson, downtown (505-989-8226). Women's clothing and jewelry with flair.

Tom Taylor. 100 East San Francisco, downtown (505-984-2231). Custom boots, belts, and buckles.

Vi Vi of Santa Fe. 117 Galisteo, downtown (505-984-3114). Contemporary Southwestern sweaters and other knitwear.

New Mexico Food Products

Chile Shop. 109 East Water, downtown (505-983-6080). Chiles and more, including tableware. Mail order available.

Coyote Cafe General Store. 132 West Water, downtown (505-

982-2454). Retail outlet for the famous restaurant. Mail order available.

Santa Fe Farmer's Market Store. 500 Montezuma in Sanbusco Center, off Guadalupe (505-984-1010). Some of the same items sold at the farmer's market, described in Chapter 6.

Santa Fe School of Cooking. 116 West San Francisco in the Plaza Mercado, downtown (505-983-4511). Strong selection of local products in addition to Southwestern cooking classes. Mail order available.

For Any of the Above and Who Knows What Else

Trader Jack's Flea Market. Highway 84/285, just beyond the Santa Fe Opera. One of the great bazaars in the Southwest, Trader Jack's attracts savvy locals and visitors alike for its value-priced, often unusual merchandise. Even if you're not searching for used cowboy boots, Guatemalan fabrics, buckles, bangles, or beads, the flea market makes for fine people-watching, especially on weekend mornings.

PART THREE

Taos

CHAPTER TEN

The High Road to Taos

WHEN THE Spanish arrived in New Mexico to stay in the seventeenth century, some of the more independent and adventurous settlers pushed on beyond Santa Fe to the north. They established farms on both sides of the Rio Grande Valley, all along the 75-mile stretch between Santa Fe and the large Indian pueblo in Taos. Santa Fe was a small, isolated frontier village in this period, but compared to the northern settlements it was a busy, cosmopolitan metropolis. A common punishment for crimes in the early centuries was banishment to one or another of these remote villages, where life was invariably hard and lean.

Santa Fe courts no longer exile convicts to Chimayó or Las Trampas, but little else has changed substantially in these places. If anything, survival may be tougher today in the northern villages than it was in the early centuries, and the towns have certainly lost ground to Santa Fe in contact with the outside world. Taos is, and always has been, a special case among the northern communities, but the others remain frontier outposts of the Old World, rustic, pastoral, and still thoroughly Spanish.

Two superb books provide wonderful insights into the villages' confrontation with "progress." Robert Coles describes

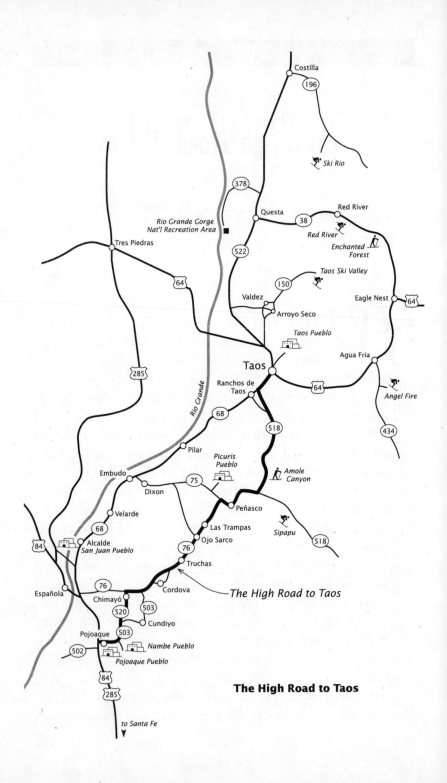

The High Road to Taos

the persistence of their traditional values and mores in *The Old Ones of New Mexico* (Harcourt Brace Jovanovich, 1989). Taos writer John Nichols creates a fictional but authentic mountain community, populated with splendid characters, in *The Milagro Beanfield War* (Ballantine, 1987), one of the most delightful American novels of the 1970s, translated to film by Robert Redford in 1988.

The fabled "High Road" to Taos from Santa Fe passes through several of the Old World villages, described below. The towns and the spectacular mountain scenery make the drive one of the most fascinating in the United States.

Chimayó

The High Road starts in Pojaoque, where N.M. 503 intersects U.S. 84/285 and heads east toward the Sangre de Cristos. After winding through the peaceful countryside of Nambé, the road climbs into the village of Chimayó, the center of Spanish weaving in New Mexico.

Chimayó families such as the Ortegas and the Trujillos have been weaving for centuries. Many years ago they developed a design pattern, named for the town, that is characterized by a background of one solid color with stylized diamond figures in the center and stripes on the ends in different colors.

A good place to see examples of the weaving today is at the Ortega family shop, where artisans work daily at their looms. The Ortegas stopped using homespun yarn in the 1930s, and now employ some weavers from outside the family, but the essence of their craft hasn't changed much since the eighteenth century. The Trujillo family shop, Centinela Weavers, features excellent work by Irvin Trujillo, his wife, Lisa, and other fine artisans from the area.

The major attraction in Chimayó is El Santuario de Nuestro Señor de Esquípulas, a small chapel that's one of the most revered places in the Southwest. The facade and the religious folk art inside are simple and unpolished but intensely expressive, typical of Spanish frontier churches of the early nineteenth century.

The ground under and around the chapel is reputed to have miraculous healing powers. Pilgrims visit Chimayó as they do Lourdes in France, to cure their afflictions through faith. In a tiny back room they crouch over a hole in the middle of the floor and scoop up holy earth to rub over their arms and faces. In an adjoining room many of the cured have left their crutches, leg braces, and other testimonies of their faith.

Culinary pilgrims look for their succor at the Restaurante Rancho de Chimayó, one of the best-known restaurants in New Mexico. Described in Chapter 8, the Rancho serves some of the most authentic traditional cooking in the state in a lovely adobe hacienda just up the road from the Santuario. If you prefer a quick, casual meal or snack, Léona's de Chimayó, a stand immediately next door to the Santuario, offers hearty and delicious tamales and other native dishes. Léona's flour tortillas may be the best in the country.

Three local B&Bs provide delightful and affordable accommodations in a pastoral setting midway between Santa Fe and Taos. The Hacienda Rancho de Chimayó shares ownership and ambience with the acclaimed Restaurante, directly across the street. Built as a home in the late nineteenth century, the inn lost nothing of its comfort or authenticity in the conversion to a B&B. The spacious rooms open onto an enclosed courtyard, in the traditional manner, and come with private baths, fireplaces, and regional antiques, mostly from the Victorian era. Rates start around $60 for the smallest single and go up to $105 for the largest double. P.O. Box 11, Chimayó 87522. 505-351-2222. Major credit cards.

La Posada de Chimayó offers four rustically romantic rooms, two in an adobe guesthouse and two in a nearby nineteenth-century farmhouse. Each features Southwestern and Mexican furnishings, a fireplace, and a private bath. Owner Sue Farrington serves a bountiful breakfast, perhaps French toast oozing cheese or a Spanish omelet topped with green chile. Rates are $80 to $90 for two. P.O. Box 463, Chimayó 87522. 505-351-4605. MC, V.

The newest of the B&Bs, Rancho Manzana is in the oldest hacienda, directly on the village's historic fortified plaza. Chuck and Jody Apple welcome you warmly with your own fireplace, terry robes, fluffy towels in the private bath, and a hot tub for a soothing soak. The hosts, who also offer cooking classes, serve a full breakfast in the country kitchen or outside on a deck overlooking their apple orchard and chile farm. For $75 to $85, it's quite a value. HCR 64, Box 18, Chimayó 87522. 505-351-2227. MC, V.

Cordova

A few miles east of Chimayó, Cordova sits serenely just off the High Road in a heavily tilled valley. It is known primarily for its woodcarving, particularly a style of carefully incised, unpainted santos named for the village.

The founder of the modern carving tradition in Cordova was José Dolores López, born in 1868. Like his father before him, López was a carpenter and furniture maker by trade who used his skills in his free time to help beautify the local church.

During World War I, anxious about a son who had been drafted, López began carving small wooden figures, mainly animals, for relaxation. Members of the Santa Fe art colony "discovered" his work shortly afterward and convinced López that he should begin making some carvings to sell, which must have been a startling idea in Cordova at the time. López taught his techniques to his children, including the talented George López, who was honored by the National Endowment for the Arts as a national treasure. George and his siblings passed along the tradition to their children, including Sabanita Ortiz, Gloria López Cordova, and Eluid L. Martínez.

The local artists welcome visitors to their homes to see and buy carvings. Just follow the handlettered signs in the village.

Truchas and Las Trampas

Truchas, the next community along the High Road, enjoys magnificent views across miles of mountain and desert. Another center of New Mexico weaving, the town is known for a design scheme that varies a little from the Chimayó style. Local weavers, such as the Cordova family, often use a pattern called Vallero, developed about a century ago by the Montoya sisters in the nearby town of El Valle. Other fine crafts are showcased at Hand Artes Gallery, and an ambitious selection of contemporary paintings, drawings, and sculpture can be seen at Cardona-Hine Gallery, both found along the village's main road.

For sustenance, try the local fare at the Truchas Mountain Cafe, perhaps the stuffed sopaipillas or any of the other New Mexican dishes. While you're there, ask directions to the meadow nearby that served as the beanfield in Robert Redford's film version of *The Milagro Beanfield War,* which was shot in Truchas and used many residents as extras.

A few miles farther, Las Trampas is the site of a beautiful Spanish colonial chapel, San José de Gracias, built in the mid-eighteenth century. The chapel is sometimes open on summer days, but if it's locked, check with local residents, who can usually find the key if you're persistent and respectful. The religious folk art of the interior is superb. Donations are welcomed and needed.

Ranchos de Taos

At Peñasco the High Road goes east several miles along a fertile valley and then turns north for Taos on N.M. 518. It connects with N.M. 68, the main route between Santa Fe and Taos, in the town of Ranchos de Taos, home of one of the most photographed churches in the United States. Though the San Francisco de Assisi Church is a small chapel, it has massive adobe walls and buttresses that cast grand shadows in the New Mexico sun. Georgia O'Keeffe, among many other artists, felt the lure of the light and captured its spell in a number of paintings.

CHAPTER ELEVEN

The Plaza, the Pueblo, and Other Historic Places

W HEN THE Spanish founded Taos in 1617, they built the town around the plaza. It's been the center of community life ever since, a gathering spot for colonial soldiers, French trappers, American mountain men, artists, and now, droves of visitors each day.

As you might expect, the contemporary businesses that rim the historic common serve the tourists more than the town's 6,000 residents and, unfortunately, few of them do it with much style or felicitous character. Still, the plaza remains the heart of Taos and the starting point for everything, including a walking tour of the downtown. Our suggested stroll encompasses many of Taos's primary attractions, but don't overlook the places mentioned at the end of this chapter that require a short drive or the art museums described in the next chapter.

Kit Carson Home

A block east of the plaza on Kit Carson Road, the street's namesake mountain man and scout purchased a twelve-room adobe in 1843 as a wedding gift for his bride, Josefa Jaramillo. Born in Kentucky, Carson came west at the age of 17 and adopted Taos as his hometown in 1826, a year after his future residence had been built. He spent much of his time away from

Central Taos Attractions

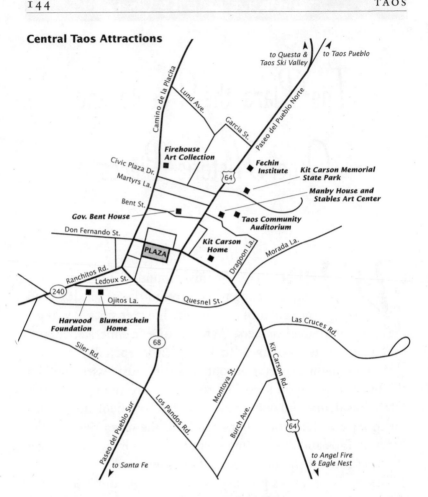

his family on various ventures and missions—often romanticized in the dime novels of the nineteenth century—but he and Josefa lived in this house for twenty-five years, until they died within a month of each other in 1868. Now a museum, three of the rooms display typical Taos furnishings of the period and the others contain Indian and Spanish artifacts, a gun exhibit, and relics of the mountain-man era.

The Carson Home (505-758-4741) is open daily, 8:00 to 6:00 in the summer and 9:00 to 5:00 in the winter. Admission is $4 for adults and $2.50 for children. Consider a combination ticket that includes visits to the Blumenschein Home and the Martínez Hacienda, or a more inclusive deal that covers most of the Taos museums described in this and the following chapter. Both are fine values available at any of the participating institutions.

Kit and Josefa Carson are buried a short distance from their home in a cemetery that sits between two other historic houses. After seeing their abode and browsing the nearby shops on Kit Carson Road, backtrack a few steps to Paseo del Pueblo Norte and turn north to the Manby House, just beyond the Taos Inn.

Manby House

Now the Stables Art Center, this was the grandest residence in Taos at the turn of the century and the home of the town's most notorious character. Englishman Arthur Manby, who moved to New Mexico in the 1880s, made a fortune as a speculator. A good part of the profit resulted from shady deals that earned him a reputation for both cunning and conning. Widely despised in his latter years, he became a hermit in his house, keeping a mean dog to protect himself from his enemies.

Manby's murder in 1929 became one of the most famous unsolved mysteries in the state. He was found at home decapitated, with his head so badly mutilated that it wasn't recognizable. Investigators said someone probably took revenge for being swindled, but many Taoseños believed that the killing was the most heinous Manby fraud of all. They claimed he murdered another man who looked similar, disfigured the head to make people think it was him, and then fled the region to start a new life.

Kit Carson Memorial State Park

The body and head found in Manby's House lie at the back of the park next door, which was once part of the Englishman's estate. Wander through the peaceful park, site of many local events, back to the small cemetery. Markers and plaques identify the graves of Kit and Josefa Carson, Mabel Dodge Luhan, the popular Padre Antonio José Martínez, and other notable figures in Taos history. The Manby remains are buried beyond the fence, outside the consecrated grounds.

Fechin Institute

A little farther north, famed Russian artist Nicolai Fechin built a monumental home, in some ways his greatest artistic achievement. Already recognized as a master architect, painter, and sculptor when he moved to Taos in 1923, he applied all his talents in designing and embellishing the adobe mansion. Fechin carved the elaborate woodwork and many of the furnishings, blending Russian and New Mexican traditions, and he put his personal touch on everything from the fireplaces to the windows. The intricate detail makes you wonder how he had time to produce the artwork on the walls.

Now the home of the Fechin Institute (505-758-1710), which hosts educational and cultural programs, the residence is open to the public from May to October on Wednesday through Sunday, from 1:00 to 5:00. It's definitely worth seeing for the suggested donation of $3. The house sits well back from Paseo del Pueblo Norte, which has provided the institute with the opportunity to raise money by building a luxury hotel on the property directly in front of the street. Scheduled for completion by 1997, it's likely to be the most elegant inn in town.

Governor Bent House

Returning toward the plaza on Paseo del Pueblo Norte, turn west on Bent Street, the most fashionable shopping promenade in Taos. The first U.S. territorial governor of New Mexico, Charles Bent, lived on the street at number 117 when it was just a dusty horse trail. Like Arthur Manby, he gained historical significance partially as a result of his death.

Local Pueblo and Spanish leaders opposed the forced American annexation of New Mexico in 1846, preferring to remain a part of Mexico. With the probable support of the Taos priest, Padre Antonio José Martínez, they launched a rebellion against U.S. rule by storming the governor's home and killing him.

Artifacts of the early Southwest are displayed in the house today, but the overall tone is as commercial as it is historical. Visiting hours are 9:00 to 5:00 daily in the summer and 10:00 to 4:00 in the winter. Admission is $1 for adults and less for kids. Call 505-758-2376 for additional information.

Blumenschein Home

On the other side of the plaza from Bent Street, about three blocks away, tiny, picturesque Ledoux Street couldn't be more different in temper. You leave the tourism boom behind and step back in time to the old Taos of decades ago. The spirit of the original art colony still pervades the atmosphere, particularly in the Blumenschein Home.

Ernest Blumenschein and his friend Bert Phillips arrived in Taos accidentally around the turn of the century and stayed to become the first eastern artists in the town. "Blumy" bought this rambling old adobe, which dates to 1797, and he, his wife, Mary, and their daughter Helen all lived and painted in it as a combination home and studio.

Now open to the public as a museum, the house immerses you in the world of the Taos Society of Artists, a realm both simple and genteel, deliberately provincial and inescapably cosmopolitan. The furnishings are much as the family left them, a delightful combination of traditional woodwork from the area and European antiques.

We like to linger in three rooms in particular. The large dining room was the main gathering spot in the house and you can still sense the swirl of activity that occurred here. The bedroom exudes a similar period feel and the drawings on exhibit illustrate Mary's substantial talent, which was on a par with her husband's. Just down the hall, beyond the library, the studio is our favorite spot. It's easy to imagine Blumy behind the erect easel, savoring the play of light and shadow coming through the surrounding windows.

At 222 Ledoux Street, the Blumenschein Home (505-758-0505) is open daily, 9:00 to 5:00. If you don't have a combination ticket for Taos museums, sold here and elsewhere, the admission is $4 for adults and $2.50 for children.

Harwood Foundation Museum and Library

You can see a few of Blumenschein's paintings in his home, but don't miss the ones on display at the Harwood Foundation, two doors down the block at 238 Ledoux. A library and museum overseen by the University of New Mexico, the old adobe home harbors an extensive collection of work from the founders of the Taos art colony as well as Spanish crafts from the area.

In the early decades of the century, Burt and Elizabeth Harwood's house was a major gathering spot for artists, partially because it enjoyed electricity before most other residences. After Burt's death, Elizabeth made its status official by creating the Foundation as a community arts center. Take the staircase to the second-floor gallery to see some of the seminal pieces in the collection, which includes paintings by Andrew Dasburg and Victor Higgins, contemporary work by Larry Bell and Fritz Scholder, nineteenth-century retablos, and Mabel Dodge Luhan's personal trove of santos.

The Harwood Foundation (505-758-9826) is open Monday through Friday from 10:00 to 5:00 and on Saturday from 10:00 until 4:00. Admission costs $2 unless you have a combination ticket from the Museum Association of Taos.

Taos Pueblo

A short drive from the plaza, the pueblo is the most striking spot in Taos and perhaps all of New Mexico. Virtually unchanged in appearance since the Spanish first saw it, it speaks of a proud heritage in hushed, reverential tones.

Some of the pueblo residents continue to live in one of the two enormous adobe communal buildings—divided into many separate rooms—that reach five stories into the sky. The mountain creek running between the two apartment compounds flows from sacred Blue Lake, high in the surrounding mountains. The river provides water for the ancient dwellings, which don't have plumbing or electricity to this day.

Visitors can wander through the central section of the pueblo, where some people open their homes as tourist shops, though large "restricted" signs keep you well away from the kivas. Since this is a living community, many travelers feel awkward about looking around, a sense often reinforced by residents who understandably resent the zoo-like atmosphere. You may want to admire the pueblo quietly from the creek bank and leave the camera in the car.

Even better if possible, time your visit for one of the many traditional ceremonies scheduled throughout the year, when the celebratory mood is more welcoming and the event itself adds multiple layers of magic to your experience. The San Geronimo Feast Day is worth a special trip. It starts with a sunset dance on September 29 and reaches full force the next day with rituals that include a foot race, pole climbing, and more dances. Pueblo artists sell their work and food booths ply local specialties. See Chapter 21 for more information on Feast Days.

Christmas Eve and Day also sparkle, with a procession on the night of December 24 and a Deer Dance or Matachines rite on the 25th. Other events occur on January 1 (Turtle Dance), January 6 (Buffalo or Deer Dance), May 3 (Corn Dance), June 13 (Corn Dance), June 24 (Corn Dance), and the second weekend of July, when the pueblo invites other Native Americans for its annual Pow Wow.

The pueblo charges a $5 parking fee for cars and $10 for larger vehicles. A permit to carry a still camera costs $5 and the fee goes up to $10 for a video camera. Photography is not permitted during dances. The Taos Indian Horse Ranch (505-758-3212) provides guided trail rides across pueblo land beyond the village. Rates vary depending on the size of the group and the length of the ride.

Martínez Hacienda

Another don't-miss, particularly for history buffs, this two-hundred-year-old hacienda vividly illustrates life in the Spanish colonial era. Severino Martínez built the home in fortress style, with massive adobe walls and no windows on the outside, to provide protection against Apache and Comanche raids. The twenty-one rooms open onto two *placitas,* or courtyards, where the family secured their livestock in times of danger.

Carefully restored period rooms provide insight into the lifestyle of a prominent family in a period when everything was made locally or brought from Mexico on the arduous "Journey of Death" up the Camino Real. Artisans work regularly in other rooms, demonstrating the skills and crafts that sustained households in the colonial era.

In late September the Martínez Hacienda hosts the annual Old Taos Trade Fair. The two-day event reenacts the fall fairs of the nineteenth century, when the Spanish and the Pueblos called a temporary truce with their Plains Indian enemies and invited them, trappers, and anyone else in the area to Taos to trade goods. It's quite a party these days.

Two miles south of the Taos plaza on N.M. 240 (Ranchitos Road), the hacienda is open daily from 9:00 to 5:00. If you don't have a combination ticket for Taos museums, sold here and elsewhere, the admission is $4 for adults and $2.50 for children. Phone 505-758-1000 for additional information.

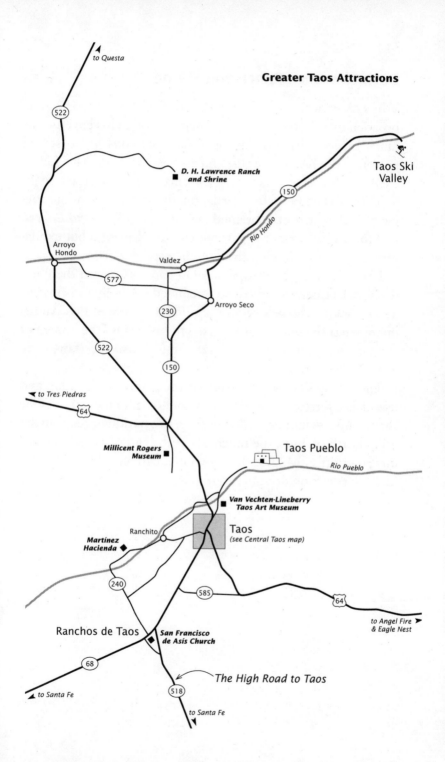

Greater Taos Attractions

to Questa

522

D. H. Lawrence Ranch
and Shrine

150

Taos Ski
Valley

Rio Hondo

Arroyo
Hondo

Valdez

577

230

Arroyo Seco

522

150

to Tres Piedras

64

Millicent Rogers
Museum

Taos Pueblo

Rio Pueblo

Van Vechten-Lineberry
Taos Art Museum

Ranchito

Taos
(see Central Taos map)

Martínez
Hacienda

240

585

64

to Angel Fire
& Eagle Nest

Ranchos de Taos

San Francisco
de Asís Church

The High Road to Taos

68

518

to Santa Fe

to Santa Fe

D. H. Lawrence Ranch and Shrine

While American writers flocked to Paris in the 1920s to broaden their horizons, D. H. Lawrence found his haven—and much bigger horizons—in the Taos mountains. A possessive patron of the British novelist and essayist, Mabel Dodge Luhan tried to give this ranch to Lawrence but he refused to be indebted to her. His wife, Frieda, finally accepted it for the couple in exchange for the original manuscript of *Sons and Lovers,* and for several years the pair enjoyed an elemental but exhilarating life in the simple cabins on the property.

Lawrence died in Europe in 1930 and was buried there initially, but Frieda exhumed and cremated the body to bring the ashes back to the beloved mountains. Concerned that Mabel might covet the remains, she mixed the ashes into the cement of a small shrine, now a pilgrimage site for Lawrence fans from around the world.

The University of New Mexico owns the ranch today and uses it as a retreat center. The only spot open to the public is the shrine, up a winding walkway from the parking area. Fifteen miles north of Taos, the ranch sits at the end of a well-marked dirt road off N.M. 522. In the winter, call ahead to 505-776-2245 to check on driving conditions.

CHAPTER TWELVE

The Art Colony Today

T HE COLORFUL DAYS of D. H. Lawrence, Mabel Dodge Luhan, and Ernest Blumenschein may be gone, but the arts still thrive in Taos, and still in a big way for such a small town. If you're in pursuit of the muses, or just looking for fun, check out the following art museums, events, and galleries. Also, don't overlook places covered in the downtown walking tour in the previous chapter, particularly the Fechin Institute, the Blumenschein Home, and the Harwood Foundation.

Van Vechten–Lineberry Taos Art Museum

You leave this magnificent new museum feeling like you have a Ph.D. in Taos art history. Edwin C. and Novella Lineberry built the gallery on their private estate and dedicated it to the late artist Duane Van Vechten, whose 1929 studio serves as the entrance hall. Grand exhibition areas branch off from the foyer, leading visitors through a century of local creativity. Though a number of living artists are represented in the collection, the focus is on the Taos Founders, whose work has never been brought together so extensively for public display. From Joseph Henry Sharp to Kenneth Adams, from Bert G. Phillips to Andrew Dasburg, they share a splendid spotlight.

At 501 Paseo del Pueblo Norte, the museum is on the road
to the Taos Pueblo, just beyond its intersection with N.M. 522.
Closed on Monday, it's open other weekdays from 11:00 to
4:00 and on weekends from 1:30 to 4:00. Admission is $5 for
adults and $3 for children and seniors unless you're using a
combination ticket from the Museum Association of Taos, sold
here and at six other participating institutions. Call 505-758-
2690 for additional information.

Millicent Rogers Museum

A wealthy socialite, passionate designer, and beautiful model,
Millicent Rogers moved to Taos in 1947 and became fascinated
with Southwestern Indian art. Within six short years she
amassed a stunning collection of work, which her family gave
to this museum as a founding gift after her death in 1953.

Now considerably expanded with the acquisition of newer
pieces and an additional emphasis on colonial and contemporary Hispanic art from the area, the Millicent Rogers has
become one of the top museums of its kind in the region. Don't
overlook it just because of the isolated location—the exhibitions, the sprawling adobe home, and the gift shop are each
worth a detour.

The Millicent Rogers (505-758-2462) is four miles north of
the Taos plaza, off N.M. 522 near the intersection with the
road to the ski basin. Open daily, 9:00 to 5:00, the museum
charges $3 for adults and $1 for children unless you're using a
combination ticket from the Museum Association of Taos.

Firehouse Art Collection

It may sound unlikely, but the Taos Volunteer Fire Department
has one of New Mexico's best art collections, a trove of over
250 works by some of the most famous artists who ever lived
in town. The collection started in 1953–54, when the firemen
built a recreation room. To decorate the new space, they sought

help from their artist friends, who contributed as generously with their work as the firemen did with their time. The system works for everyone, including the public, who get to see the paintings free.

Open daily, the fire station (505-758-3386) is downtown, two blocks north of Bent Street, near the corner of Civic Plaza Drive and Camino de la Placita.

Meeting the Artists

If you visit Taos in the spring or fall, it can be difficult to avoid a tête-à-tête with an artist even if you wanted to. Between the heavy tourism seasons of the winter and summer, the town relaxes by reveling in its cultural heritage. Artists showcase their work in a variety of venues and media over many weeks, bringing the local residents out of hiding and enticing plenty of visitors as well.

The spring season starts with the Taos Art Celebration, held during the first two weeks of May. In addition to an annual invitational and juried art exhibition, it features openings at almost every gallery in town, children's activities, and community music and theater performances. Call 800-732-8267 or 505-758-3873 for exact dates and a calendar of events.

As soon as the Celebration ends, the Taos Inn opens the spring rendition of its "Meet the Artist" Series. A local institution since the early 1970s, the program offers intimate evenings with artists who share the inspiration behind their work in slide shows, demonstrations, lectures, studio tours, and informal discussions. The downtown hotel hosts the gatherings on Tuesday and Thursday evening from mid-May to mid-June and then resumes the series in October, when it continues into the early part of the ski season. For details, phone 800-TAOS INN or 505-758-2233.

In the fall, the Taos Arts Festival kicks off another round of activities that eventually wind down with the year's final "Meet the Artist" presentation. From mid-September until early October, the event centers on two exhibitions of local artists, Taos Invites Taos (an invitational show) and the Taos Open (a juried show). Galleries stage major openings again, artisans display their work at the Plaza Arts and Crafts Fair, and near the end, the Wool Festival offers everything from weaving demonstrations to regional lamb specialties. Call 800-732-8267 or 505-758-3873 for a complete schedule.

Taos Poetry Circus

Since its founding in the early 1980s, the Taos Poetry Circus has relished its role in taking poetry off an academic pedestal and bringing it down to earth. One of the liveliest literary events in the country, it makes verse a different type of tune.

The highlight of the weeklong June festival comes on the last Saturday evening, when two nationally known poets square off in the World Heavyweight Championship Poetry Bout. The match goes ten rounds, as the contestants battle each other through feisty readings from their work. Gregory Corso, Andrei Codrescu, Victor Hernandez Cruz, and Anne Waldman have all danced to victory in the past.

New in 1995, The nXt Generation Poetry Slam features young poets competing for the favor of the crowd. Other activities include workshops, discussions, and less combative readings. Call 505-758-1800 for details.

The Performing Arts

The Taos School of Music Summer Chamber Music Festival forms the foundation of an active summer concert season. Started in the 1960s, the school brings in major professional string quartets and pianists to coach advanced young artists from around the world in an intensive eight-week training program. Both the teachers and the students perform regularly during their residency, offering over a dozen concerts between June and August at the Taos Community Auditorium and at the Hotel St. Bernard in the Taos Ski Valley. Phone 505-776-2388 for the schedule and tickets.

When the Chamber Music Festival wraps up, Music from Angel Fire (505-377-3233) begins to heat up. Staged in late August and early September about twenty-five miles from Taos in the ski village of Angel Fire, it features artists of international standing, a composer-in-residence, and a varied program of chamber music.

South of Taos at the Fort Burgwin Research Center, the Lette Hutchinson Concert Series presents free performances by faculty and students participating in a summer program run by Southern Methodist University. Professors in other fields also offer colloquia on topics ranging from Pueblo pottery to local geology. Call 505-758-8322 for details.

The Taos Art Association (505-758-2052) sponsors arts events on a regular basis year-round at the Taos Community Auditorium. From creative cinema to ballet, jazz to theater, the bill of fare ranges broadly.

Art Galleries and Arty Shops

Like Santa Fe, Taos has its share of touristy souvenir stores but also abounds in good galleries and fascinating shops. The following is a selective list of some places in the downtown area that carry high-quality art or other handmade work, usually with a Southwestern orientation. Shops come and go, of course, and also change personalities, so you have to expect both disappointments and new delights. Wander around and look everywhere, but if you're following the suggested walking tour in Chapter 11, you'll encounter most of these businesses along the way.

Brazos Fine Art. 119 Bent Street (505-758-0767). Contemporary art, mainly representational.

Brooks Indian Shop. 108-G Cabot Plaza Mall, on Kit Carson Road (505-758-9073). Pottery, jewelry, and more.

Clay and Fiber. 126 West Plaza Drive (505-758-8093). A solid collection of fine crafts.

Collins-Pettit Gallery. 1 Ledoux Street (505-758-8068). Contemporary work, mainly figurative.

Coyote Moon. 120-C Bent Street in the John Dunn House shopping plaza (505-758-4437). Folk art, mainly from Mexico.

Dwellings Revisited. 10 Bent Street (505-758-3377). Traditional New Mexico crafts and a range of architectural accessories.

El Rincón Trading Post. 114-A Kit Carson Road (505-758-9188). If it's Western, you might find it here.

Fenix Gallery. 228-B Paseo del Pueblo Norte (505-758-9120). Contemporary paintings and sculpture, mostly by Taos artists.

Gallery A. 105–107 Kit Carson Road (505-758-2343). Traditional and contemporary paintings, sculpture, and graphics.

Hirsch Fine Art. Call 505-758-5460 for an appointment. Works on paper by early Southwestern artists.

La Chiripada Winery & El Bosque Garlic Farm. Plaza Real Mall on East Plaza Drive (505-751-1311). Handcrafted wines, garlic ristras, and more from family farms in Dixon.

Lo Fino. 201 Paseo del Pueblo Sur (505-758-0298). Handcrafted furniture.

Lumina of New Mexico. 239 Morada Road, three blocks from the plaza. Contemporary photography, painting, and sculpture in the historic Victor Higgins home.

Maison Faurie Antiquités. 1 McCarthy Plaza, just off the main plaza (505-758-8545). Always fun for a hodgepodge of collectibles.

Mission Gallery. 138 Kit Carson Road (505-758-2861). Perhaps the best-established and most respected gallery in town. Represented Andrew Dasburg before his death.

Navajo Gallery. 210 Ledoux Street (505-758-3250). Paintings and prints by Taos artist R. C. Gorman, who owns the gallery.

New Directions Gallery. 107-B North Plaza (505-758-2771). Represents innovative New Mexico artists, presenting some of the most exciting shows in town.

Old Taos Shop. 108 Teresina Lane, just off the plaza (505-758-7353). Local collectibles, ranging from Spanish folk art to fishing memorabilia.

The Parks Gallery. 106 Doña Luz, on Guadalupe Plaza (505-751-0343). Represents four talented area artists.

Perna Gallery. 203 Ledoux Street (505-751-3300). Wide-ranging collection of contemporary paintings and sculpture.

Pueblos & Plains. 110 Paseo del Pueblo Norte (505-758-0211). Small selection of American Indian art.

Emily Benoist Ruffin, Goldsmith. 119 Bent Street (505-758-1061). Creative jewelry by American and European artists.

Second Phase Gallery. 110 Doña Luz, on Guadalupe Plaza (505-751-0159). Antique Indian art.

Southwestern Arts. John Dunn House shopping plaza on Bent Street (505-758-8418). Historic and contemporary Indian and Hispanic work.

Stables Art Center. 133 Paseo del Pueblo Norte (505-758-2036). Represents a wide range of Taos artists.

Tally Richards Gallery. 118 Camino de la Placita, near Ledoux Street (505-751-3427). Vibrant and sometimes playful contemporary art. A personal favorite.

The Taos Company. 124-K Bent Street in the John Dunn House shopping complex (505-758-1141). Handcrafted home furnishings and accessories.

Total Arts Gallery. 122-A Kit Carson Road (505-758-4667). Enticing blend of traditional and contemporary work.

12 x 12 Gallery. 1 Ledoux Street (505-751-7210). Small pieces that display well in a 12-foot-by-12-foot space.

Twining Weavers. 135 Paseo del Pueblo Norte, behind the Stables Art Center (505-758-9000). Fine weavings and other crafts.

Worth Gallery. 112-A Camino de la Placita, near Ledoux Street (505-751-0816). Contemporary sculptural forms in various media.

CHAPTER THIRTEEN

Skiing and Other Outdoor Adventures

TAOS IS ONE of the outdoor recreational capitals of the country, a superb spot for skiing, hiking, river rafting, fishing, and more. Santa Fe and Albuquerque also offer good skiing and other mountain adventures (see Chapters 6 and 18, respectively), but if you're seeking the biggest challenges and the heaviest concentration of activities, Taos soars to the summit. Even when you stay in another New Mexico city, you may want to play here. The map in Chapter 10 indicates the top spots discussed below.

Don't go anywhere in the state, though, expecting breadth or depth in conventional resort sports such as golf and tennis. You can enjoy both games in Taos, Santa Fe, and Albuquerque—check our hotel descriptions and the yellow pages—but this is an area to chase the wind and water instead of balls. In this country, you want to be looking up and out, not down and around.

Taos Ski Valley

A Swiss-German native of the Alps, Ernie Blake spent two years searching the southern Rockies by small plane for skiing terrain that matched the magnificence of his homeland mountains. He found what he wanted at an abandoned mining site high above Taos and opened a primitive version of his ski resort there in 1955. Since then, the Taos Ski Valley has bloomed into one of the best in the West, building its reputation with solid service, exhilarating trails, committed family management, an absence of Aspenesque glitter, and an abundance of Alpine ambience.

About thirty minutes north of town, surrounded by the majestic Carson National Forest, the Ski Valley flaunts sublime scenery. Even nonskiers love the sights, though you have to head up the mountain for the most expansive views. If you're a newcomer to the sport, or even a grizzled pro, tune up at the world-class ski school. Sign up for a group lesson on a weekday morning during a nonholiday period and you may end up with a private or semiprivate lesson for a bargain price.

Expert skiers love the bowls, the great powder, and the wide variety of black-diamond runs, which make up more than half of the 72 trails. The less-skilled get plenty of challenges of their own in navigating down the 2,600-foot vertical drop from the 11,800-foot summit. Along the way and at the bottom, eleven lifts (including four quad chairs) quickly carry you back up to the high altitudes for another try at a graceful descent.

Everyone enjoys the lively, intimate base area, home to a score of restaurants and shops. Settle back with a hot chocolate, bask in the warm winter sun, and watch the hotdoggers schuss down Al's Run. Lodging is limited right on the slopes (see Chapter 14), but it's a delightful place to stay for the accommodations, the food, and the chance to avoid the minor hassles of the parking lot. For up-to-the-minute facts on snow conditions, call 505-776-2916; for other information, phone 505-776-2291.

Angel Fire, Red River, and More

Several nearby ski areas offer opportunities for a change of pace, either for a day's break from Taos's demanding slopes or as an alternative destination. Each is gentler and kinder on both your knees and your wallet.

About twenty-five miles east of Taos, Angel Fire Resort (800-633-7463 or 505-377-6401) caters particularly well to families. The "Family Reunion" program provides two days of lessons for all members of the clan, geared to their individual needs, and then brings everyone together on the third day for a complimentary group class. If that's more than you want, sign up for "Family Practice," a half-day session with your household. The area operates six lifts that serve fifty-two trails, mostly beginner and intermediate runs. For information on lodging and other facilities, see the "Enchanted Circle" drive in Chapter 22, which also covers Red River.

North of Taos and east of Questa, Red River offers many of the same advantages as Angel Fire, including a family-friendly environment, door-front skiing, and a high percentage of wide, easygoing trails. It may be the differences that count, though. This is a real, fun-oriented Rockies town rather than a condominium resort development, and the snowmaking equipment reaches 75 percent of the slopes, ensuring good conditions most of the season. Call 505-754-2223 for details.

To escape the crowds entirely, consider a day trip to Sipapu (505-587-2240), 25 miles southeast of Taos, or the Ski Rio area (505-586-9949), about twice as far north and more than twice as large. With just three lifts and nineteen runs, tiny Sipapu keeps its prices in line with its size. Ski Rio also entices with bargains but attracts people partially because of its combination of downhill and cross-country trails.

Cross-Country Skiing

Cross-country opportunities abound near Taos. The local Carson National Forest office (208 Cruz Alta Road, 505-758-6200) can provide maps and advice on public trails, and any of the many ski rental companies will do the same.

The best maintained of the public paths is at Amole Canyon, off N.M. 518 between Taos and Sipapu. A Nordic ski club and the forest service cooperate in caring for a well-marked three-mile loop where snowmobiles are prohibited.

The trail system spreads more extensively at the Enchanted Forest Cross Country Ski Area, a privately operated touring center. A few miles east of Red River, it roams over 1,400 scenic acres ranging in elevation from 9,600 feet to 10,040 feet. The eighteen miles of groomed trails come complete with warming huts, patrols, instructors, and a snack bar.

Hiking and Biking

When the winter snows melt, the Carson National Forest puts on its fair-weather hat and beckons hikers, backpackers, and mountain bikers to some of the same arteries that skiers just crossed. Over three hundred miles of trail stretch in all directions, from Georgia O'Keeffe's Ghost Ranch country up to the Alpine tundra of the Wheeler Peak Wilderness. For maps and solid suggestions on where to head, contact the Taos office of the Forest Service (208 Cruz Alta Road, 505-758-6200) or Taos Mountain Outfitters (114 South Plaza, 505-758-9292), which sells or rents any gear you might need.

Hikers and campers should also consider a trip to Bandelier National Monument (505-672-3861), south of the Carson National Forest between Taos and Santa Fe. Described more fully in Chapter 23, the fifty-square-mile park encompasses a wealth of trails, most probably walked by the ancient Anasazi.

River Rafting

As the Rio Grande approaches the Taos area from its source in Colorado, the river spills into a rugged, angular gorge formed by a rift in a massive lava flow. You can see the canyon from 650 feet above at the Rio Grande Gorge Bridge on U.S. 64, 10 miles west of Taos, but the perspective is much better from the water.

Three sections of the river provide entirely different rafting, canoeing, and kayaking experiences. To the far north, the Taos

Box takes you through dramatic landscape and thrilling Class 4 whitewater action. Ranked as one of the premier rapids rides in the West during May and June, the full-day trip is guaranteed to get you wet.

The river slows down substantially in the Lower Gorge, where relaxed half-day family rafting continues through most of the summer. Scenic and relatively serene, the float is usually suitable for small children, who shouldn't attempt the rougher routes. As the Rio Grande leaves the gorge, it picks up momentum again at the Pilar Racecourse, which splashes over Class 3 rapids at Albert Falls, Big Rock, Godzilla, and other spots on the half-day trip.

A few rafting companies also run the Rio Chama farther west, and all vary in the ways they package the Rio Grande excursions, with some specializing in longer trips that involve overnight camping. Among the many operators, all listed in the yellow pages, three that span the range of approaches are Far Flung Adventures (800-359-2627 or 505-758-2628), Rio Grande Rapid Transit (800-222-RAFT or 505-758-9700), and Rio Grande River Tours (800-525-4966 or 505-758-0762).

Don't try the river on your own unless you're truly an expert. Check with the Taos office of the Bureau of Land Management (505-758-8851) about the experience and equipment required.

Fly-Fishing

You can use bait or ordinary lures, of course, in New Mexico's high lakes and rivers, but fly-fishing is the adventure of choice in the state. For everything you need to know and carry, contact the experts at Los Rios Anglers in Taos (226-B Paseo del Pueblo Norte, 505-758-2798) and High Desert Angler in Santa Fe (435 South Guadalupe, 505-988-7688). Both can arrange instruction, guides, and gear, or just point you in the right direction for the best action at a particular time of the year.

$\mathcal{A}$rtful $\mathcal{A}$ccommodations

$\mathcal{N}$O TOWN in the country boasts a better collection of B&Bs than Taos. You can find almost anything you want in a local B&B and you'll usually be rewarded with much more than you expect.

Regular hotels offer less on the whole, though some of them are exceptional too for atmosphere, recreational facilities, convenience, and other factors. As long as you pick accommodations according to your style and needs, you're likely to relish your stay in town.

If you book late and have trouble getting a room, try Taos Central Reservations (800-821-2437 or 505-758-9767) or the Taos Bed and Breakfast Association (800-876-7857 or 505-758-4747), which represents some but not all of the best B&Bs in town. For lodging at or near the ski valley in the winter, call the Taos Valley Resort Association (800-776-1111 or 505-776-2233). If you're interested in renting a vacation home or condominium, contact Taos Vacation Rentals (800-788-8267 or 505-758-5700).

The rates quoted in the lodging reports are accurate at press time for the high seasons, which are summer and winter both in Taos, but prices do change and fluctuate on a regular basis. The costs often drop in the spring and fall.

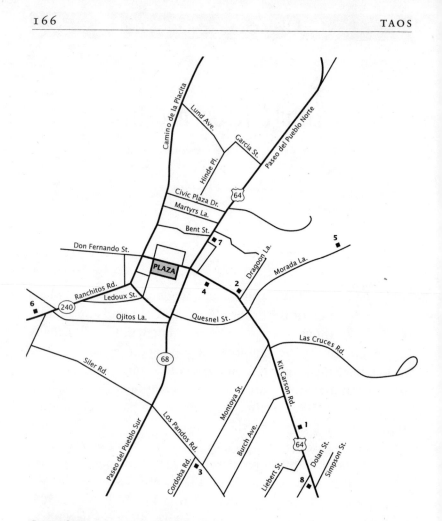

Central Taos Accommodations
1. Adobe Wall
2. Casa Benavides
3. Casa de las Chimeneas
4. El Rincón Inn
5. Mabel Dodge Luhan House
6. Taos Hacienda Inn
7. Taos Inn
8. The Willows Inn

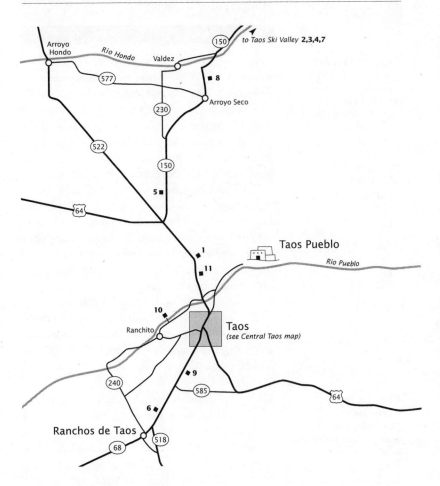

Greater Taos Accommodations
1. Hacienda del Sol
2. Hotel Edelweiss
3. Hotel St. Bernard
4. Inn at Snakedance
5. Quail Ridge Inn
6. Sagebrush Inn
7. St. Bernard Condominiums
8. Salsa del Salto
9. Sun God Lodge
10. Taos Country Inn
11. Touchstone Inn

BEST B&BS

Casa Benavides.
You can get in the door for as little as $80 but you can spend up to $195 to make a grand entrance.
137 Kit Carson Road, Taos 87571.
505-758-1772.
Major credit cards.

Less intimate than most Taos B&Bs, and more varied in style, Casa Benavides thrives on a great downtown location and immense diversity in its 28 rooms. Barbara McCarthy, who runs the inn with her husband, Tom, grew up in one of the five homes and other buildings that comprise the sprawling property, so she's certainly a seasoned guide to the neighborhood.

The least expensive quarters are small rooms in Barbara's childhood residence, the Benavides Home, but it may be worth spending a little more for extra space and charm. In the moderate price range, we like the Doña Tules room, named for the famed nineteenth-century madam and decorated in a manner she might have relished for an amorous rendezvous. It has a fireplace, as many of the chambers do, and along with all the others, it comes with a private bath, TV, use of a hot tub, and a big breakfast that includes Mexican eggs and "drop-dead" granola.

Casa de las Chimeneas.
The Willow and Blue rooms, both large and luxurious, cost $118 for two people, the sky-lighted Garden Room goes for $130, and the Library Suite opens its covers for $143.
405 Cordoba Road, Box 5303, Taos 87571.
505-758-4777.
MC, V.

Built as a humble two-room adobe in the 1920s, a few blocks from the plaza, the "House of Chimneys" bloomed over time into a grand hacienda. It was already a special place when Susan Vernon purchased the property in 1987, but she gilded the lily in a magnificent manner, creating one of the loveliest gardens in New Mexico and one of the most refined B&Bs in the Southwest.

Susan prides herself on attention to the details, and properly so. You can see her conscientious care in the brilliant floral palette of the walled grounds, the 200-thread sheets on the beds, the breadth of the bathroom amenities, and the elegant breakfasts bursting with regional flavor. Her special morning frappé, a blend of juices and fruit, made it into the pages of *Gourmet*.

The four guest rooms feature kiva fireplaces, viga ceilings, private baths and entrances, TVs, phones, and a compact fridge stocked with complimentary beverages. All are wonderful, but the Library Suite takes the grand prize. It may be the most alluring chamber in town—though hardly the most expensive—because of its namesake parlor, a perfect place to read and relax.

El Rincón Inn.
Rates start at $59 for a room with a low ceiling, rented only to people shorter than six feet two inches, and go up to $125 for a lofty suite.
114 Kit Carson Road, Taos 87571.
505-758-4874.
Major credit cards.

The most joyfully eclectic of the Taos B&Bs, El Rincón celebrates the enduring eccentricity of the town. Just a block from the plaza, it's close to the core in all ways.

The dozen rooms are dazzlingly different— from each other and from most accommodations you'll find anywhere. Sonrisa shines in its Garden of Eden bath, covered with handmade tiles and murals depicting the biblical paradise, and Los Angelitos soars with a collection of angels from around the world. Deriving its theme from host Paul "Paco" Castillo's Pueblo name, the Yellow Bird Deer Room abounds in American Indian decor, while the Paisley Room flaunts an East Indian motif. Many of the chambers enjoy a kiva fireplace and all come with a private bath, TV, VCR, stereo, and a basic breakfast served on a sunny patio or in a colorful dining room.

Hacienda del Sol.

The least expensive double—filled with light and two handcrafted double beds—costs $65. For $120, at the top of the rate scale, Los Amantes gives you a spacious chamber with a fireplace and a double-size Jacuzzi tub under a skylight positioned for stargazing.
P.O. Box 177, Taos 87571.
505-758-0287.
Credit cards for deposits only.

Truly a sunny spot, as the name suggests, the B&B won recognition from *USA Today* as one of the ten most romantic inns in the country. Proprietors John and Marcine Landon earn the distinction in many ways, from their attentive landscaping of the garden grounds to their hearty and delicious breakfasts, served beside a roaring fire in the winter, and in the summer on a patio peering out to the hot tub.

The Landons' rooms are their ultimate treat for guests. Spread through a historic 1804 adobe and two newer casitas, just a mile from the Taos plaza, the quarters exude Southwestern charm. Each is different but most enjoy a kiva fireplace, viga ceiling, regional antiques, a colorful quilt, and original art on the walls. All come with a private bath and a cassette player with a collection of tapes chosen to provide a little romantic night music.

Mabel Dodge Luhan House.

Prices in the original house start at $75 for rooms with twin beds and a shared bath and go up to $150 for Mabel's own suite, with her handcarved double bed, private bath, kiva fireplace, and patio entranceway. We would avoid the more modern quarters in a new guesthouse, which share little of the character you're looking for.
240 Morada Lane,
P.O. Box 3400,
Taos 87571.
800-84 MABEL,
505-758-9456. MC, V.

During her four-decade residency, the flamboyant grande dame of Taos made this the town's "Big House," a magnificent Pueblo-style hacienda that welcomed a world of eminent guests. Carl Jung dreamed here, D. H. Lawrence painted some windows, Willa Cather wrote in one of the rooms, and Georgia O'Keeffe came to contemplate a move to New Mexico. After Mabel's death, actor Dennis Hopper bought the estate and hosted another generation of celebrities. Now a B&B, the house allows you to snuggle up with legends.

Don't jump too quickly at the opportunity, though. The B&B hasn't lived up to its enormous potential in the early years, providing personality for sure but neglecting some of the basics. The owner apparently wants to sell the property, which could put the B&B out of business or, on the other hand, result in substantial improvements. Ask before you leap.

Salsa del Salto.
Rates range from $85 to $160.
P.O. Box 1468,
El Prado 87529.
505-776-2422.
MC, V.

Built by acclaimed architect Antoine Predock, this stunning contemporary Southwestern home sits in a small luxury development midway between the Taos Ski Valley and the town, within ten miles of each. Innkeepers Dadou Mayer and Mary Hockett, from the French Riviera and New Mexico, respectively, dreamed for years of hosting guests in such a house and that goal shows in every aspect of their design and operation.

A professional chef (Dadou) and a talented baker (Mary), the proprietors start the day with an elegant breakfast and then encourage you to join them in the late afternoon in front of the majestic stone fireplace for salsa and more. In between, you can swim in the heated outdoor pool, soak in the hot tub, or play tennis on the private court.

The eight guest rooms feature views of mountains or the Taos mesa, handcrafted New Mexico furniture, king beds with goose-down comforters, and private baths. The ultimate abode, The Master's Suite, opens onto a covered portal and boasts a handsome fireplace with copper detailing.

Taos Country Inn.
High-season rates run from $110 to $150.
P.O. Box 2331,
Taos 87571.
505-758-4900.
MC, V.

The B&B is just two miles from the Taos plaza, but it definitely means the "country" in its name. Situated along a mountain stream, the Rio Pueblo, the inn nestles under the shelter of two-hundred-year-old willows and cottonwoods.

Some parts of the home are almost as old as the trees, yet it projects a contemporary countenance. New Mexico nuances shine throughout, but all the comforts are up-to-date. Each of the nine rooms has a private bath, fireplace, TV, phone, leather sofa, and handcarved furniture. Some enjoy their own entrances and Jacuzzi tubs. Yolanda, the personable hostess, serves a full breakfast in the morning, starting with a bread and fruit buffet and then a hot entrée. Her hospitality is genuine, just like the country milieu.

Taos Hacienda Inn.
Rates start at $95 for a small room and go up to $185 for Cary's Studio.
315 Ranchitos Road, Box 4159,
Taos 87571.
800-530-3040,
505-758-1717.
Major credit cards.

Atop a small hill just three blocks from the Taos plaza, the inn sprawls serenely through a magnificent historic home. Thick adobe walls surround the park-like grounds, where you can relax in a hot tub, and inside, a spacious living room and sunny dining room welcome you warmly with kiva fireplaces, viga-and-latilla ceilings, a gurgling fountain, and walls of local art.

Each of the seven guest quarters is distinctively different, though all come with their own fireplaces and baths, king or queen beds, phones, and TVs. Of the regular double rooms, we particularly like Georgia's Garden, which features O'Keeffe prints, a private entrance, and French doors that lead out to a secluded corner of the courtyard. Two artists' studios provide extra space, sleeping up to five people. The largest and most expensive, Cary's Studio, enjoys lots of light and grand vistas. All guests get a full breakfast in the morning, hors d'oeuvres in the afternoon, and a memorable escape from the ordinary.

Touchstone Inn.
The Library and Tony rooms cost $85 and suites run from $115 to $135.
P.O. Box 2896,
Taos 87571.
800-758-0192,
505-758-0192.
MC, V.

When D. H. Lawrence stayed here in the 1920s, before the B&B days, he called it "a gay little adobe house" and found it such a perfect hideaway that he didn't go out to "see much of the 'world'." The home has grown larger over time, but the setting remains as the novelist described, a bucolic retreat on a brook just one mile from the Taos plaza.

Touchstone emphasizes luxury in its rooms and luscious cornucopia in its breakfasts. Each of the six chambers comes with a private bath made for pampering, TV, VCR, tape player, oriental rugs, and original art. Most open to patios and outside entrances, and half have kiva fireplaces. Even one of the smallest and least expensive rooms, the Miriam Hapgood Library, enjoys all those virtues plus a canopied bed.

The Willows Inn.
The regular double rooms cost $95 and the Hennings Studio goes for a bargain $130.
Corner of Kit Carson Road and Dolan Street, NDCBU 4558, Taos 87571.
505-758-2558.
MC, V.

Perhaps our personal favorite among the many fine B&Bs, the inn takes its name from two of the largest living willow trees in North America, massive old-timers that greet you gracefully as soon as you pull in the gravel drive of the walled compound. The adobe hacienda just beyond, on the National Register of Historic Places, flows gently with the same organic form as the billowing branches. Once the home and studio of E. Martin Hennings, a major Taos painter early in this century, it now provides accommodations as artful and well priced as any in town.

The four spacious double rooms are all superb values. Admirably appointed to match their names—Cowboy, Anasazi, Conquistador, and Santa Fe—each has a private bath and entrance, a kiva fireplace, wood floors, and viga ceilings. The fifth guest room, Hennings's former studio, offers the same allures and much more. A suite in size, it features a grand queen bed with a seven-foot headboard, a sofa sleeper, an enclosed patio, and a whirlpool tub in the bath. A painting stands on an easel, other original art adorns the walls, and pigment splashed by Hennings dots an area of the floor.

Innkeepers Janet and Doug Camp cater to their guests with personable hospitality. They invite you to their living room to watch TV, listen to a CD, make a phone call, or pick up a game to play. In the morning the Camps prepare an elegant breakfast and dine with you, suggesting possible activities or shops on the plaza, a half-mile away. As the day winds down, they ask you to join them again for wine and freshly made snacks such as smoked trout and piñon brownies. When you have to check out, you'll

leave with new friends and enduring memories
of the Willows.

BEST INNS

Adobe Wall.
A double room goes
for $56 in the winter
and $50 the rest of
the year. Some
adjoining rooms serve
as suites for families
or friends traveling
together.
227 Kit Carson Road,
P.O. Box 1081,
Taos 87571.
505-758-3972.
MC, V.

Taos has a number of chain motels, but if you're
looking for individual style and true Southwestern flavor, opt instead for one of the town's renovated motor-court classics. The Sun God Lodge,
described below, offers more frills than the Adobe
Wall, but the latter compensates with lower rates
and a prime country setting under the shade of
towering cottonwoods just east of downtown.

An art gallery greets you at the entrance to
the nonsmoking motel, offering a sculpture-dot-
ted courtyard for guest contemplation. Ask for a
room facing the patio, away from the road. All
the quarters are comfortable, though usually
cozy in size except for special chambers such as
number 17. A refreshment room provides coffee,
sodas, and snacks, but the closest restaurant is a
short drive or brisk walk away.

Sagebrush Inn.
In peak season,
double rooms start at
$95, but we would
spend an additional
$15 to get a fireplace.
Suites with a living
room are $125 to
$140 for two.
N.M. 68, Box 557,
Taos 87571.
800-428-3626,
505-758-2254.
Major credit cards.

With more attention to the details, this historic
hotel could rival any in New Mexico. As is, the
Sagebrush is worth considering for its extraordinary Taos character, but you have to rein in your
expectations. Many people who stay elsewhere
get an ample measure of the mood just by visiting the bar (see Chapter 15).

Built in 1929 with traditional adobe techniques, the hotel served as a home and studio for
Georgia O'Keeffe for six months in the 1930s. In
the decades since, the Sagebrush has gradually
grown to one hundred rooms and condominiums, acquired an outdoor pool and indoor hot
tubs, and added more steaks to the menu at Los
Vaqueros. Guests today get some of the hotel's
venerable spirit in their quarters, but it doesn't
always mesh well with the modern improvements.

Sun God Lodge.
Refurbished doubles from the old days cost $67, and newer, larger deluxe doubles go for $75, a better overall value. Suites and rooms with kitchenettes are $95. 919 Paseo del Pueblo Sur, P.O. Box 1713, Taos 87571. 800-821-2437, 505-758-3162, fax 505-758-1716. MC, V.

Sparkling fresh today, this renovated 1950s motel offers old-fashioned motor-lodge hospitality with all the modern conveniences. The original rooms, which line a landscaped central courtyard, look brand-new except for their tiny baths. A hot tub and a second wing in the back of the property are indeed new, added in 1993.

All the 55 rooms and suites boast a bright, colorful Southwestern style, with handcrafted furniture and prints on the walls. Some come with a kitchenette, and each has a coffeemaker, TV, and phone. The suites offer a kiva fireplace in the separate living room.

Taos Inn.
Rates start at $70 and peak at $155. 125 Paseo del Pueblo Norte, Taos 87571. 800-TAOS INN, 505-758-2233, fax 505-758-5776. MC, V.

Billing itself as "an adventure for visitors, a tradition for locals," the Taos Inn is that and more. A downtown landmark, a building on the National Register of Historic Places, the host of the "Meet the Artist" Series, the most popular watering hole in town—it's simply the living room of the community.

In the nineteenth century the current lobby was an open courtyard that connected a cluster of separate residences. The town's first physician, Paul Martin, bought the complex after he moved to Taos in 1895, and his widow converted it to a hotel on his death in 1935. Where Doc Martin's restaurant (see Chapter 15) now serves fine wines, the namesake doc used to pour cod liver oil.

The 39 rooms vary considerably in size and features, though each is steeped in the inn's Southwestern spirit, with handcrafted local furniture, custom-made Zapotec bedspreads, and usually a kiva fireplace built by adobe artist Carmen Velarde. The TVs and carpets can look incongruous, but they supposedly serve a purpose. Even if you don't get the full enchantment of the town's best B&B quarters, you have all of Taos in your living room.

BEST SKI LODGES AND CONDOMINIUMS

Hotel Edelweiss.
Ski-package rates are
$2,860 per week for
two people in a
double room.
P.O. Box 83, Taos Ski
Valley 87525.
800-I LUV SKI,
505-776-2301,
fax 505-776-2533.
Major credit cards.

Just a schuss away from the lifts at the Taos Ski Valley, this 21-room Alpine inn enchants in all ways, from the traditional European atmosphere to the recently renovated rooms. A big stone fireplace greets you in the lobby and proprietors Tim and Ann-Marie Woolridge maintain the warmth of the welcome throughout your stay.

Like other prime spots near the slopes, the Edelweiss likes to uphold the Taos tradition of "Ski Better Weeks," a Saturday-to-Saturday package plan that includes accommodations, daily meals, lift tickets, and morning ski lessons. In this case, the rate covers breakfast and dinner in a hotel restaurant that serves a variety of fine food, from American regional to continental cuisine. Other deals for fewer nights may be available at the very beginning or end of the season, depending on conditions. You can also enjoy Edelweiss on a more limited scale from June to October, when it operates as a B&B for $65 a night.

Hotel St. Bernard.
Two people pay
$2,700 for one week
(Saturday to Saturday)
for a double room and
everything else.
P.O. Box 88, Taos Ski
Valley 87525.
505-776-2251.
No credit cards.

This could be your skier heaven, at least if you're interested in a week's stay, fancy food, and daily ski lessons. The owner of the 28-room hotel, Jean Mayer, is also the technical director for the world-class Taos Ski Valley Ski School, and he only accepts guests on a full package that includes classes, lift tickets, and all meals. The rooms are attractively Alpine, though simple in some respects, and the dinners are decidedly French, ambling through multiple courses.

The St. Bernard isn't for everyone and makes no pretense to be. If it doesn't strike a chord instantly, go elsewhere, but if you fantasize about a true European ski experience in the Rockies, book it early. The hotel fills up quickly, mainly with repeat guests who can't get enough of the coddling. The rest of us mortals make do with a drink in the atmospheric Rathskeller bar, right at the bottom of the slopes.

Inn at Snakedance.

At slow periods of the ski season, the basic double rates dip as low as $125, but they go up as high as $230 during Christmas week. Though the hotel offers week-long ski packages, it doesn't require them. P.O. Box 89, Taos Ski Valley 87525. 800-322-9815, 505-776-2277, fax 505-776-1410. Major credit cards.

A new sixty-room hotel at the center of the Ski Valley, Snakedance strives to maintain the mountain aura of the inn it replaced, the turn-of-the-century Hondo Lodge, a hunter's hideaway long before anyone in Taos skied. The architects accomplished the goal handily in the cozy library, warmed by a large stone fireplace, and in the Hondo Restaurant and Bar, where massive old beams support the ceiling.

The designers didn't capture the feel quite as well in the rooms, but they did provide plenty of contemporary comforts. All the quarters come with TVs, phones, tub-shower combos, queen or king beds, wet bars, and compact refrigerators. For only $20 extra, you can have a fireplace and sitting area. Everyone gets use of the fitness center and hot tub as well as good, quick access to the ski lift.

St. Bernard Condominiums.

For the required seven-night stay (Saturday to Saturday) accommodations only, with no package enhancements, cost $2,600 for up to six people. A ski lift, school, and dinner package is $1,175 per person if you have four people in your party and $1,000 per person for a group of six. P.O. Box 676, Taos Ski Valley 87525. 505-776-8506. Major credit cards, but checks or cash preferred.

On a hill overlooking the Ski Valley, this small operation boasts the most luxurious condos in the area, handsome two-bedroom, two-bath apartments that accommodate up to six people. Individually decorated by the owners in stylish ways, each has a fully equipped kitchen, TVs, VCRs, phones, and balconies that peer directly out to the ski trails.

The rooms are a short walk to the lifts, but you don't need to worry about carting your equipment. You stow it in a room reserved for the use of condo guests at the Hotel St. Bernard, where you can also use the fitness center and hot tub. Package plans even include dinners at the hotel's renowned restaurant.

Quail Ridge Inn.
Rates range between
$85 and $220 in the
summer and go as
high as $350 in the
winter.
P.O. Box 707, Taos
87571.
800-624-4448,
505-776-2211,
fax 505-776-2949.
Major credit cards.

Advertising itself as a family resort, conference center, and tennis ranch, Quail Ridge can be all of those things if you want, but it's basically a condominium development. The individually owned units, simply but adequately appointed, can be configured as standard hotel rooms (with a queen bed, sleeper sofa, and fireplace), studios (which add a kitchen and terrace to the package), and one- or two-bedroom suites (combining hotel rooms and studios).

The recreational facilities are the highlight at Quail Ridge, set in a quiet rural area four miles north of town. Two of the eight well-maintained Laykold tennis courts enjoy protection from the elements inside an all-weather bubble. The heated twenty-meter pool, fitness center, and hot tubs stay open throughout the year. In the winter, a shuttle carries skiers to the slopes. Before or after a day of play, you can get eat in the Renegade Cafe, an aptly sporty spot.

CHAPTER FIFTEEN

Creative Cooking and Carousing

*T*AOS'S artistic heritage finds its way into food in the town's top restaurants. With a few notable exceptions, the cooking lacks the refinement of Santa Fe—which has ten times the population base—and the tempting diversity of Albuquerque—a true metropolis—but it boasts an imaginative and expansive spirit. Eating out in Taos can teach your taste buds novel tricks.

In other respects, what we said about Santa Fe restaurants in the introduction to Chapter 8 applies in Taos too. In both places, our main criterion in the recommendations is talented cooking, but we also look for superior value, sympathetic service, and an agreeable atmosphere.

The cost categories remain the same as well. "Expensive" means entrées cost over $18. Under $8 is "inexpensive," and in-between is "moderate." Whatever your budget, you can eat creatively in Taos if you choose your table with crafty sensibility.

AMERICAN AND
CONTEMPORARY SOUTHWESTERN

Apple Tree.
123 Bent Street,
downtown.
505-758-1900.
Open daily for dinner,
for lunch Monday
through Friday, and
for brunch on the
weekend.
Reservations advised.
Moderate.
Major credit cards.

A local favorite for many years, the Apple Tree takes the "melting-pot" approach to American cooking, blending flavors from around the world into a merry melange of its own. In our experience, the inventive ferment works best at the weekday lunches and weekend brunches, but many people love the daily dinners as well.

The starters on the changing menu always include sumptuous salads and soups, which can make a fine and filling meal ordered together. Among the lunch sandwiches, consider the Veggie Burger or the Shrimp Quesadilla. For an entrée in the evening, you can go global with mango chicken enchiladas or vegetarian green curry, or stick closer to home with a steak or grilled lamb chops. At any time of the day, the dining rooms and patio of the old downtown adobe sparkle, setting an appetizing country-inn mood.

Doc Martin's.
125 Paseo del Pueblo
Norte, in the Taos Inn.
505-758-1977.
Open daily for
breakfast, lunch, and
dinner.
Reservations advised
for dinner. Moderate
for breakfast and
lunch, expensive for
dinner. Major credit
cards.

Wine lovers converge on Doc Martin's like bears on a beehive. A consistent *Wine Spectator* award-winner, the Taos Inn restaurant showcases one of the best cellars in the Southwest, soaring to the stars in quality and price both. Even the selection by the glass can be outstanding.

Over the years the contemporary Southwestern cooking has reached similar peaks at times and then taken big dips in other periods. The food is usually a reasonable foil for the vino at least, but it can come off as pricey and pretentious for the town. The seasonal dinner menu opens with appetizers such as chiles rellenos, salmon gorditas, and smoked chicken tostadas. Main courses might include chile-braised rabbit, or cider-soaked pork tenderloin. If you're tempted by the fare, give the kitchen a try first at breakfast or lunch to see how the pans are clicking.

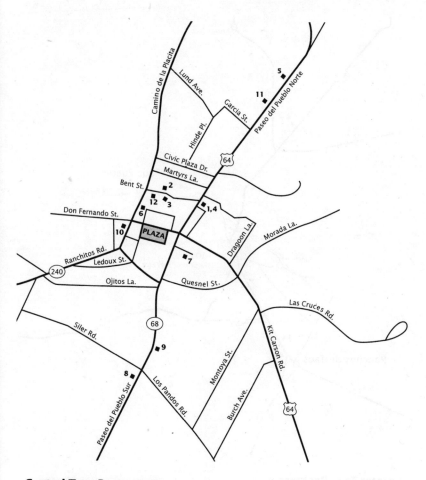

Central Taos Restaurants
1. Adobe Bar
2. Apple Tree
3. Bent Street Deli
4. Doc Martin's
5. Dori's and Tony's
6. El Patio de Taos
7. Eske's Brew Pub
8. Fred's Place
9. Lambert's of Taos
10. Mainstreet Bakery & Cafe
11. Michael's Kitchen
12. Tapas de Taos

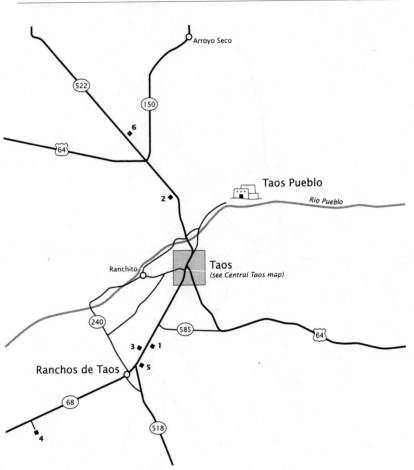

Greater Taos Restaurants
1. Jacquelina's Southwestern Cuisine
2. The Outback
3. Sagebrush Inn
4. The Stakeout
5. Trading Post Cafe
6. Villa Fontana

Jacquelina's Southwestern Cuisine.

1541 Paseo del Pueblo Sur, about four miles south of the Taos plaza.
505-751-0399.
Closed Monday. Lunch and dinner.
Reservations advised for dinner. Moderate.
Major credit cards.

A refugee from the kitchen of the beloved and bemoaned Brett House, a first-rate restaurant in its day, Jacquelina brings similar Southwestern style to her newer, simpler cafe. The changing seasonal menu roams the contemporary landscape, tendering hearty salads (such as a Caesar de Pollo), nouvelle enchiladas (perhaps a blue corn variation with long-roasted duck leg), tastes of the sea (like Fresh Ahi Tuna with Mango-Serrano Chili Salsa), and the bounty of the range (certain to include a cowboy steak). The best choice of all may be the pork marinated in chipotle chile and honey, one of the most dependable dishes in the occasionally overreaching repertory.

Lambert's of Taos.

309 Paseo del Pueblo Sur, a few blocks south of the Taos plaza.
505-758-1009.
Open daily for dinner and on weekdays for lunch.
Reservations advised.
Moderate.
Major credit cards.

Zeke Lambert came to Taos from California years ago and helped to build the repute of Doc Martin's during one of its most successful periods. In 1989 he moved again, just a mile or so this time, down the road to the historic Randall Home. Now the chef seems firmly ensconced in his own intimate, elegant restaurant and in his own local reputation as a culinary master.

The menu shifts gears gently every week, evolving with the availability of fresh ingredients but maintaining a fine balance between the classic and the contemporary. The starters always include salads and soup, perhaps marinated artichoke hearts on young greens and a roasted pepper and spaghetti squash soup. The grilled dishes shine, both as appetizers (such as radicchio with a blue cheese vinaigrette) and as main courses, when Lambert puts the flame to pork tenderloin, lamb chops, fish steaks, and beef filet. You'll usually find a game specialty among the entrées and you can count on a chance to wrap up any meal with a richly rewarding dessert.

Michael's Kitchen.
304 Paseo del Pueblo
Norte, just north of
downtown.
505-758-4178.
Open daily for
breakfast, lunch, and
dinner.
No reservations.
Inexpensive to
moderate. MC, V.

You can get a hearty breakfast all day at Michael's, which is a good thing since that's the kitchen's forte. The menu offers a plethora of sandwiches, steaks, New Mexican platters, and more, but the lunch and dinner dishes seldom rise above the mundane. Whether it's morning, noon, or night, set your sights on something like an omelet, the granola pancakes, or the breakfast burrito, stuffed with scrambled eggs, bacon, hash browns, and green chile. A funky longtimer that now seems as quaint as free love, the restaurant captures the essence of laid-back in a town renowned for the trait.

The Outback.
On Paseo del Pueblo
Norte, about one-and-
a-half miles north of
the Taos plaza.
505-758-3112.
Open daily for lunch
and dinner.
Reservations not
needed. Inexpensive.
MC, V.

It is "outback," behind a video store on the fringes of town, but it's upfront in claiming to be "a slice above." The dozen specialty pizzas range from a Primavera (mushrooms, artichoke hearts, olives, sun-dried tomatoes, feta cheese, and walnuts) to a Carnivore (with a choice of four meats). If the pizzas don't match your mood, you can opt instead for homemade soup, a full-meal salad, pasta, or a chicken Parmesan sandwich made with slices of marinated breast and stir-fried vegetables.

The Stakeout.
On Stakeout Drive, off
N.M. 68 about eight
miles south of the
Taos plaza.
505-758-2042.
Open daily for dinner
and on Sunday in the
summer for brunch.
Reservations advised.
Moderate to
expensive.
Major credit cards.

South of town, a mile up a dusty dirt road, the Stakeout sits atop Outlaw Hill, named for its perspective on the horizon. Desperadoes and diners alike get a good long-range view of Taos, alerting the one to approaching adversaries and enchanting the other with magical mountain sunsets.

The cooking has improved considerably in recent years under new management. The menu offers selected specialties, from Trout en Papillote to Duck Cumberland, but the kitchen really excels with venison preparations and the half-dozen steaks. If you're bursting with hunger, saddle up for the Steak Fiorentina, a mammoth cowboy cut accented with Alpina sauce. Pasta plates satisfy smaller appetites, and nibblers can make do with two or three of the appetizers, which include baked brie, carpaccio, and escargots. In the warmer months, enjoy your dinner on the panoramic patio, and in the winter, snuggle up closely to a roaring fire.

BAKERIES, COFFEEHOUSES, AND DELIS

Bent Street Deli.
120 Bent Street, downtown.
505-758-5787.
Closed Sunday.
Breakfast, lunch, and dinner.
No reservations.
Inexpensive to moderate. MC, V.

A downtown resting spot all day for a cappuccino or freshly baked croissant, the deli is also a dependable stop for full meals. Come in the morning for a veggie or Spanish omelet, at lunch for the biggest sandwich selection in town, or in the evening for a light but satisfying supper. The moderately priced dinners feature large salads and entrées such as a New Mexican chicken *mole* and Prima Vera Sumatra, stir-fried vegetables tossed with pasta and an Indonesian *satay*. Enjoy your selections on the pleasant patio or on a mountain picnic.

Dori's and Tony's.
402 Paseo del Pueblo Norte, a few blocks north of the Taos plaza.
505-758-9222.
Open daily for breakfast, lunch and dinner.
No reservations.
Inexpensive. MC, V.

Dori used to do it on her own, and only in the morning, but now she has a partner and they do it all day. The founder's breakfast menu, served through lunchtime, features her Hash Brown Heaven, potatoes (or brown rice if you wish) covered with cheese, green chile, and a fried egg. She'll also serve you fruit with a freshly baked muffin, a bagel and lox, or scones and an espresso. Tony's Manly Burrito will keep your stomach on hold until the evening, when he trots out an array of straightforward Italian specialties. If your mind reels from the ferment of flavors, you'll feel right at home in a Taos institution that remains a tribute to individual inspiration.

Mainstreet Bakery & Cafe.
Guadalupe Plaza, one-half block west of the Taos plaza.
505-758-9610.
Open daily for breakfast, lunch, and dinner.
No reservations or credit cards.
Inexpensive.

The counterculture bounces back with gusto at this downtown hangout *cum* hideaway. Advertising that the food is "all organic–all natural almost," the cramped cafe starts the day with choices such as scrambled tofu, buckwheat pancakes, homemade granola, a variety of garlic-laced egg dishes, and toasts that run the gamut from chile anadama to cinnamon raisin. At lunch, tackle a bowl of the black beans, green chile, red onions, and tomatoes served with the house cornbread. The dinners grow larger but stay just as elemental.

BARS

Adobe Bar.
125 Paseo del Pueblo Norte, in the Taos Inn.
505-758-2233.
Open daily.
Major credit cards.

Long a popular hangout for residents and visitors alike, the bar at the Taos Inn gets crowded quickly on busy days, even with seating that sprawls through the lobby, a library, and a street-front patio. The people-watching is always enjoyable but the entertainment broadens several nights a week when local musicians perform. Order hors d'oeuvres from Doc Martin's, or come back later in the evening for one of the desserts and an espresso.

Eske's Brew Pub.
106 Des Georges Lane, one-half block east of the Taos plaza.
505-758-1517.
Open daily.
No reservations.
Meals inexpensive.
MC, V.

Brewmaster Steve "Eske" Eskeback developed his love for full-bodied beers in Europe, but he felicitously translates the Old World taste to the Taos setting in classics such as 10,000-Foot Stout and Green Chile Ale. He always has a half-dozen handcrafted specials on tap, ready to drink by the pint in the former adobe home or outside on a beer-garden patio. To soak up the suds, Eske offers a limited selection of pub fare, from traditional Bangers and Mashers to the singular potato and egg medley called Tapa de Tortilla Española.

Sagebrush Inn.
N.M. 68, a few miles south of the Taos plaza.
505-758-2254.
Open daily.
Major credit cards.

A combination honky-tonk and Southwestern monument, the lobby bar at the Sagebrush Inn may have you two-stepping with delight even before the band begins to warm up midevening. Massive beams support old vigas, a fire blazes in the winter, and the cluttered walls flaunt enough regional icons to stagger a museum curator. Navajo rugs, paintings, and a local carving of Christ on the cross watch over you while you sit and sip or dance to the music, usually country-and-western in beat.

ITALIAN

Trading Post Cafe.
N.M. 68 in Ranchos de Taos, about four miles from the Taos plaza.
505-758-5089.
Open daily for lunch and dinner.
No reservations.
Moderate.
Major credit cards.

The best thing to hit Taos since skiing, this is superb succor. At least it is at press time, when the brand new cafe is bowling over people like a serial killer on a snowboard. The kitchen hasn't been tested by time, but even a few stumbles will leave it on a level seldom seen in the area.

Don't think conventional sophistication or conventional anything. The three conspiring chef-partners—"just call us René, Kimberly, and Marco"—simply know good food, and that's what they fix in a pleasant but inauspicious cafe. What can you say about a menu that separates nothing into separate courses or categories, and ranges in choices from chicken noodle soup to osso buco Milanese? We say hooray.

The base of the cooking is Italian, but it has no national boundaries or any faddish fusion pretensions either. Escargots come with crispy pasta and the Sonoma lamb chops with a tomato mint salsa, while the penne *arrabbiata* and the fettuccine *alla carbonara* are exactly what the Roman gods always intended. Go figure, if you wish, but do go eat.

Villa Fontana.
N.M. 522, five miles
north of Taos.
505-758-5800.
Closed Sunday. Lunch
Tuesday through
Friday and dinner
Monday through
Saturday. Reservations
advised. Moderate to
expensive.
Major credit cards.

This is the other side of Italian inspiration from the Trading Post Cafe, a well-honed, refined rendition of the cuisine's Northern classics. In an elegantly attired country adobe just outside town, the restaurant wins laurels from experts of international stature, including the Distinguished Restaurants of North America organization and Italian food and wine critic Luigi Veronelli.

Chef Carlo Gislimberti, who hails from the Italian Dolomites, and his wife Siobhan love wild mushrooms. They select them personally to flavor a variety of dishes, including a luscious pâté and their magnificent Crema di funghi Porcini, among the best appetizers. If your wallet is thinner than you wish, choose an entrée from the list of pastas, available in first- and main-course portions. If you're feeling flush, head instead for the specialties, perhaps the glorious osso buco or the changing fresh fish and game dishes. You might take a wrong turn finding Villa Fontana, but you won't anywhere on the menu.

MEXICAN AND NEW MEXICAN

El Patio de Taos.
Teresina Lane,
between the Taos
plaza and Bent Street.
505-758-2121.
Open daily for lunch
and dinner.
Reservations advised
for dinner. Moderate.
Major credit cards.

The closest place to the plaza to eat well, El Patio has drawn crowds for decades. Part of its allure comes from the setting, in a handsome adobe with portions of walls that date back to the seventeenth century. The menu is less venerable, shifting over the years with changes in the kitchen. Recently, the cooking settled comfortably into a combination Mexican and New Mexican mode, featuring a variety of enchiladas, flautas, burritos, and similar dishes at both lunch and dinner. In the evening, the main-course choices also include "significant others," such as margarita shrimp and pork in a *mole* sauce. It's stalwart fare, if not exactly stellar, and it offers a soothing respite from downtown sightseeing.

Fred's Place.
332 Paseo del Pueblo Sur, just south of downtown.
505-758-0514.
Open daily for dinner.
No reservations or credit cards.
Inexpensive.

A simple storefront cafe, Fred's serves the best authentic New Mexican cooking in town right now. The namesake proprietor is still new at the business at our press deadline, but he's already won the affection of many locals for going back to the basics with gusto.

Pass over the more common salsa and guacamole appetizers in favor of old home kitchen favorites such as *chicos* (specially processed corn kernels) or squash stew. Among the main courses, consider the enchiladas, a carne adovada burrito, pork tamales, or a combination plate that packages several of the options. It's all tasty and true to the source.

Tapas de Taos.
136 Bent Street, downtown.
505-758-9670.
Open daily for dinner, for lunch Monday through Friday, and for brunch on the weekend.
Reservations usually not necessary.
Inexpensive to moderate. MC, V.

The name may mislead you at this mainly Mexican cafe, a cheerful spot decorated in a festive Day of the Dead motif. The menu presents a wide selection of dishes called "tapas," but they are really appetizers, ranging from a jazzy version of *queso fundido* to savory pork and ginger potstickers. Follow one at lunch with tacos or a burrito filled with a grill specialty—either carne asada (beef), chicken, or pork *al pastor*—and garnish the plate to your taste at the salsa bar. You have the same option in the evening among the varied choices, which include vegetarian tamales, a Yucatecan *pooc chuc,* and shrimp sautéed in garlic and chile. The portions tend to be small relative to price—the most noticeable nod to a tapas inspiration—but the flavor is often big.

PART FOUR

Albuquerque

CHAPTER SIXTEEN

Old Town Sightseeing

and Shopping

SPANISH COLONISTS established Albuquerque in 1706, a century after their ancestors settled Santa Fe and Taos. The founders named the town for the then Viceroy of New Spain, the Duke of Alburquerque, whose only claim to historic honor comes from the modern city that misspells his once-revered title by dropping the first "r."

Albuquerque remained a small and somnolent village until 1880, when the railroad roared into town. Santa Fe was still much larger at the time and more of a commercial hub, but the capital spurned the Atchison, Topeka & Santa Fe Railroad, sending the namesake line south instead. That quirk of fate turned Albuquerque into the transportation axis of the state and stimulated a steady growth of industry and population.

The city's downtown grew up around the railroad depot, which the Atchison, Topeka & Santa Fe deliberately built a couple of miles east of the original village, now known as Old Town. An area bounded by Central Avenue, Rio Grande Boulevard, and Mountain Road—see the map in Chapter 17— the neighborhood retains much of its architectural integrity and many vestiges of historic character.

Old Town Plaza

Settled in the traditional Spanish style, Old Town features blocks of low adobe buildings surrounding a central plaza. The lovely San Felipe de Neri Church, dating to 1793, graces one side of the plaza, maintaining its dignity despite the touristy bustle on the nearby streets. Named to honor King Philip V of Spain, the church initially had a simple facade that was altered in the late nineteenth century to include the distinctive twin spires, added to give an air of European refinement.

With the exception of the rectory next door, similar in age to San Felipe de Neri, the other historic buildings around the plaza come from the same territorial time period as the spires. Now occupied by shops and restaurants, the structures hide some of their old character behind commercial gloss, but it's easy to look beyond the modern embellishments into the village past.

The Sister Blandina Convent, on the west side of the church, was erected in 1881 to house the nuns who taught at Albuquerque's first school, located in the adjacent adobe at 320 Romero Street. Farther west, directly across from the plaza, nineteenth-century merchants constructed the four buildings at 121, 201, 205, and 301 Romero. The distinctive El Parrillán, on the northwest corner of Romero and South Plaza, dates to the 1890s, when it served as a saloon and barbershop.

On South Plaza, the Manuel Springer House at 2036 and the Cristóbal Armijo House at 2004 originated as elegant Queen Anne mansions. Across the street on San Felipe, the long, low adobe that runs the width of the plaza developed as Ambrosio Armijo's combination residence and store. German-American farmers, the Bluehers and the Stueckels, founded their homesteads in the same period just up the block at 302 and 306 San Felipe.

Strolling and Shopping

A warren of placitas, portals, and narrow passageways, about four blocks square, Old Town is wonderful for wandering in an unhurried way. You'll definitely want to browse the shops as you stroll, though it's easy to get discouraged by the number of places stuck in the trinket-and-T-shirt rut. To help you sort through the scads of shops, we mention some that may be worth a stop, depending on your personal interests.

If you're a natural-history buff or have children in tow, start your tour at the American International Rattlesnake Museum, just south of the plaza at 202 San Felipe. A "museum" mainly in name, it charges a small admission to see an extraordinary private collection of rattlesnakes from all over the Americas. The gift shop stocks rattlesnake-related curios.

Directly north on San Felipe, Native American artisans sell jewelry, pottery, and more under the portal of the Ambrosio Armijo House and Store, now La Placita restaurant. Nearby shops carry work of higher quality, but it may be more fun to buy from the source.

As you continue up the street, poke into the arcades and alleyways that meander off toward the Albuquerque Museum. In a courtyard at 328 San Felipe, the Chile Pepper Emporium avows that it has "the hots for you." Farther back on the same garden terrace, at 324-C, Ortega's offers a small selection of handloomed weavings from Chimayó.

In the next block, Grey Tones (404 San Felipe) represents talented Navajo weavers and sculptors. Behind the gallery, the Patio Escondido rambles back to the small Chapel of Our Lady of Guadalupe, graced with a vivid and prominent painting of the beloved patroness at the entrance. The shaded sitting area outside is a pleasant spot to pause for rest or contemplation.

Across Mountain Road from San Felipe, a branch of the Maxwell Museum Store features a broad range of Native American crafts and folk art, chosen to reflect the spirit of the University of New Mexico's Maxwell Museum of Anthropology. In the same area, next to the Albuquerque Children's Museum, well-known cookbook author Jane Butel serves up chiles and spices as well as classes at her Southwestern Cooking School (800 Rio Grande, 800-473-TACO).

On the northern end of Romero Street, at 413, the Antonio Vigil House now shelters the historic and contemporary Indian art of the Adobe Gallery and the cowboy memorabilia at Rio West. The territorial-style home dates back to 1879.

On the other side of the street, the Tanner Chaney Gallery (410 Romero) offers an extensive collection of Native American pottery, jewelry, and weavings. In the next block south, the Navajo Gallery (323 Romero) represents the work of Navajo painter R. C. Gorman.

The mini-mall at 303 Romero contains an Albuquerque Visitor Information Center as well as Footsteps Across New Mexico, which has a strong selection of New Mexico books and a small theater that presents a film about the state. In the same complex, PotPourri sells kitchenware with a Southwestern accent and regional food products.

If you like to save the best for last, you might want to wrap up your wanderings at the Mariposa Gallery (113 Romero). It handles an excellent range of contemporary crafts, including many pieces made by New Mexico artists.

The Albuquerque Museum

On the northwest edge of Old Town, the Albuquerque Museum houses the most extensive collection of Spanish Colonial artifacts in the United States. The trove includes some of the first maps of the Southwest, arms and armor used in the conquest of the region, and domestic goods that exemplify everyday life. A permanent exhibit, "Four Centuries: A History of Albuquerque," traces the development of the city from those early years to the present.

Art gets its due too. The museum focuses primarily on New Mexico work, presenting shows in both indoor galleries and a sculpture garden.

The official address is 2000 Mountain Road Northwest, though many visitors enter the grounds from San Felipe Street as they're exploring Old Town. Closed Monday, the museum charges no admission but appreciates donations. Call 505-242-4600 for additional information.

New Mexico Museum of Natural History and Science

Just steps down the street from the Albuquerque Museum, two bronze dinosaurs welcome visitors to the New Mexico Museum of Natural History and Science. Built for excitement, it's one of the most stimulating and fun institutions of its kind in the country.

The adventure starts with a trip on the Evolator time machine, a high-tech journey through 38 million years of the state's geologic past. From there you can step into a hissing volcano, wander through an Ice Age cave, bone up on the Brachiosaurus, or join the big-screen action at the Dynamax Theater. Hands-on exhibits in the Naturalist Center introduce children to the inner workings of beehives and ant farms.

At 1801 Mountain Road Northwest, the museum is open daily, charging $4 for adults and only $1 for children under 12. The Dynamax Theater is extra. For other details, call 505-841-8837.

Albuquerque Children's Museum

The Children's Museum bounded to life in recent years to encourage creativity, imagination, and discovery in the arts and sciences for kids between ages 2 and 12. It features a variety of hands-on exhibits and participatory activities for youngsters and their parents, who must accompany their charges.

Near the Sheraton Old Town Hotel at 800 Rio Grande Boulevard Northwest, the museum is open daily, with shortened hours on Sunday. Kids pay $3 and adults $1. Call 505-842-5525 for program or other information.

Indian Pueblo Cultural Center

Just outside Old Town on the other side of I-40, a short drive
from the museums described above, the Indian Pueblo Cultural
Center provides a good introduction to Pueblo life in New
Mexico. The museum portion of the facility is rather spare,
though informative in explaining commonalities and differences among the various pueblos. Indian dancers perform frequently during the year, and artisans demonstrate their skills
and techniques on weekends.

The center devotes most of its space to an enormous gift
shop offering jewelry, pottery, and other crafts. All the work is
guaranteed authentic, and it's generally moderate in price as
well as quality.

At 2401 12th Street Northwest, the Indian Pueblo Cultural
Center is open daily and charges $3 admission for adults and
$1 for kids over 4. For details on dances and other events,
phone 505-843-7270.

CHAPTER SEVENTEEN

Route 66 and Beyond

ALBUQUERQUE consolidated its position as New Mexico's urban center in the early decades of the twentieth century. One of the nation's first airlines, TWA, made the city an overnight stop on its inaugural cross-country flights, and America's "Mother Road," the famed Route 66, brought several generations of highway travelers directly through downtown.

The old Route 66 is Central Avenue, still Albuquerque's main street. Several of the city's most interesting areas are along the historic highway and, appropriately enough, you need a car to get between them or to see much else of the town.

Downtown Albuquerque

The short stretch of Central Avenue in the modern downtown is a quick walk from the convention center, the focal point of activities for many people staying in the city. The highlight of the neighborhood is the flamboyant KiMo Theater (423 Central Avenue Northwest, 505-764-1700), built in 1927 as a movie house and vaudeville stage. Native American motifs inspired the fanciful art-deco facade and interior, an exuberant ferment of clever and kitschy design elements. The Hollywood architect even painted the radiators to look like Navajo rugs.

Home now to special performing arts events (see Chapter 18), the KiMo is open weekdays for a free look.

The theater opened in the heyday of downtown Albuquerque, just a year after Route 66 came through the city. Originally called "New Town," to distinguish it from the old Spanish settlement, the area grew up around the railroad depot in the late nineteenth century. Route 66 produced a boom that lasted for several decades, until suburbs and shopping centers began drawing residents away from the center. The downtown remains the financial and government hub of the city but now attracts many more business travelers than other tourists.

Much of the commerce downtown is oriented toward the area's work force, though a smattering of galleries and shops appeal to visitors. Just down the street from the KiMo Theater, Cafe (216 Central Avenue Southwest, 505-242-8244) offers contemporary exhibitions, performances, and events with an avant-garde edge. Next door, the Richard Levy Gallery (514 Central Avenue Southwest, 505-766-9888) features contemporary prints and other fine art. Two blocks to the south in St. John's Episcopal Church (318 Silver Southwest, 505-247-1581), the Cathedral Shop sells folk art from around the world.

University of New Mexico

Just east of downtown, the University of New Mexico dominates a long section of the old Route 66. The campus itself is a major attraction for its architecture and museums, and the shops and restaurants that line Central Avenue in the neighborhood offer that combination of funk and fascination you often find around major colleges.

Famed Santa Fe architect John Gaw Meem set the design standards for UNM's buildings in the 1930s, establishing the Spanish Pueblo style as the universal norm. One of his first projects, the Zimmerman Library, features massive ceiling vigas carved with abstract Native American images. Later additions now blur some of Meem's original vision of the library, but his work still stands undiluted at the Alumni Memorial Chapel, completed in 1962. The massive walls, flat roof, recessions, vigas, and corbels reflect the Spanish Pueblo motif at its purest.

The university also houses three important museums, including two devoted to fine art. The Jonson Gallery (1909 Las Lomas Northeast, 505-277-4967), in the home of the late painter Raymond Jonson, shows his work, that of the transcendentalist painting group, and other contemporary art. The University Art Museum (Central at Cornell, 505-277-4001) hosts changing exhibitions of nineteenth- and twentieth-century American and European art. Both are free and open during the day Monday through Friday, as well as Tuesday night. The University Art Museum also opens on Sunday afternoon.

The Maxwell Museum of Anthropology (University and Grand Northeast, 505-277-4405) displays artifacts from its enormous international collection, which has a special emphasis on the native cultures of the Southwest. Also free, it's open during the day Monday through Saturday and on Sunday afternoons.

Just off campus, on the other side of Central, UNM operates the Tamarind Institute (108 Cornell Southeast, 505-277-3901). A printmaking studio as well as a sales gallery, Tamarind has been a significant fixture on New Mexico's art scene since 1970. It may be the best place in the state to buy prints done by excellent artists—many of whom come for residencies—at reasonable prices. Tamarind is open during the day Monday through Friday and by appointment.

Nob Hill

Albuquerque's trendiest and most off-beat neighborhood, Nob Hill starts on the eastern edge of the UNM campus and continues a half-dozen blocks along Central Avenue to Carlisle. Between Girard Boulevard and the old Nob Hill Shopping Center, an eclectic array of businesses offer some of the best food in town, creative and kinky clothes, budget bric-a-brac,

Central Albuquerque Attractions

out-of-the-mainstream films, and more. From door to door, the atmosphere ranges from smart to spacy, from vital to banal.

The focal point of the district, the Nob Hill Shopping Center at 3500 Central was one of the first auto-oriented malls west of the Mississippi River, built right after World War II in an area then on the fringes of the city along busy Route 66. It seems tiny today compared to its contemporary counterparts, but the renovated Southwest Moderne facade is quaintly authentic for the era.

Rio Grande Zoo

In the opposite direction from downtown, just west of the city center and a few blocks south of Central Avenue, the Rio

Grande Zoo is Albuquerque's premier family attraction. Shaded by giant cottonwoods, the park spreads expansively over sixty acres of riverside bosque. Many of the thousand-plus animals live in naturalistic settings, including an African savannah, a tropical rain forest, a primate island, and lobo (wolf) woods.

At 903 10th Street Southwest (505-843-7413), the zoo is open daily. Admission is $4.25 for adults and $2.25 for children.

The North Valley and Corrales

Up the river from the zoo, the Rio Grande flows lazily through Albuquerque's north valley and the neighboring village of Corrales, still pastoral enclaves in the modern city. The river continues to water a variety of nurseries and horse farms, and the area retains some of its old Spanish charm, particularly in parts of Corrales.

From Old Town, head north on Rio Grande Boulevard, skirting the river's east bank. Jog left at Candelaria Road to reach the Rio Grande Nature Center State Park. Designed to introduce residents and visitors to the flora and fauna of the cottonwood bosque along the river, the park features trails that wind through the natural habitat of migratory birds, roadrunners, beavers, and other denizens of the area. The delightful visitor center, built partially underground, provides views over and under a large pond brimming with birds, frogs, ducks, and turtles.

Continuing north, you come to the Anderson Valley Vineyards (4920 Rio Grande Boulevard, 505-344-7266), just beyond Montaño Road. Founded in 1973, the winery was a pioneer in reviving an agricultural industry that once thrived in New Mexico. Spanish priests planted the first grapes in the state four centuries ago, inaugurating wineries that reached a peak of production a few decades before Prohibition shut down the presses.

Anderson Valley offers free tours and tastings each afternoon except Monday. Other Albuquerque wineries open to the

Greater Albuquerque Attractions

public include the exceptional Gruet (along I-25 between Paseo Del Norte and Alameda Road, 505-821-0055), Sandia Shadows (11704 Coronado Northeast, 505-856-1006), and just up the road in Corrales, Las Nutrias (4627 Corrales Road, 505-897-7863).

On the west side of the Rio Grande, farther north, Corrales provides a glimpse of the old New Mexico. Still a rural hamlet, like Albuquerque and Santa Fe in the past, it sprawls lazily for several miles along Corrales Road, lined with aging adobes, off-beat businesses, horse stables, and farms.

Coronado State Monument

If you continue north through Corrales to the nearby town of Bernalillo, the Coronado State Monument takes you further back in history. The park preserves the ruins of the Kuaua pueblo, where Francisco Vásquez de Coronado probably camped with his twelve hundred soldiers during the winter of 1540–41. In searching for the fabled Seven Cities of Gold, the army alighted in the Albuquerque area instead. The highlight of the excellent interpretative trail is a restored kiva open to the public. The walls contain reproductions of unusual frescoes depicting sacred Pueblo rituals—the originals hang in the visitor center.

The Coronado State Monument (505-867-5351) is one mile northeast of Bernalillo off N.M. 44. Adults pay $2 admission and children are free.

Petroglyph National Monument

Going another step back into the past, the Petroglyph National Monument offers the world's largest accessible collection of prehistoric rock art. More than fifteen thousand ancient images adorn a seventeen-mile escarpment rimming five extinct volcanoes. Ancient hunting parties camped at the base of the lava flow for thousands of years, carving images from their culture into the basalt. The four trails that wind through the petroglyphs range from easy to challenging in terrain.

West of the Rio Grande a few miles, off Unser Avenue Northwest, the park (505-897-8814) is open daily and costs $1 per vehicle.

Sandia Peak Tramway

The planet's longest aerial tramway climbs 2.7 miles from the base of Sandia Peak to the summit, transporting passengers through four of the earth's seven life zones. You start in the desert on the northern outskirts of the city and ascend over canyons and jagged promontories to a verdant pine forest at an elevation of 10,400 feet. The observation deck at the top provides views—particularly stunning at sunset—that encompass eleven thousand square miles out to Santa Fe, Los Alamos, and beyond. The nearby High Finance Restaurant (505-243-9742) enjoys some of the same panorama, allowing it to boast of a dining experience "above them all."

From I-25 take the Tramway Road exit, number 234, east about five miles to the tramway terminal. The tram operates daily from morning until night except on Wednesday, when hours are shorter. The usual cost is $12.50 for adults and a little less for children, but depending on your interests, you may be able to get better package rates by calling 505-856-7325.

CHAPTER EIGHTEEN

The Cultural and Entertainment Calendar

*A*LBUQUERQUE is known across the country for its International Balloon Fiesta in early October, but the annual extravaganza is just one of many special activities in the city. Whether you're trying to time a visit around something of personal interest or just want to know what might be happening when you're already in town, the following synopsis of major events, fairs, and arts attractions covers the most appealing possibilities. For a more detailed day-by-day calendar of things to do, get a copy of the current Albuquerque Official Visitors Guide from the Albuquerque Convention and Visitors Bureau (800-284-2282, 505-842-9918).

Albuquerque International Balloon Fiesta

The largest hot-air ballooning event in the world, the Fiesta fills Albuquerque's autumn skies with a kaleidoscope of color. The organizers schedule special activities throughout the nine-day festival, but the major thrills for the general public are the mass ascensions of six-hundred-plus balloons, staged the first two Saturdays and Sundays of October. A spectacular sight, the launchings will dazzle even the most jaded travelers. Plan to arrive before dawn and mingle with the crews as they prepare to lift off shortly after daylight.

When the balloons are grounded in the evening, because flying conditions become precarious, catch the "Balloon Glow," usually set for the first Sunday. Pilots light the propane burners in their tethered airships, turning the envelopes into giant light bulbs that cast a magical glow over the city. Later in the Fiesta, the Special Shapes Rodeo features a mass ascension of the most unusual balloons, imaginatively rigged to look like elephants, penguins, polar bears, and even bourbon bottles.

Pilots from around the world flock to the Fiesta because of the superb flying conditions. The "Albuquerque box effect" allows balloons to glide over the city in different directions at varying altitudes, catching currents that move within the box of air created by the surrounding mountains. Visitors can check out the phenomenon personally in flights offered by a number of ballooning companies that sell their services at the Fiesta, or during other times of the year, through offices listed in the yellow pages.

The event takes place at Balloon Fiesta Park on the city's far north side. The minimal admission fees vary according to the activities. Call 505-821-1000 for more information.

New Mexico State Fair

Just a few weeks before the Balloon Fiesta, starting the weekend after Labor Day, New Mexico's State Fair is one of the largest and liveliest of its breed in the country. It encompasses everything from a major professional rodeo to a forty-acre midway, from old-fashioned cooking competitions to a trove of modern junk food.

The highlight for most of the one million attenders is the nightly entertainment, staged in the rodeo arena between the bull riding, calf roping, and other PRCA events. The featured stars are generally country-and-western recording artists, but other nationally prominent musicians appear frequently enough to satisfy most local interests.

Other attractions include a miniseason of thoroughbred and quarter-horse racing, a junior livestock auction, Indian and Spanish "villages," a painting exhibition, and much more. Like state fairs elsewhere, it's as corny as it is fun.

The State Fairgrounds are in the heart of the city, bordered by Central Avenue, San Pedro Drive, Lomas Boulevard, and Louisiana Boulevard. Parking costs more than admission, but neither approaches expensive. Call 505-265-1791 for additional information.

Fiery Foods Show

It's not as monumental or well known as the State Fair or the Balloon Fiesta, but the "Hottest Show on Earth" does spice up life in early March. Vendors of chile products and other zesty foods come from all regions of the Americas to introduce their goods to retailers and restaurateurs. The sponsors open the trade show to the public most of one weekend for tastings and food demonstrations. You can try and buy hundreds of treats ranging from salsas and sauces to chile-laced chocolate and peanut brittle.

Held in the Albuquerque Convention Center, the Fiery Foods Show charges a nominal admission. For more information, contact Sunbelt Shows, 505-873-2187.

Skiing and Biking Sandia Peak

Not as grand or snowy as the Santa Fe and Taos ski basins (see Chapters 6 and 13, respectively), Sandia Peak still supplies a stellar recreational break from business or other activities. Part of the pleasure is the ride up to the slopes in the world's longest aerial tramway, described in the previous chapter. You can also drive to the base area from the other side of the summit, but it's harder to admire the scenery through a steering wheel.

Of the 25 runs, more than half are rated intermediate and only 10 percent get tagged as expert. That makes Sandia good for learners, who usually benefit quickly from the capably taught classes at the ski school. In the summer the trails are turned over to mountain bikers, who navigate the 1,700-foot vertical drop up, down, and in loops. For additional information on either skiing or biking, call 505-242-9133 or 856-6419.

Performing Arts Series

Albuquerque's two major concert and performance venues, Popejoy Hall and the KiMo Theater, both offer a year-round schedule of activities. In addition to providing homes for most of the major local arts groups, they sponsor a variety of traveling shows and special events, keeping their stages live most of the time.

One of the foremost architectural attractions of downtown, described in Chapter 17, the KiMo is the more eclectic of the pair. It might host a ballet folklorico company from Mexico one night and a body-building championship the next, but the arts are the primary focus. For what's on the docket, call the box office at 505-764-1700.

The larger but architecturally less interesting Popejoy Hall is near the center of the University of New Mexico campus, just north of Central Avenue at Cornell. It books a broad range of arts programs, from avant-garde dance performances to classic theater, as well as popular entertainment. Call 505-277-3121 for information on concerts and other events.

Though not as active as the KiMo and Popejoy, the South Broadway Cultural Center (505-848-1320) also offers a wide variety of performances, often geared to local community interests. It's located near downtown at 1025 Broadway Southeast.

Music

Older than most of modern Albuquerque, the New Mexico Symphony Orchestra began following the baton in 1932. Still vigorous at its advancing age, the orchestra performs a daunting schedule of classical, pops, and chamber concerts. When the musicians aren't touring the state, doing programs in schools, or playing under the stars at the Rio Grande Zoo, they're usually sharing the spotlight at Popejoy Hall. Popular enough to need a toll-free number, the orchestra can be reached at 800-251-NMSO or 505-881-8999.

The Albuquerque Civic Light Opera Association also calls Popejoy home, presenting five Broadway musicals in the hall each year between March and December. One of the largest community-based producers of musical theater in the country, the group usually stages hits with popular appeal. Phone 505-345-6577 for the bill of fare.

The June Music Festival of Albuquerque (505-294-2468) actually kicks off in May, hosting a series of chamber concerts by nationally known string quartets and other ensembles. Around the same time, the Albuquerque Convention and Visitors Bureau sponsors "Magnifico!," a broad-ranging arts festival with a heavy music component.

For great jazz, check out who the Outpost (505-268-0044) has booked into town. A storefront performance space, the nonprofit operation has its headquarters at 112 Morningside Drive, just off Central Avenue east of Nob Hill.

Theater

La Compania de Teatro de Alburquerque produces a full season of bilingual theater at the KiMo. Under professional direction, the group develops most of its own scripts in a participatory process to address issues and values in Hispanic New Mexican culture, sometimes using one of Shakespeare's plays as a framework. Anyone who understands only English or Spanish can follow the action. Call 505-242-7929 for more information in either language.

Another community company with professional leadership, the Albuquerque Little Theater (505-242-4750) presents more conventional comedies, musicals, and dramas. The production quality is high, but the troupe is worth seeing for its theater alone, built by Santa Fe architect John Gaw Meem in the 1930s. Near Old Town, the playhouse is at 224 San Pasquale Avenue Southeast.

New Mexico Arts & Crafts Fair

Other than Indian Market in Santa Fe, the New Mexico Arts & Crafts Fair in June is the largest and oldest juried show in the state. Held outside under the trees and stars at the State Fairgrounds, the event limits the number of booths to 214 as a means of maintaining quality standards. The work ranges from abstract paintings to whimsical masks. Call 505-884-9043 for details.

ArtsCrawl

Once a month art lovers gather in a different area of the city for an organized tour of galleries in the neighborhood. Sponsored by the Albuquerque Art Business Association (800-284-2282, 505-842-9918), the exhibits, open houses, and demonstrations are free and fun. The stops on the tour are clustered conveniently for walking or driving, depending on the district.

The Albuquerque Dukes

On many nights during the spring and summer, the Dukes baseball stadium is the most relaxing and rejoicing spot in the city. An intimate and attractive park that puts you right on the field, it's home to the Los Angeles Dodgers' triple-A farm team. For many of the players, this is the last stop before the major leagues, and their level of competence and competition shows it. Call 505-243-1791 for schedule and ticket information or drop by the box office at the corner of Stadium Road and University Boulevard, near the airport.

Ways to Wager

If you're looking to lay down a bet, thoroughbreds and quarter horses race on the State Fairgrounds at the Downs at Albuquerque (505-262-1188) from the winter through the spring and then again in September during the State Fair. For Las Vegas games, the largest Pueblo casinos near Albuquerque are along I-25, on the north and south fringes of the city at Sandia (Tramway Road exit, 505-897-2173) and Isleta (Broadway exit, 505-869-2614).

CHAPTER NINETEEN

Great Places to Stay

*A*LBUQUERQUE accommodations on the whole are typical of cities across the country, a mix of high-rise hotels and sprawling motels, often dully standardized. We describe the best of these options along with a selection of smaller and more charming spots. Rates stay about the same year-round except for moderate increases during the State Fair and the Balloon Fiesta, and substantial reductions on weekends at places oriented to business travelers. The downtown hotels are a ten-minute drive from the airport and the rest of the recommendations are scarcely twice as far.

BEST HOTELS AND MOTELS

Doubletree Hotel. Rates start at $145 during the week but drop sharply on nonconvention weekends. 201 Marquette Northwest, Albuquerque 87102. 800-222-TREE, 505-247-3344, fax 505-247-7025. Major credit cards.

Next door to the Convention Center, the fifteen-story Doubletree is built for business travelers. The hotel provides opportunities to play, in an outdoor pool and at an inside fitness center, but most guests come for the convenience of the location and the standard, no-surprises comfort of the rooms. The signature feature of the marbled lobby is a two-story waterfall that tumbles into La Cascada, a casual all-day cafe with an airy, patio feel.

Central Albuquerque Accommodations

1. Casa de Sueños
2. Doubletree Hotel
3. Hyatt Regency Albuquerque
4. La Posada de Albuquerque
5. W. E. Mauger Estate
6. Monterey Motel

Barcelona Court.
Regular weekday rates
begin at $74 and go
up to $129 for a
specialty suite with a
fireplace and extra
amenities.
900 Louisiana
Boulevard Northeast,
Albuquerque 87110.
800-222-1122,
505-255-5566.
Major credit cards.

An all-suites hotel cleverly converted from an
apartment complex, the Barcelona Court gives
you more space for your money than any hotel
in town. Every guest gets a one-bedroom suite
with a living room and well-equipped kitchenette. Furnished in a plain but contemporary
style, with multiple phones and TVs, the quarters make you feel right at home.

In the morning the staff serves a complimentary breakfast in the Fountain Court, an inviting
atrium that may entice you back in the evening
for a free cocktail. If you don't want to go out
for dinner, or cook for yourself, a nearby restaurant provides room service. Just off I-40 near the
State Fairgrounds and two of New Mexico's
largest shopping malls, the sprawling low-rise
hotel doesn't look special from the street, but it
begins to impress just as soon as you step inside
the gracious Mexican-accented lobby.

**Holiday Inn
Pyramid.**
Regular double rates
start at $118 except
on slow weekends,
when prices drop.
5151 San Francisco
Road, Albuquerque
87109.
800-HOLIDAY,
505-821-3333,
fax 505-828-0230.
Major credit cards.

Much more compelling than most of its roadside
cousins, this Holiday Inn in the shape of an
Aztec pyramid soars up a ten-story atrium with
a fifty-foot waterfall. The two restaurants and
two lounges offer plenty of variety in food and
entertainment, and the staff sincerely strives for
good service. For recreation, the hotel provides a
pool, Jacuzzis, a sauna, and a fitness center.

Glass elevators carry guests up the atrium to
the three-hundred-plus rooms, more upscale
than you expect for the chain but not unusual in
other ways. They are certainly worth their rates
compared to similar downtown hotels because
of the Pyramid's location, away from the city
bustle on I-25 at Paseo del Norte near the
Balloon Fiesta Park.

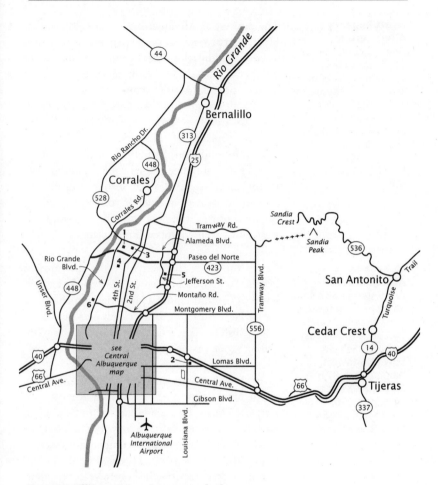

Greater Albuquerque Accommodations
1. Adobe and Roses
2. Barcelona Court
3. Casa del Granjero
4. Casita Chamisa
5. Holiday Inn Pyramid
6. Sarabande Bed and Breakfast

Hyatt Regency Albuquerque.
Double rooms start at $145 and suites at $325. Inquire about weekend discounts. 330 Tijeras Northwest, Albuquerque 87102. 800-233-1234, 505-842-1234, fax 505-766-6710. Major credit cards.

The poshest of Albuquerque's major hotels, the Hyatt soars twenty stories above downtown into a pair of landmark peaks. Designed primarily to pamper business travelers, it also attracts vacationers looking for full urban amenities.

The 395 rooms and 14 suites mix the tasteful and the trendy, offering all of Hyatt's usual upscale touches. Downstairs, where a palm-shaded fountain gurgles in the lobby, McGrath's serves some of the best hotel cooking in the city, featuring classic American dishes dressed up with Southwestern accents. If you need to work off the calories, the hotel provides an outdoor pool and a well-equipped fitness center.

La Posada de Albuquerque.
Rates start at $82 and go up to $250 for the most expensive suite. Executive rooms cost $92. 125 Second Street Northwest, Albuquerque 87102. 800-777-5732, 505-242-9090, fax 505-242-8664. Major credit cards.

Easily the most distinctive of the downtown hotels, La Posada opened in 1939 as the crown jewel of Conrad Hilton's just-emerging chain. A native New Mexican, Hilton built it to showcase Southwestern style, filling the lavish lobby with ceiling vigas, carved corbels, tin chandeliers, and Mexican tile.

In 1984 new owners refurbished the 114-room hotel, now on the National Register of Historic Places. La Posada doesn't try to match contemporary hotels in luxury, but it offers a wealth of local character to compensate. Even if your bathroom is a little cramped, and the old windows don't exactly glide open, you can count on regional fabrics, furnishings, and even art. Avoid the least expensive quarters, which tend to be small, and pay slightly more for a spacious executive room.

Before retiring in the evening, enjoy a cocktail in the delightful lobby and consider a dinner at Conrad's, the hotel restaurant. The menu features contemporary interpretations of traditional dishes from Spain and the Yucatan, including tapas and paella.

Monterey Motel.
The year-round rates run $39 to $45.
2402 Central Avenue Southwest,
Albuquerque 87104.
505-243-3554.
MC, V.

For personality at a pittance, try an original Route 66 motor court. Built in 1932, just a short walk from Old Town, the Monterey Motel is the best of its breed in Albuquerque and enjoys the distinction of being one of the oldest AAA-rated "Mother Road" motels anywhere between Chicago and Los Angeles. The well-kept rooms are modest in size and appointments, but they come with queen beds, TVs, phones, and air conditioning, as well as use of a heated pool and laundry facilities. You won't find an ashtray anywhere because the Bugg family proprietors take pride in keeping butts off the property.

BEST B&Bs

Adobe and Roses.
Rates for two people range from $59 to $79, including a full breakfast. Families and couples traveling together can rent the entire guesthouse for $115.
1011 Ortega Northwest,
Albuquerque 87114.
505-898-0654.
No credit cards.

As the name implies, the walls are adobe and the two-acre grounds abound with flowers at this north-valley B&B. The name doesn't reference good value and hospitality, but hostess Dorothy Morse provides that as well.

Each of the three guest rooms features a private entrance and bath plus a kiva fireplace, kitchenette, plants, books, and comfortable furnishings. The most expensive chamber is a suite in the main house with a piano and TV in the parlor, windows overlooking a horse pasture, and a spacious bath with an old-fashioned tub and separate shower. The other quarters are in a detached guesthouse. The larger and more desirable of the two comes with a living room, TV, stereo system, and skylights.

Casa del Granjero.
Rates range from $89 to $129, reaching a peak for two suites in the guesthouse.
414 C de Baca Lane Northwest,
Albuquerque 87114.
800-701-4144,
505-897-4144.
MC, V.

You may wonder where you're going when you turn down C de Baca Lane to the "Farmer's House," but you'll be delighted when you arrive. At the end of the dusty north-valley street, a magnificent old territorial adobe sprawls across a verdant ranch. Horses, goats, and other farm animals keep you company during your stay, though the rest of your surroundings are as palatial as they are pastoral.

Victoria and Butch Farmer offer four rooms in the main house and another four across the street in a guesthouse. Each is wonderfully distinctive, with a kiva fireplace and a wealth of Southwestern allure. Cuarto Allegré, one of our favorites, is characteristic in some ways and special in others, with a canopied king bed, a garden patio, and a bathroom featuring massive beams, corbels, an antique wardrobe, and Mexican tiles. The bath is actually grander in Cuarto Grande, but the private facilities are spacious and colorful in all cases, even in the two instances where they are down the hall from the room.

The hosts serve a full breakfast in the large dining room or outside under a portal, overlooking a lovely lawn with a lily pond. Guests share use of a hot tub, a TV room with a 52-inch set, and a living room filled with Western artifacts, books, and the aura emanating from a massive, sculptured adobe fireplace.

Casa de Sueños.
Rates begin at $85 and reach a peak of $250.
310 Rio Grande Southwest, Albuquerque 87104.
800-242-8987, 505-247-4560, fax 505-842-8493.
Major credit cards.

Artist J. R. Willis designed and built this delightful garden compound in the 1930s in fulfillment of a personal dream. In addition to his own home and studio, the complex contained fifteen charming cottages rented to other artists, making it a communal retreat for creative spirits. When attorney Robert Hanna purchased the property and converted it to an inn, he maintained the mood, naming it the "House of Dreams" and commissioning noted architect Bart Prince to erect a fanciful snail-shaped structure that greets guests at the entrance.

Just two blocks from Old Town, bordering the Albuquerque Country Club golf course, Casa de Sueños ranges all over the map in accommodations. Some of the quarters are elegantly English, some Oriental, some Southwestern. You can get a standard-size double room or a two-bedroom suite with a parlor.

One of the original artist's studios serves as the dining room, and it still looks the part, full of light and local paintings. The complete breakfast might feature pumpkin empanadas or an asparagus cheese soufflé, and it always includes home-baked goods and fine coffee.

Casita Chamisa.
The price for two people is $85. Children cost an additional $10 each in the guesthouse. 850 Chamisal Road Northwest, Albuquerque 87107. 505-897-4644. Major credit cards.

When Arnold and Kit Sargeant decided to build their indoor swimming pool, they discovered a prehistoric trove—thousands of pottery shards and other artifacts from a succession of Pueblo villages that occupied the property as far back as 1300 A.D. A professional archaeologist herself, Kit is happy to explain the significance of the site and may even show you a video of the excavation.

In addition to an education and a pool, Casita Chamisa offers a pair of pleasant and private accommodations, an excellent continental breakfast and a serene north-valley setting brimming with gardens, horses, and chickens. One of the quarters is a large bedroom attached to the main house, with its own entrance and bath, and the other is a two-bedroom, one-bath guesthouse with a kitchenette that's ideal for families. Both come with a TV, phone, and cushy robes.

Sarabande Bed and Breakfast.
The Iris Room costs $75, the Garden Room goes for $90, and the Rose Room is $110. 5637 Rio Grande Boulevard Northwest, Albuquerque 87107. 505-345-4923. Major credit cards.

A lovely north-valley estate close to the Rio Grande, Sarabande invites its guests to swim in the 50-foot lap pool, stargaze in the outdoor Jacuzzi, relax in the Japanese garden, or huddle around the country fireplace in the guest living room. Wherever you alight, innkeepers Margaret Magnussen and Betty Vickers make it a treat.

They offer only three guest chambers, keeping everything intimate, from the ambience to the generous breakfasts. The Garden and Iris Rooms are pretty and plush, but the Rose Room wins the laurels with its four-poster bed and deep soaking tub that's separate from the shower. Each enjoys a private bath and opens onto a landscaped patio.

W. E. Mauger Estate.
Rates start at $65 for
a small single and go
up to $115 for two in
the large and lovely
Brittania Room.
701 Roma Avenue
Northwest,
Albuquerque 87102.
505-242-8755,
fax 505-842-8835.
Major credit cards.

Just on the edge of downtown, this 1897 Queen Anne house provides an air of stately elegance that contrasts sharply with the modern business hotels nearby. It's just a short walk to the convention center and the rest of downtown, but a quaint step back in time at the end of an active day.

The eight rooms vary considerably in size and style. Some maintain the Victorian feel of the house, while others offer a flavor of their own. All come with private baths, small TVs, coffeemakers, use of the cheerful period parlor, afternoon refreshments, and a big breakfast.

CHAPTER TWENTY

Albuquerque's Global Kitchen

ALBUQUERQUE restaurants top their counterparts in Santa Fe and Taos in two ways—diversity and value. In the past decade, Albuquerque's culinary horizons have broadened expansively to encompass every corner of the globe. Today, you can find a felicitous version of almost any cuisine, usually at a price that's well below levels in other American cities.

You will have to search the side streets, however, and venture into some inauspicious places that don't look promising on the surface. Albuquerque has its share of elegant, fine-dining restaurants—such as Prairie Star and Stephens—but even some of the classiest continental fare comes out of kitchens in unpretentious storefront locations. When you branch out to less familiar foods, or authentic local home cooking, you're often going to be eating in a strip shopping center or a fading neighborhood.

Skeptical perhaps when you open the door, you'll probably be greeted like a long-lost cousin. In most of the recommended restaurants, despite the low prices, service is almost too solicitous and the chef is genuinely eager to please. The proprietors probably decorated the place themselves, obtaining a lot of cheer out of a tight budget. You instantly forget any limitations of the location and settle in for an enjoyable experience.

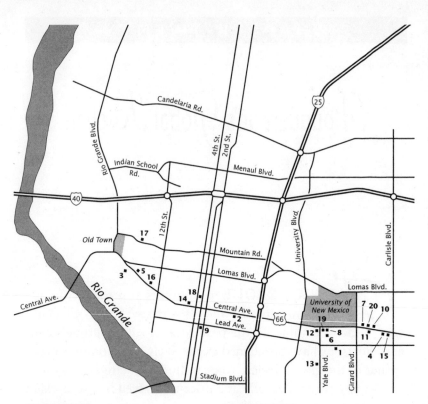

Central Albuquerque
Restaurants
1. Amerasia
2. Artichoke Cafe
3. Chef du Jour
4. Double Rainbow
5. Duran Central Pharmacy
6. El Patio
7. Fred's Bread and Bagel
8. Frontier
9. M&J Sanitary Tortilla Factory
10. Monte Vista Fire Station

11. Nob Hill Bistro
12. Perico's
13. The Quarters
14. Rio Bravo Restaurant & Brewery
15. Scalo
16. Stephens
17. W.C.'s Mountain Road Cafe
18. Wolfe's Bagels
19. Wolfe's Bagels
20. Yanni's Mediterranean Bar
    and Grill

Greater Albuquerque
Restaurants (facing page)
1. Assets Grille & Brewing
   Company
2. Bangkok Cafe
3. Cafe Spoletto
4. El Norteño
5. El Pinto
6. Huong Thao

7. India Kitchen
8. Joey's Famous Pizza
9. Malaysia Bay Oriental Seafood
10. Mary & Tito's Cafe
11. Middle East Bakery
12. Prairie Star
13. Sadie's
14. Weck's
15. ZuZu

As in Santa Fe—see the introduction to Chapter 8—be sure to sample the New Mexican food. It's one of several strong suits in the city, along with Asian home cooking and personalized chef-owner styles.

For the sake of consistency in the reviews, we use the same cost categories that we apply in Santa Fe and Taos. "Expensive" means entrées cost over $18. Under $8 is "inexpensive," and in-between is "moderate." Since prices are considerably lower on the whole in Albuquerque, few of the recommended restaurants reach the high end of the scale and most barely nudge into the moderate range.

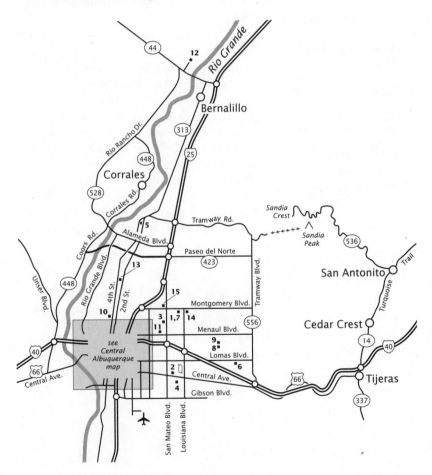

AMERICAN AND
CONTEMPORARY SOUTHWESTERN

Chef du Jour.
119 San Pasquale
Southwest.
505-247-8998.
Open Monday through
Friday for lunch only.
No reservations or
credit cards.
Inexpensive.

Chef Connie Allgood keeps her concentration on the cooking by opening only for lunch on weekdays and serving just a handful of tables. The casual and cheerful cafe offers simple dishes with tasty touches, such as a gazpacho pasta, a calabacitas burrito, and a chicken-breast sandwich on whole wheat–fruit-nut bread with the house's signature Jamaican banana ketchup. For desserts, the menu suggests that you check the blackboard for what's "fresh and inspired this week."

Monte Vista Fire Station.
3201 Central Avenue
Northeast, in the Nob
Hill neighborhood.
505-255-2424.
Open daily for lunch
except Sunday and for
dinner nightly.
Reservations advised.
Moderate.
Major credit cards.

Here, there, and around the world with flavors, the Monte Vista Fire Station focuses primarily on contemporary American dishes with Southwestern accents. The changing lunch and dinner menus start with a similar selection of appetizers, salads, and pastas, including options such as a quesadilla with shrimp and sun-dried tomatoes, crab cakes with goat cheese on baby greens, and green chile cilantro linguini. Lunch offers sandwiches as well—say, a vegetarian club and a "fire" burger—while dinner provides a greater range of entrées, perhaps grilled lamb loins surrounding polenta diamonds, seared yellow-fin tuna with basil oil, and roasted duck with a grapefruit sauce.

The name of the restaurant comes from its location in a restored 1936 fire station, a classic adobe building listed on the National Register of Historic Places. As spiffy now as a freshly waxed fire engine, the cafe seats you inside in a dining room dressed with art-deco accents or outside on a spacious terrace.

Prairie Star.
Off Jemez Dam Road, north of N.M. 44 in Bernalillo.
505-867-3327.
Open daily for dinner only.
Reservations necessary. Expensive.
Major credit cards.

Perhaps the most elegant restaurant on Native American land anywhere in the country, Prairie Star occupies a lovely 1940s-vintage mission-style adobe now owned by Santa Ana Pueblo. It's a moderate drive north of Albuquerque, in the town of Bernalillo, but you're rewarded for your effort with intimate local charm, grand views of the Sandia Mountains, and reputable contemporary cooking with a Southwestern slant.

We skip the first courses here, often pedestrian. The entrées on the seasonal menu can excel, though the multiple daily specials are usually a better choice. One wonderful spring dinner revolved around Venison Osso Bucco, which was lusciously lean, and Raviloni, an onion-tarragon pasta stuffed with smoked sirloin and cheeses. Select desserts from a cart, continental-style.

The Quarters.
905 Yale Boulevard Southeast, between the airport and the University of New Mexico.
505-843-7505.
Closed Sunday. Lunch and dinner.
No reservations.
Inexpensive to moderate.
Major credit cards.

Albuquerque is not a Memphis or Kansas City when it comes to the caliber of the barbecue, but several places do know what the "Q" is all about. Of these, the original branch of the Quarters on Yale Boulevard stands out for a combination of cooking and atmosphere. The pitmasters tackle ribs, beef brisket, and other favorites, but they're really smoking with the pork and turkey. Get the meat in a sandwich or on a platter and enjoy it with a beer or margarita from the busy bar.

Stephens.
1311 Tijeras Avenue Northwest, at the corner of Central Avenue between downtown and Old Town.
505-842-1773.
Open daily. Lunch weekdays, dinner nightly. Reservations necessary. Moderate to expensive.
Major credit cards.

Modestly calling itself "An American Cafe," Stephens is the place in the city for a power lunch or an elegant anniversary dinner. The restaurant radiates style in its smartly renovated territorial hacienda, built around a colorful courtyard, and the cooking shines by applying worldly inspiration to American and Southwestern classics.

At lunch, the choices range from a Reuben sandwich to smoked salmon quesadillas. In the evening, start with the baked brie or the hearty French onion soup. Entrée options include a

New York strip steak, seafood specialties, pastas, and lighter spa dishes. You won't ever go wrong with the lamb loin .chops grilled with rosemary and garlic and served with green chile jelly.

W. C.'s Mountain Road Cafe.
1501 Mountain Road Northwest, near Old Town.
505-243-9550.
Open daily for breakfast and lunch, and for dinner on Friday and Saturday.
No reservations.
Inexpensive at breakfast and lunch, moderate at dinner.
MC, V.

Chef-owner W. C. Longacre calls his cooking "New Hong Key" fare because it mixes influences from New Mexico, Hong Kong, and Key West, all places where he's plied his trade. It's an imaginative ferment of flavors and a perfect match for the jazzy cafe space, a brightly decorated nineteenth-century adobe that once housed a bordello and speakeasy.

For breakfast, try one of the half-dozen "Burrito Platos," perhaps the hot choice featuring the "Way South" salsa made from habaneros, poblanos, and chiltepíns. The extensive omelet list includes the Popeye (spinach, roasted garlic, and Swiss cheese) and the Sweet Heart (artichoke hearts, caramelized onions, gorgonzola, and tomato). For an eggs Benedict variation, consider the Eggs Byzantine with fresh roasted turkey instead of Canadian bacon.

Start lunch with one of the Italian sodas, or take your cue from the Jamaican Red Stripe beer carton that holds the condiments and order a brew. Among the many and varied sandwiches, salads, pastas, and burritos, we often opt for two terrific house specialties, W. C.'s Chile Mac (a heaping bowl of pasta covered with red and green chile and a couple of cheeses) and the Key West Tacos (crisp flour tortillas filled with sautéed shrimp and scallops). On Friday and Saturday night, the kitchen shifts gears a bit, offering a sophisticated selection of fresh fish and seafood in preparations that blend tropical, Asian, and Southwestern tastes.

Weck's.
7200 Montgomery
Boulevard Northeast.
505-881-0019.
Open daily for
breakfast and lunch.
No reservations or
credit cards.
Inexpensive.

The runaway favorite locally for breakfast, Weck's makes an occasion of a morning meal. The shopping-center setting may not stir your appetite, but the menu will, extending enough unusual possibilities to keep your mouth watering for a week. Try a plate of the *papas,* a huge pile of hashbrowns with a choice of meats, eggs, and chile, or a burrito with the same basic fixings.

The kitchen maintains the pace at lunch, when the eclectic selection includes serious salads, creative sandwiches, and solid New Mexican specialties. Make sure your order comes with potatoes, either the homemade chips or the freshly cut French fries.

ASIAN

Amerasia.
301 Cornell
Southeast, a few
blocks from Central
Avenue.
505-266-8400.
Closed Sunday. Lunch
Monday through
Saturday, dinner
Friday and Saturday
nights. Reservations
advised for dinner.
Moderate.
Major credit cards.

The New Chinatown Restaurant (5001 Central Avenue Northeast, 505-265-8859) wins most local awards for Chinese food, but for our money it tops Amerasia only in rococo aura. Barely a bungalow, and open most days just around noon, Amerasia understands the subtleties of the cuisine. The specialty is authentic dim sum, served traditional-style at lunch. On Friday and Saturday evenings, the kitchen prepares more elaborate meals in classic Cantonese, Hunan, Mandarin, and Szechuan styles.

Bangkok Cafe.
5901 Central Avenue
Northeast.
505-255-5036.
Open daily. Lunch
weekdays, dinner
nightly. Reservations
advised for dinner.
Inexpensive to
moderate.
Major credit cards.

The most dependable of several Thai restaurants in town, the Bangkok Cafe takes pride in preparing each dish to order. That helps to keep the ingredients fresh and allows the kitchen to adjust the heat level to your liking, from mild to fiery. Everything on the long menu exudes zesty Thai flavor, from the traditional Tom Yum Gai soup to the wok-fried specialties. The Pad Prig Pla Muk (spicy squid) always puts us in the pink, matching the simple but pretty cafe decor.

Huong Thao.
1016B Juan Tabo
Northeast.
505-292-8222.
Closed Monday. Lunch
and dinner.
Reservations usually
not necessary.
Inexpensive.
Major credit cards.

The Vietnamese cooking at Huong Thao is as straightforward as its shopping-strip location and just as inexpensive. The French side of the country's cuisine takes a back seat to the original basics, particularly rice and noodle plates flavored with grilled shrimp, barbecued pork, sliced beef, tofu, mung beans, and more. The "special dinners" on the menu, a fine bargain, feature catfish and chicken in a variety of preparations, from soups to stir-fries.

India Kitchen.
6910 Montgomery
Northeast, near
Louisiana Boulevard.
505-884-2333.
Open daily for dinner.
Reservations advised.
Inexpensive to
moderate.
Major credit cards.

A dozen years ago Ajay Gupta gave up an engineering career to introduce Albuquerque to the delightful tastes of his native Indian food. It was slow going at first, as a pioneer of exotic flavors in the city, but now his restaurant wins raves in all quarters.

Though Ajay will tailor any dish to your preference of spice and fire, he's not too timid to tell you how an experienced palate usually prefers it. Ask advice, always provided with empathetic expertise.

The kitchen knows things about cooking mustard greens that would be the envy of any Southerner. Try them curried or in the sag paneer, where they are combined with spinach and homemade cheese. If you want meat, and aren't afraid of heat, go for the lamb or chicken vindaloo. The *pakoras* and *samosas* start a meal right, and the stuffed paratha bread tantalizes either as an appetizer or accompaniment.

**Malaysia Bay
Oriental Seafood.**
1826 Eubank
Boulevard Northeast.
505-293-5597.
Open daily for lunch
and dinner.
Reservations usually
not necessary.
Inexpensive to
moderate. MC, V.

The menu offers an abundance of beef, poultry, pork, and vegetable dishes, but this storefront Taiwanese cafe really excels with seafood. The daily specials, dependably fresh and flavorful, might include a tea-smoked whole sea bass, steamed mussels in a sizzling sauce, or crispy frog legs. Among the regular dishes, shrimp shines in two preparations, covered with a garlic sauce and in a Malay stir-fry with a hot, spicy tang. For an appetizer, try the sesame dumplings, charged with a chile, soy, and ginger sauce.

BAKERIES, COFFEEHOUSES, AND DELIS

Double Rainbow.
3416 Central Avenue Southeast.
505-255-6633.
Open daily from early in the morning until late at night.
No reservations or credit cards.
Inexpensive.

A coffeehouse, ice cream parlor, and munchies magnet, the Double Rainbow brings more people to Nob Hill than any other business in the neighborhood. Grab a cappuccino and pastry, or tea and quiche, and head to the "hassle-free magazine zone" to read one of the many periodicals on the rack. Afterwards, indulge in one of the rich and renowned desserts, perhaps the chocolate mousse cake.

Fred's Bread and Bagel.
3009 Central Avenue Northeast.
505-266-7323.
Open daily from early morning until late afternoon.
No reservations or credit cards.
Inexpensive.

Another popular Nob Hill hangout, Fred's specializes in bagels, sandwiches, and bohemian bonhomie. Even New Yorkers love the classic bagels, though the green-chile version tends to shock them out of their socks. For breakfast, try one of the dozen varieties with lox or perhaps a Fred's Spread. The mountainous sandwiches roam the globe in tastes, from Cajun roast beef to hummus.

Middle East Bakery.
5017 Menaul Northeast.
505-883-4537.
Open daily, usually from midmorning to early evening.
No reservations or credit cards.
Inexpensive.

The pita bread is fresh daily and so are the meat and spinach pies. You can take them home or enjoy them in the small cafe, filling the pita with falafel perhaps, and then wrap up a meal with baklava and Turkish coffee. The shelves along the walls are lined with Mediterranean foods, many of them difficult to find elsewhere in the state, and the counter cabinets contain imported olives, homemade yogurt, and other treats.

Wolfe's Bagels.
Closed Saturday. Open other days from the early morning until the late afternoon. No reservations or credit cards. Inexpensive.

Advertising "the best bagels above sea level," Wolfe's goes for quantity as well as quality, making so many different varieties that a deli devotee may go delirious with the choices. The kitchen also exults in its cream-cheese Shmears, homemade tuna, egg and chicken salads, the fish platters, and a range of fine coffees.

Among the four locations across the city, the two that are most convenient for visitors are downtown at 201 Third Street (505-243-4801) and at 2318 Central Avenue Southeast (505-254-9866), across from the UNM campus.

BARS

Assets Grille & Brewing Company.
6910 Montgomery Northeast, near Louisiana Boulevard. 505-889-6400. Open daily from noon until late. Reservations advised for meals. Moderate. Major credit cards.

Brewmaster Mark Matheson makes award-winning beers for this trendy suburban hangout. Order a Duke City Amber or an Albuquerque Pale Ale and soak up the suds with good pizza and pasta. You can relish the fare in moderate peace on the patio or join the crowd inside, where twentysomething singles and older wannabes meet and mingle.

Rio Bravo Restaurant & Brewery.
515 Central Avenue Northwest, downtown. 505-242-6800. Closed Sunday. Open other days from noon until late. Reservations advised for meals. Moderate. Major credit cards.

Easily the best place downtown for a beer, this brew pub is also a good spot for other drinks or a taste of contemporary Southwestern cooking. A short walk from the convention center and the major business hotels, Rio Bravo greets you with a Route 66–style Western neon sign hanging brightly above the door. Inside, the casually upbeat bar serves an assortment of its own microbrewery beers, mainly European ales that range in hue and heft from light to dark.

CONTINENTAL AND MEDITERRANEAN

Artichoke Cafe.
424 Central Avenue
Southeast.
505-243-0200.
Closed Sunday. Lunch
(except Saturday) and
dinner. Reservations
advised. Moderate.
MC, V.

The classy cooking at the Artichoke Cafe creeps into all corners of Continental cuisine, and beyond, but chef-owner Patty Keene really reaches her stride these days with Mediterranean dishes. At lunch some of the best selections might include a grilled eggplant sandwich on foccaccia and a spinach linguine. In the evening, consider the Calamari Provencal and the veal or fish specials. The steamed artichoke with three sauces is always a worthy starter.

Between downtown and the university, the small, popular cafe shares inspirations from both areas. It's sleekly urban in decor, accented with neon art, but also as casually congenial as a student hangout.

Cafe Spoletto.
2813 San Mateo
Northeast.
505-880-0897.
Closed Sunday and
Monday. Dinner only.
Reservations advised.
Moderate. MC, V.

Chef-owners Bruce Folkins and Roch Shillings came to Albuquerque from the San Francisco Bay area and brought along a good measure of California flair. Their cooking reflects influences from France and Spain, but the tone is mainly nouvelle Italian.

The changing menu focuses on a limited number of dinner specials. Caesar salad is always among the half-dozen starters and always a dependable way to begin. Several pasta and risotto options might include dishes such as far-falle with artichokes, sun-dried tomatoes, flakes of chile, and manchego cheese. The main course choices could range from a spicy gumbo with Spanish chorizo, chicken, and basmati rice to braised lamb with fresh fava beans and grilled portobellos. On a good night, the kitchen can send you home in bliss.

Nob Hill Bistro.
3118 Central Avenue
Southeast, in the Nob
Hill neighborhood.
505-255-5832.
Closed Monday.
Dinner only.
Reservations advised.
Moderate to
expensive. MC, V.

The best spot in Albuquerque for French finesse, this intimate, elegantly attired cafe seldom falters with challenging preparations. The pan-seared sweetbreads with crispy bacon, fried shallots, and pecans made a knock-out appetizer one night, and, on another occasion, the tea-smoked mussels packed similar punch. Our favorite entrées have included salmon roulade flavored with olives and caviar, and sauteed duck breast stuffed with smoked duck.

Chef-owner Barry Strauss prides himself on an intimate knowledge of his ingredients, even studying horticulture at the University of New Mexico to gain a deeper understanding of local produce. He favors light, contemporary sauces based on herbs rather than butter and cream, and presents his dishes with the kind of artistic exuberance symbolized by the Rousseau painting that dominates the cafe decor.

Scalo.
3500 Central Avenue
Northeast, in the Nob
Hill Shopping Center.
505-255-8782.
Open daily. Lunch
weekdays, dinner
nightly.
Reservations advised.
Moderate.
Major credit cards.

The kitchen here prepares its northern Italian dishes with a flair that matches the urbane sparkle of the restaurant. Eat on the covered patio or on one of the multiple levels in the light-filled dining room overlooking the open grill.

The heaping plate of fried calamari is a popular antipasto, though you can also start lighter with a salad or the soup of the day. Almost a dozen pastas and pizzas cross courses, but don't neglect the house specialties, which include dishes such as veal scaloppine with toasted almonds and sun-dried cranberries, and grilled chicken breast with creamed spinach, crispy sweet potatoes, and goat cheese. The cooking always satisfies and often excels.

Yanni's Mediterranean Bar and Grill.
3109 Central Avenue Northeast, in the Nob Hill neighborhood.
505-268-9178.
Open daily for lunch and dinner.
Inexpensive to moderate. MC, V.

For solid but simple cooking, primarily Greek in origin, this sparkling bistro satisfies your appetite without even denting your wallet. Start with dolmathes, spanakopita, or tabbouleh. Move on to the moussaka (in standard and vegetarian versions), pastitsio or pizza, and wrap up a hearty meal with the homemade baklava.

FAST FOOD

Frontier.
2400 Central Avenue Southeast.
505-266-0550.
Open daily all day.
No reservations or credit cards.
Inexpensive.

A barn both in its facade and its internal dimensions, the Frontier can hold half the student body of the University of New Mexico, directly across the street, and often seems to pack that many people into its orange naugahyde booths. Grab a seat under a wagon-wheel chandelier or in front of a "Duke" Wayne painting and munch down with the masses on a bargain burger, burrito, or butter-laden cinnamon roll. Just staying open twenty-four hours sets the Frontier apart from almost every other eatery in town, and makes it convenient if you've arrived at the nearby airport hungry at an odd hour.

Joey's Famous Pizza.
Open daily. Lunch and dinner. Inexpensive to moderate. MC, V.

If you want a pizza delivered to your door, this is the place to call. Joey's builds them in three dimensions, with the standard flat crust, in a pielike deep dish, and as a double-layer stuffed deep dish. You can create your own pizza in any of the styles with a large selection of toppings or choose one of the house combos, such as the chicken cacciatore, made with roasted chicken breast, zucchini, eggplant, red onions, black olives, mushrooms, and garlic.

The downtown branch, which delivers to the central part of the city, plans to relocate in the near future and may change phone numbers, but for now call 505-768-1121. In other parts of town, phone 505-293-7210 for the branch at 1716 Eubank Boulevard Northeast.

Perico's.

109 Yale Southeast,
just off Central
Avenue.
505-247-2503.
Closed Sunday. Lunch
and dinner.
No reservations or
credit cards.
Inexpensive.

We stumbled onto Perico's one night when we arrived back at the Albuquerque airport after a long trip in need of quick chile fix. The food fit the bill to perfection and still does any time we're on the run around the University of New Mexico campus. The menu says "our famous homemade burritos built our business" and it's easy to understand why. The two dozen choices offer the standard fillings as well as fajitas, fish, chicharrones, potatoes, and guacamole. You can also get a six-pack of tacos to go.

MEXICAN

El Norteño.

6416 Zuni Road
Southeast, just east of
San Pedro.
505-255-2057.
Open daily for
breakfast, lunch, and
dinner.
Reservations usually
not necessary.
Inexpensive. MC, V.

In Mexico, *norteño* cooking is fare from the northern borderlands, particularly the states of Chihuahua, Nuevo León, and Sonora. This is it in a form as authentic and tasty as you'll find anywhere, including the mother country.

Jump-start the morning with the Hungry Burro, a big burrito brimming with scrambled eggs and potatoes and topped with a red or green salsa. Later in the day the menu features soft tacos filled with a wide choice of regional favorites, such as carne asada, carnitas, pork al pastor, chorizo, fish, and *nopales* (delicious strips of prickly pear cactus). The same foods appear in other dishes too, alongside steaks, seafood, and vegetarian specialties. Try the *queso fundido* (baked cheese) for an appetizer, and if you've never had *cabrito* (baby goat), you simply shouldn't pass up the opportunity here.

ZuZu.

4411 San Mateo at
Montgomery.
505-837-1669.
Open daily for lunch
and dinner.
No reservations.
Inexpensive.
Major credit cards.

Opened in 1995, this Montgomery Plaza cafe is the first of several projected New Mexico branches of an inspired Dallas-based chain. ZuZu cofounder Espartaco Borga created the food concept, developing "handmade" dishes based on the authentic regional cuisines of Mexico. The cooks prepare everything to order, rather than in large batches, and they use only fresh, wholesome ingredients, which glisten from the open kitchen.

The gordita, quesadilla, fajita, and burrito platters offer a choice of chicken or steak, but we favor the former, marinated overnight in an *achiote*-lime sauce and then grilled. If you're really hungry, put the dishes together in a combination plate or order them in a "mucho" version. Whatever you get, top it with one of the treats from the salsa bar, based mainly on roasted tomatillos and poblanos. Wrap up the cheap feast with a Cajeta Nacho Sundae, as zany a dessert as you'll find anywhere.

NEW MEXICAN

Duran Central Pharmacy.
1815 Central Avenue Northwest.
505-247-4141.
Closed Sunday.
Breakfast and lunch.
No reservations or credit cards.
Inexpensive.

A local institution since 1912, the drug store attracts a devoted clientele for its New Mexican specialties, offered here with old-fashioned lunch-counter atmosphere. Located these days in a modern faux-adobe building close to Old Town, the pharmacy sells all the contemporary cures plus medicinal herbs and the kind of chile that clears the sinuses.

Don't look for dainty egg dishes when the cafe opens for breakfast at 9:00 in the morning. You can get huevos rancheros, but the serious eaters here start the day with a blue corn enchilada plate or a bulging burrito. For the full experience, wash down your meal with a shake.

El Patio.
142 Harvard Southeast, one block from Central Avenue.
505-268-4245.
Open daily. Lunch and dinner.
No reservations.
Inexpensive. MC, V.

Just across from the UNM campus in a converted house, El Patio packs in the professors and students for tasty New Mexican home cooking. The kitchen excels with chiles rellenos and carne adovada, but also offers vegetarian options such as an avocado burrito. If you have trouble choosing, you won't go wrong with a combination plate.

El Pinto.
10500 Fourth Street
Northwest, just west
of the Alameda and
Tramway exits from
I-25.
505-898-1771.
Open daily for lunch
and dinner.
No reservations.
Inexpensive to
moderate.
Major credit cards.

A grand restaurant in size and atmosphere, El Pinto boasts the best setting in Albuquerque. Away from the city bustle in the pastoral north valley, the restaurant sprawls through a stately, flower-filled hacienda and outside to an enormous garden patio. Mellow live music enhances the gracious mood, keeping your attention off the so-so food.

The problem for the kitchen is the nine hundred chairs that the restaurant tries to fill, a cooking challenge that would daunt the world's top chef. The lineage of the recipes couldn't be better; they come from the grand dame of southern New Mexican cooking, Josephine Chavez-Griggs, the founder of La Posta restaurant in La Mesilla and the grandmother of El Pinto owners Jim and John Thomas. The heritage helps us to like the bland dishes, but it's the setting that brings us back and enchants everyone who comes.

M&J Sanitary Tortilla Factory.
403 Second Street
Southwest, on the
fringes of downtown.
505-242-4890.
Closed Sunday.
No reservations or
credit cards.
Inexpensive.

New Mexican home cooking doesn't get any better than this in the entire state. As the old-fashioned name implies, the business opened its doors years ago to produce and peddle fresh tortillas. Meals developed as a sideline, and even today—despite immense popularity—they are secondary in terms of operating hours, usually 9:00 to 4:00. Occasionally, M&J's decides it's really a restaurant and starts serving dinner a few nights a week, but so far the lure of the nightlife has always faded fast.

Everything on the limited menu radiates local heat and flavor. After grazing through the choices over many years, we've locked in on several personal favorites, especially the chiles rellenos and the "House Special," carne adovada enchiladas made with blue corn tortillas. Complimentary fresh chips from the tortilla factory and a sassy salsa start every meal with a bang.

Mary & Tito's Cafe.
2711 Fourth Street
Northwest.
505-344-6266.
Closed Sunday.
Breakfast and lunch.
No reservations or
credit cards.
Inexpensive.

Don't be put off by the fraying neighborhood or the aging adobe facade. For over thirty years, Mary and Tito's family has served some of the best home cooking in the city. The proprietors haven't changed the decor much over that period, except to add more photos of the clan to the walls, but the cafe remains as tidy and friendly as ever.

The specialty is carne adovada, cooked in a sumptuously spicy red chile. The kitchen offers it in enchiladas, flautas, omelets, and big, puffy turnovers from 9:00 in the morning until the early evening. The rest of the New Mexican menu must be good too, but we wouldn't know from personal experience. With this many ways to enjoy great carne adovada, we're stuck in a heavenly rut.

Sadie's.
6230 Fourth Street
Northwest, in the
north valley.
505-345-5339.
Open daily for lunch
and dinner.
No reservations.
Inexpensive to
moderate.
Major credit cards.

Some people swear the cooking was better when Sadie's operated out of a bowling alley, but you would never know it from the crowds that pack the much more attractive and spacious current quarters. This is big-business New Mexican food, infused with a few tasty outside influences though still close to the core. We would stay away from the steaks ourselves, but we're always content with the chiles rellenos, enchiladas, and burritos, and we crave the fried potatoes called *papitas*.

PART FIVE

Off the Beaten Path

CHAPTER TWENTY-ONE

Pueblo Feast Days and Dances

*W*HILE MOST of the New Mexico pueblos welcome courteous and respectful visitors, they are living communities, not places seeking to become tourist attractions. Many of the villages have a crafts cooperative or a few individually owned shops, and some operate a small museum, but that is usually the extent of visitor services. Acoma (see Chapter 23) and Taos (Chapter 11) warrant a detour for their extraordinary historic character, and San Ildefonso (Chapter 22) may be worth a stop near Santa Fe, but generally the pueblos have limited appeal to travelers most of the year.

Special ceremonial days are the exception, and a major one, times that justify dropping anything else on an itinerary to get to a pueblo. The dances and other events amaze visitors with their ritualistic intensity, so rare in modern society, and carry an empathetic observer back to the spiritual roots of human civilization.

Be aware, however, that the community is not staging the activities for outsiders. One Pueblo publication explained it this way:

> Pueblo ceremonies have been continually performed for centuries as vital cultural acts. As a very generous people, the Pueblos have in recent decades opened up some of their cere-

monies to the public, as an invitation to partake, if even in a small way, of their cultural experience. An observer's presence should be understood as a privilege. The ceremony is not a performance for the benefit of the viewer, not a Disney-like presentation. It has been faithfully performed much the same over the centuries to benefit not only the Pueblo people but all of us who share the planet.

Feast Days

The best time to visit a pueblo is on the annual Feast Day, held to commemorate the patron saint of the village. By tradition it's a day of hospitality, when friends of the residents come for communal celebration and feasting. Don't assume you will be invited to eat unless you know someone in the pueblo, but if asked, you should accept politely without lingering over the meal.

Since each community, with one exception, has a different patron saint, Feast Days fall throughout the year. The majority happen to occur between June and September, during the busy tourism season, but they definitely are not intended to draw tourists. Visitors should remain respectfully quiet during dances, refrain from applause or other outbursts, and strictly adhere to local laws, which prohibit drinking, approaching or getting close to a kiva, parking in an unauthorized area, and (in most cases) photographing, sketching, or recording any of the activities. A sign in one of the pueblos would apply to all:

> We welcome you. We have always been friendly to visitors who appreciate that they are guests in our villages and respect our privacy. You will attend one of our ancient religious ceremonies. This ceremonial is as sacred to us as your church services are to you. We ask only that you always keep in mind the sacred nature of this ceremonial dance and be guided by the rules of our village government.

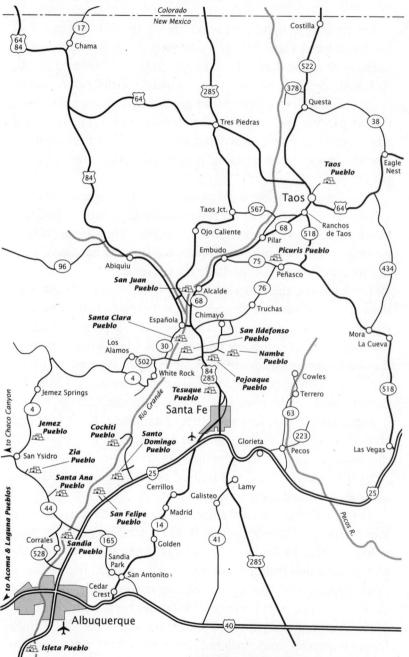

Pueblos of Northern New Mexico

Events vary in significant ways among the different pueblos, but most Feast Days follow a common pattern. The morning opens with a mass, usually sometime between 7:00 and 10:00. Residents carry a sacred santo, an image of the patron saint, from the church in a procession around the village plaza, ultimately placing the icon in a shrine on the plaza. Ceremonial dances start soon afterward and continue off and on until the late afternoon, when another procession returns the santo to the church.

The dances form the focal point of the day for residents and visitors alike. They bear no resemblance in nature or purpose to what most Americans regard as dancing. They are prayers in motion, a demonstration of reverence for and harmony with the spiritual forces that pervade the universe.

To observers, the dances seem highly repetitive, almost hypnotically monotonous. Drums and a chorus provide a pulsing rhythm that changes in tempo and sometimes pauses abruptly. Most of the dances involve dozens or even hundreds of people, dressed in clothing traditional for the particular ceremony, which can vary from breechcloths to full animal costumes. Often the dancers wear headdresses and the men paint their bodies.

Different pueblos feature different dances on Feast Day and sometimes change them from year to year. The Corn Dance is the most common. Its presentation at Santo Domingo on August 4, when some five hundred residents may participate, assumes dramatic dimensions.

The San Ildefonso celebration on January 23 may be even more striking. The pueblo's Buffalo Dance begins the evening before, lighted by log bonfires, and resumes at dawn with animal dancers descending from nearby hills, guided by the Game Priest dancer, who spreads sacred cornmeal to form a path. As the Corn Dance pays homage to what has been the main staple of the Pueblo diet for the past four thousand years, the Buffalo Dance expresses unity with the game hunted for meat over the same millennia.

An ancient element of Pueblo religious ceremonies, clowns play a prominent role in some but not all Feast Days. When they participate, they're often the most colorfully dressed and painted of the celebrants. At Picuris on San Lorenzo Day, August 10, the clowns wear stripes of gray and black body paint, breechcloths, skull caps with corn-husk horns, and necklaces made of plastic fruit or glazed doughnuts.

Special Feast Day customs also vary widely. Jemez brings out the playful Pecos Bull on August 2, when residents commemorate the patron saint of the extinct Pecos Pueblo, whose survivors moved to Jemez. A man wearing a wooden frame covered with black cloth, with a roll of sheepskin for a face, charges around the village, pursued by boys whose faces are painted black. Taos features a relay race to sacred stones on San Geronimo Day, September 30, along with a ritual pole climb.

Dates for the Feast Days are:

January 23	San Ildefonso
May 1	San Felipe
June 13	Sandia
June 24	San Juan
July 14	Cochiti
July 26	Santa Ana
August 2	Jemez
August 4	Santo Domingo
August 10	Picuris
August 12	Santa Clara
August 15	Zia
August 28	Isleta ("Big Feast")
September 2	Acoma
September 4	Isleta ("Little Feast")
September 19	Laguna
September 30	Taos
October 4	Nambe
November 12	Jemez and Tesuque
December 12	Pojoaque

Other Pueblo Dances

While Feast Days provide the most special occasion to visit a pueblo, any dance will do. Many of the villages have dances on Kings' Day (January 6), Easter, and Christmas, and one or more celebrate a ceremonial event almost weekly during the rest of the year, though some are closed to nonresidents and others are scheduled only a short time in advance.

For information on dances planned for particular days, call the Eight Northern Indian Pueblos Council (505-852-4265), the governor's office at individual pueblos, the Santa Fe Convention and Visitors Bureau (800-777-CITY or 505-984-6760), or the Indian Pueblo Cultural Center in Albuquerque (505-843-7270), which stages dances itself on most weekend days. Expect starting times to be approximate and be prepared to wait patiently.

CHAPTER TWENTY-TWO

Scenic Highways and Colorful Byways

*I*F YOU'RE looking for just one special drive, head to the High Road between Santa Fe and Taos, described in Chapter 10. The meandering mountain route isn't the only way to go, though, even from one of those towns to the other. The following car tours cover a range of fascinating country and enticing stops, mostly well off the usual tourist beat. Some of the options link Santa Fe, Taos, and Albuquerque, providing alternative means of access, and the others make a loop back to the starting point. In presenting the excursions, we move from north to south, both in the sequence of appearance and in the direction of noncircular treks.

The Enchanted Circle

A ninety-mile loop tour starting and ending in Taos, this popular drive is an official National Forest Scenic Byway. You may wonder why the feds want to show off what Questa's molybdenum mine did to public lands, but the question won't distract you long because you pass the scarred slopes quickly.

Take N.M. 522 north from Taos, considering a stop on the way at the D. H. Lawrence Ranch and Shrine (see Chapter 11). Turn east at Questa on N.M. 38 for the climb into **Red River,** a turn-of-the-century boom town that flaunts its Wild West aura

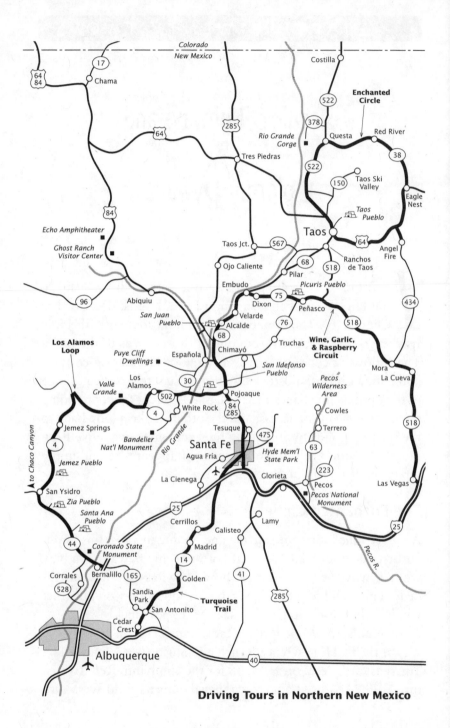

Driving Tours in Northern New Mexico

with an abandon that manages to combine greed with guile in a fun-loving way.

The spirit harks back to the local gold-rush era, when the population soared to ten times the present level and so did the number of red lights, none exactly meant to stop street traffic then. Smaller and more wholesome today, though still filled with saloons, Red River now looks for its lode in skiing, snow-mobiling, fishing, river rafting, and other outdoor pursuits discussed in Chapter 13.

Numerous Main Street hotels cater to those interests during the summer and winter seasons, providing quick, direct access to ski lifts and other facilities. The oldest establishment, the **Lodge at Red River** (800-915-6343 or 505-754-6280), refurbished the rooms recently with fresh pine walls and country fabrics. Its next-door nightclub, almost as large as the hotel, jumps with honky-tonk exuberance.

A more contemporary woodsy style reigns at the **Riverside** (800-432-9999 or 505-754-2252), which offers a broad selection of different cabins, condos, and standard rooms. The **Alpine Lodge** (800-252-2333 or 505-754-2952) dresses the part suggested by the name, but under the garb it's simply a cheerful, value-priced motel. Both places are a short walk from the **Red River Inn** (800-365-2930 or 505-754-2930), where Taos singer Michael Martin Murphey performs regularly.

Continuing east, you cross Bobcat Pass at almost 10,000 feet before descending to the town and lake called **Eagle Nest.** N.M. 38 meets U.S. 64 here and the Enchanted Circle route takes the west fork toward Angel Fire. Between the burgs you pass a privately sponsored Vietnam Veterans Memorial, built by a father in memory of his slain son. A stirring high, wing-like wall welcomes visitors to a chapel.

Angel Fire thrives as a secluded, self-contained resort community. Golf dominates social life in the summer and skiing in the winter (see Chapter 13), but residents and guests also enjoy ample opportunities for tennis, racquetball, and horseback riding. The **Legends Hotel & Conference Center,** which lives up to the last half of its name better than the first half, provides its own standard quarters and also a check-in service for the plethora of rental condominiums in the valley. Call 800-633-7463 to reserve accommodations or anything else from a tee time to a Texas T-bone.

U.S. 64 continues back to Taos from Angel Fire, scaling the 9,000 feet of Palo Flechado Pass and snaking its way scenically through a canyon into the town.

Wine, Garlic, and Raspberry Circuit

A long loop tour from Santa Fe, as we approach it, this route starts up the main highway to Taos and can be continued to the town, if you wish, making it a shorter and more direct alternative to the High Road. You'll miss the raspberries that way, and the historic burg of Las Vegas, but you'll catch the rest of the sights and tastes.

Leave Santa Fe on U.S. 84/285 toward Española, clocking twenty miles on the odometer to alert you to the proximity of **Santa Fe Vineyards.** We gave a brief overview of winemaking in New Mexico in Chapter 17, discussing Anderson Valley and other Albuquerque wineries, so it should suffice here to say that the vintner's art has historic roots in the state. Len Rosingana adds an Italian family love of wine to the heritage, saluting both traditions with ten varietals and blends made with grapes from all over New Mexico. Santa Fe Vineyards (505-753-8100) is open daily, usually from 10:00 to 5:00.

Pause in Española for a look around and maybe a meal. The largest and most curiously contemporary of the old Spanish towns in the north, it becomes a showcase on nights and weekends for elaborate "lowrider" cars, a major focus of the community's social life. The customized machines glide down the highway through town an inch or so off the asphalt, moving at a barely discernible pace.

The place to eat, at least during the day, is **Jo Ann's Ranch-**

O-Casados (505-753-2837), in front of the Big Rock Shopping Center directly on the main highway, which becomes N.M. 68 in Española. Don't be put off by the franchise appearance, inherited from a past occupant. Jo Ann and her kitchen dish out some of the best New Mexican home cooking in the state.

For fancier food in the evening or a place to stay in town, Anthony Garcia provides the only option worth considering. His hotel, the **Inn at the Delta** (800-995-8599 or 505-753-9466), offers the classiest bargain for spacious Southwestern luxury anywhere near Santa Fe and Taos. **Anthony's at the Delta** (505-753-4511), the restaurant, doesn't succeed quite as fully, but certainly does well with steak, seafood, and Spanish colonial ambience. The two establishments sit next to each other at 228 and 304 Paseo de Oñate, which is also U.S. 84 toward Abiquiu and Chama.

Just north of Española, **San Juan Pueblo** could warrant a visit for its crafts cooperative. From there, a back road paralleling the Taos highway leads to the Spanish village of **Alcalde,** the site of an unusual dance pageant each Christmas, Las Matachines. The traditional rite goes back in Spanish history to the time of the Moors.

By this point you're in the agricultural heart of the Española Valley, as you can see clearly from N.M. 68. Dixon writer Stanley Crawford, who farms with his wife, Rose Mary, has penned two insightful and sprightly accounts of the agrarian life in the area, *Mayordomo* (University of New Mexico Press, 1988) and *The Garlic Testament* (HarperCollins, 1992). Both provide as solid an introduction to northern New Mexico as you can find anywhere.

The drive through this stretch is particularly pleasant in the late summer and early fall, when the highway is lined with fruit and vegetable stands selling red-chile and garlic *ristras,* along with other local produce. Look for the business operated by Herman Valdez on the north side of **Velarde.** His wife, Loretta, makes distinctive wreaths with dried chiles, gourds, corn, and more. One of the youngest New Mexico wineries, **Black Mesa** (800-852-MESA), is nearby and open daily except Sunday.

Beyond Velarde, the Rio Grande, source of the valley's abundance, gradually begins to descend into the gorge that becomes so pronounced near Taos. Cliffs replace fields, pushing the road to the riverbank, and squeezing the water into rapids. To admire the scene, absorb a little history, and enjoy a handcrafted beer, stop at **Embudo Station** (505-852-4707), as the famed Chile Line railroad once did. You can dangle your toes in the Rio Grande while feasting on homesmoked trout or baby-back ribs washed down with the day's special brew, maybe a green-chile ale.

Three miles farther, N.M. 75 intersects the Taos highway and heads toward the hills for a dramatic climb over the Sangre de Cristos. Our driving tour takes that turn, though you can stay on N.M. 68 and follow the deepening gorge to Taos if that's your destination.

Just east of the junction of the two highways, the increasingly arty town of **Dixon** hosts a delightful studio tour early each November. In addition to artists' workshops, the open homes include a garlic farm and **La Chiripada Winery** (505-579-4437). Brothers Pat and Mike Johnson, La Chiripada's owner-vintners, grow many of their own grapes on the ten-acre estate, and they make them into a variety of lush red, white, and blush wines. Try a taste of the blended Primavera, which goes great with green chile. The Johnsons welcome visitors daily except Sunday.

From Dixon, N.M. 75 starts its ascent of the Sangre de Cristos. It's the only road over the mountains between Santa Fe and Taos, and you'll see why the higher you go. The entire fifty-mile ride to Mora is scenic, but the descent from the peaks offers some of the grandest views.

In Spanish, *mora* means "berry," and that's the area's top crop. Six miles south of the town, at the fascinating La Cueva National Historic Site, the **Salman Ranch** (505-387-2900) raises prodigious raspberries. If possible, time your visit for the September-October "Raspberry Roundup," when the juicy morsels are fresh, but any time of the year you can buy jam, syrup, and vinegar made from the fruit. The ranch store is open daily from May to October, and on a more abbreviated schedule in other months, and a new cafe hopes to maintain similar hours.

The old mill village of La Cueva dates back to the same period as **Las Vegas,** 25 miles south. Founded in 1835 in grasslands the Spanish settlers called "the large meadows on the Turkey River," Las Vegas boomed after the railroad arrived in town on July 4, 1879. As in Albuquerque, a "new town" commercial district grew up near the depot, and the historic plaza, where the town began as a fortified village, gradually went into decline.

Ironically, a business stimulated by the railroad, the **Plaza Hotel** (505-425-3591), has become the anchor for an effort to revitalize the original city center. Opened first in 1881, and then again in 1982 in restored Victorian glory, the hotel makes a superb hideaway for a night or two. The restaurant, bar, and a few rooms overlook the venerable, tree-shaded plaza, one of the most attractive in the state. Ask at the desk for a copy of the walking-tour brochure published by a local preservation group.

If you're getting hungry, consider the hearty, spicy New Mexican plates at the **Spic 'n Span Bakery & Cafe** (713 Douglas Avenue, 505-425-6481). A veritable institution in the town, the restaurant should fuel you for the rest of the day.

Returning to Santa Fe on I-25, look for the frontage-road tasting room of **Madison Vineyards & Winery** (505-421-2299),about 25 miles southwest of Las Vegas. Bill and Elise Madison produce wines in several styles, including more than one award-winning *vin ordinaire.* If you want to visit the winery itself, ask for directions at the tasting room. Both facilities are open daily from April to October.

Almost back to Santa Fe, the final stop on the driving tour is the **Pecos National Monument,** just north of the interstate on

N.M. 63. The park commemorates a fourteenth-century pueblo, abandoned in 1838, and a seventeenth-century mission, originally one of the most magnificent churches north of Mexico City. A mile-long walk encompasses both sites and some striking landscape as well.

The Los Alamos Loop

A lengthy way to get between Santa Fe or Taos and Albuquerque, or a scenic day's excursion from and back to any of the towns, this drive covers eons of geological and historical time. You see where an ancient volcano erupted and collapsed and where scientists work zealously today to develop new kinds of even more powerful manmade explosions.

Pick up N.M. 502-4 to Los Alamos in Pojoaque, between Santa Fe and Española on U.S. 84/285. In a few miles you reach the turnoff to **San Ildefonso,** just north of the highway. Park by the visitor center, which has an exhibit on the pueblo, and then wander through the old adobe village to the small museum. Several shops sell the local pottery, still inspired by the legacy of San Ildefonso masters such as Maria Martínez and Blue Corn.

From the pueblo, the road climbs the Pajarito Plateau, providing majestic vistas eastward to the Sangre de Cristo Mountains. It forks near the top, with one branch going south to **Bandelier National Monument** (see Chapter 23) and the other continuing west to Los Alamos. You can fit a brief visit to Bandelier into a day's drive on this tour, but the park may merit a longer look at another time, depending on your interests.

Los Alamos was nothing more than a secluded school for boys early this century, but during World War II it became the super-secret site for the Manhattan Project, which developed the atomic bomb. The town remained closed to visitors for years after the first big blast, but it actively encourages them today, seeking to broaden the economic base beyond the Los Alamos National Laboratory (LANL in the local lingo). The lab still dominates life in all respects, sprawling across the community in multiple facilities devoted to scientific research in a variety of fields.

To gain a little perspective on the work and the town, stop at the **Bradbury Science Museum** (505-667-4444) and the **Los Alamos Historical Museum** (505-662-4493), both downtown on Central Avenue and free. If you have time for only one, go to the Bradbury, which presents high-tech interactive exhibits on the Manhattan Project and some of the lab's current studies. It's open daily, but only in the afternoon on Saturday, Sunday, and Monday.

About fifteen miles west of Los Alamos, N.M. 4 skirts the **Valle Grande,** an enormous *caldera,* or collapsed volcano crater. It's part of a privately owned cattle ranch, but you can contemplate what happened here a million and half years ago from a scenic overlook.

If you would rather check out cascading water, take the turnoff to Jemez Falls, about five miles before the town of La Cueva, where the highway heads south through the beautiful **Jemez Mountains.** For information on hiking trails and hot springs in the area, inquire at the Jemez Ranger Station (505-829-3535). You'll find the post right before the Jemez State Monument, where you can explore the ruins of a pueblo and a seventeenth-century mission church.

Wedged into a narrow green valley, the town of **Jemez Springs** is a living religious sanctuary for many residents, home to a nunnery, a counseling center for Catholic priests, and the Bodhi Manda Zen Center. After a soak and a massage at the Jemez Springs Bath House, you may be inspired to stick around too. The **Jemez Mountain Inn** (505-829-3926) offers more creature comforts than the nearby cloisters.

Between Jemez Springs and Bernalillo, the end of the drive, the tour passes the pueblos of Jemez, Zia, and Santa Ana. None compel as much interest as San Ildefonso, but you might want to look at the crafts for sale in the first two villages. The quiet town of **San Ysidro,** where the route turns southeast on N.M. 44, also offers some shopping opportunities as well as a historic church.

In Bernalillo, don't miss the **Coronado State Monument,** described in Chapter 17. Shortly after the park, the highway dead-ends into I-25, which leads south to Albuquerque and north to Santa Fe and Taos.

Turquoise Trail

A back-roads route between Santa Fe and Albuquerque, the alternative to I-25, the Turquoise Trail meanders along N.M. 14 through old mining towns, piñon-dotted hills, striking rock formations, and mountain vistas. The highway starts as an extension of busy, commercial Cerrillos Road, but it loses the city character instantly when it pulls out of Santa Fe.

The first stop of interest, about twenty minutes away, is the village of **Cerrillos,** which sits several hundred yards west of N.M. 14. Miners dug almost everything from the hills here at one time or another, including gold, silver, lead, zinc, and high-quality turquoise. At its peak in the 1880s the rip-roaring town contained twenty-one bars and four hotels, though it's hard to figure where they fit. Today the few remaining businesses stress quaintness rather than kicks. The short main street flaunts the authentic look of an old frontier town and has indeed played that role in Hollywood shoots.

Just beyond Cerrillos, a small sign marks the turnoff to the **Iris Ranch** (505-473-3148). The privately owned spread, several miles east down a pot-holed road, grows a stunning array of irises in a profusion of colors, which seem all the more remarkable in contrast to the arid landscape. The flowers generally reach their peak between mid-May and mid-June, when you should definitely plan a visit if you're passing by.

Around the next big bend, **Madrid** displays all of its many generations simultaneously. A coal-mining community in the nineteenth century, it once bustled with three thousand residents, but everyone left after the mines closed following World War II. Madrid remained a ghost town from then until its resurgence in the 1970s, when some enterprising artists realized that the coal company's old wood-frame cabins could provide cheap housing. They bought up the one-street town piece by piece and established Madrid as a countercultural center.

Poke around the shops to check out the work of local artists and artisans. If you're looking for a snack instead, head to Maya Jones, which has an old soda fountain among its Guatemalan imports. The **Mine Shaft Tavern** will quench a thirst for stronger drink in authentic Western saloon style.

In the 1920s over a hundred thousand people came to Madrid annually during the Christmas season to see the town's array of holiday lights. The glow was so grand that airlines would reroute cross-country flights on Christmas Eve just to pass over the scene. Today's Christmas show isn't nearly so elaborate but still has its allure.

The next burg along the Turquoise Trail is **Golden,** a withering village that was the site of the first gold rush west of the Mississippi in 1825. Shortly after it, as you approach the Albuquerque metropolitan area, take a detour west on N.M. 536 up to the **Sandia Peak Ski Area,** where the views are grand year-round. See Chapter 18 for information on skiing and mountain biking at the basin.

The highway broadens after the turnoff to Sandia Peak and takes you through the thriving mountain community of Cedar Crest on the way to I-40. Go west at the interstate toward the city, entering Albuquerque along the modern version of old Route 66.

CHAPTER TWENTY-THREE

Worth a Special Detour

Acoma

Perched 7,000 feet above sea level on a sheer-walled mesa, Acoma surveys the earth from a perspective that's singular in all ways. The first European who sighted the pueblo, a captain in Coronado's 1540 expedition, reported that he had found "a rock with a village on top, the strongest position ever seen in the world." At the time, the only way up and down the 365-foot mesa was a stone stairway carved into the cliff with a system of tricky hand- and toeholds. Then as now, once you reached the crest of "Sky City," you could see forever, apparently justifying the chore of hauling food and water up the steep path.

Acoma Pueblos have lived at the seventy-acre village since at least the eleventh century, making it the oldest continuously inhabited city in the country. Residents once numbered in the thousands, but only fifty remain year-round today, with other members of the pueblo returning from nearby towns for special ceremonial occasions. A small reservoir collects rainwater for many domestic uses, but drinking water is still transported from below, where the electricity ends even now.

The architectural highlight of the ancient hamlet is the magnificent mission of San Esteban del Rey. Built in the 1630s, the church soars sixty feet high on ten-foot-thick walls. Villagers cut the huge ceiling beams in distant forests and managed to carry them back to the mesa and then to the top.

One hour west of Albuquerque and a dozen miles off I-40, the pueblo allows visitors only on guided tours. Shuttles with a capacity of sixteen people leave regularly from a visitor center at the base, where there's a museum, a restaurant, and a crafts shop that sells the distinctive Acoma pottery. Admission costs $6 for adults and a little less for seniors and children. A still-camera permit is $5. Call 505-252-1139 for additional information.

Bandelier National Monument

The site of ancient Pueblo settlements, abandoned before the founding of Santa Fe, Bandelier encompasses cliff dwellings, excavated and unexcavated ruins, sacred sites, waterfalls, a small museum, complete camping facilities, a wilderness area for backpacking, and superb hiking trails. What you can't find and do here may not be worth seeking.

Forty miles from Santa Fe, the park is off N.M. 4, a beautiful approach that sets the right mood after the road leaves U.S. 84/285 in Pojoaque and heads west toward the Jemez Mountains. As you climb the Pajarito Plateau, pull over and look back to the east for grand views of the Sangre de Cristo Mountains. From the top, the road winds its way down into Frijoles Canyon and to the park headquarters.

The Anasazi settlement in the river ravine, called Tyuonyi, probably dates back to the late twelfth century. Some of the residents lived on the cliff walls, making natural caves into habitable rooms by digging them out with stone, bone, and wood tools. Others occupied a pueblo on the valley floor, a two- or three-story circular communal structure built around a central plaza. They raised some of their corn, beans, and squash in small fields inside the canyon but farmed mainly on the expansive mesa tops, supplementing their hard-earned food supply by hunting game and harvesting wild plants. After four centuries of intense cultivation, resources probably dwindled, forcing a relocation to the present pueblos near the Rio Grande.

You can see the primary ruins of the village, including the

cliff dwellings, on a one- to two-hour walk, though serious hikers have lots of other options. The visitor center sells a back-
country trail map as well as a guidebook about the trails. One
of the best day hikes, covering thirteen miles, goes to the Stone
Lions Shrine, an ancient ceremonial carving still sacred to the
Pueblos and likely to be ringed with deer-antler offerings. The
hike is difficult at one point, but it includes fine views of
Frijoles Canyon from above, a range of vegetation, an unexcavated ruin, and mountain panoramas.

Bandelier is open daily, but fluctuations in the federal budget
can affect some services. For current information on hours and
facilities call 505-672-3861. Admission is $5 per vehicle.

Chaco Canyon

A major cultural and trade center in the prehistoric Southwest,
described in Chapter 1, Chaco is a mecca for serious scholars
and amateur archaeologists alike. Anyone with a keen interest
in early Native American life must make the trek—way, way off
the beaten path—but others will be satisfied with more accessible introductions to the subject at Acoma, Bandelier, or Puye.

Many archaeologists believe Chaco was the "capital" of the
Anasazi world, the commercial and perhaps religious hub of
the entire Southwest. At its peak of influence between 1000
and 1200, it may have been the most advanced Native
American community ever in the present-day United States.
Residents erected magnificent Stone Age buildings, laid an
extensive network of roads, studied astronomy, and likely
exchanged ideas and goods with the great civilizations of the
Valley of Mexico, some fifteen hundred miles away.

Today the Chaco Culture National Historic Park encompasses thirteen well-developed pueblos and four hundred small
settlements, all in a seventeen-mile-long canyon. It takes a day
or more to explore fully, but you can get a glimpse of the glory
more quickly by focusing on Pueblo Bonito, the grandest prehistoric dwelling in the country.

Drought may have destroyed Chaco, and it won't take you long to understand why. Bring plenty of water, even for a short visit. The only source in the barren, arid country is at the visitor center, which also has a fine museum and a campground.

The access road to the National Historic Park (505-988-6716 or 505-988-6727) is off N.M. 44 almost two hours northwest of Albuquerque. Turn south at Nageezi for a 26-mile washboard ride to the ruins on dirt and gravel tracks. After your body and car pay their dues getting there, the park charges only a nominal admission.

Georgia O'Keeffe Country

Centered along a fifteen-mile stretch of U.S. 84 that begins in Abiquiu, northwest of Española, the Ghost Ranch region provided the setting for many of O'Keeffe's best-known paintings. A working ranch when the artist moved to New Mexico, the spread took its name from the *brujas,* or witches, who supposedly haunted the brightly hued canyonlands. O'Keeffe herself called the country the "faraway."

Drive slowly through the area once before stopping, to get a sense of the whole. From Abiquiu, go west to the Echo Canyon Amphitheater, a good point to turn around and start back. While you're there, take a few minutes for a close look at the sandstone terrain. A natural bowl hollowed out of the earth by centuries of erosion, the formation fits its name.

You get another view of the landscape from a geological perspective at the Ghost Ranch Living Museum, a few miles east. Climb the unusual stairway exhibition to probe the strata in the cliffs, each representing a different eon of sediment. The museum condenses the same show in the "Up Through the Ages" rock column, a six-foot three-inch pillar illustrating when present life evolved in geological terms—just the last two inches. You can also see wildlife indigenous to New Mexico, mainly injured and orphaned animals no longer able to survive on their own.

The Presbyterian Church now owns Ghost Ranch and operates a conference center and two museums at the old headquarters. An anthropology exhibit explores the people who
inhabited the area over a span of twelve thousand years and a
paleontology display focuses on dinosaur fossils found nearby.

In the village of Abiquiu, the O'Keeffe Foundation allows a
limited number of visitors to tour the artist's home, where she
lived for decades before her death in 1986. A stunning testament to O'Keeffe's aesthetic sensibilities and ascetic soul, the
residence provides insights into her spirit that her paintings
only suggest. Call 505-685-4539 well in advance to make a
reservation for a tour. The foundation requests a minimum
donation of $15 for the experience and prohibits photography.

Puye Cliff Dwellings

Near Bandelier National Monument, on the same Pajarito
Plateau, Puye offers a similar ancient setting that's far less
crowded and developed. You may have to make some of your
own trails, but the forlorn mesa exerts a powerful spell that's
likely to linger a lifetime.

About a dozen miles uphill from Santa Clara, off N.M. 30,
the National Landmark was the former site of the pueblo
before the residents moved down to the Rio Grande. Occupied
around the thirteenth century, the mesa originally provided
housing in the hollows of the volcanic cliffs, which the settlers
dug out for dwellings that they reached from ladders. Later,
before abandoning the area in the sixteenth century, the villagers built a 740-room pueblo on the top of the bluff, now in
ruins. The mountain and valley views they enjoyed from the
homestead are breathtaking.

Administered by the Santa Clara people, Puye (505-753-
7326) is open daily. For a self-guided tour, adults pay $5 and
seniors and children slightly less.

Practical Travel Tips

Visitor Information

Planning a trip may not be half the fun, but it certainly can consume plenty of pleasant hours and build the anticipation properly. We may be gluttons for information, but we always seek out government tourism booklets, Chamber of Commerce promotional pieces, and advertising-based publications, even knowing that the information is unfiltered or slanted.

If you're looking for that kind of background, start with the New Mexico Economic Development and Tourism Department (800-545-2040 or 505-827-0291). The agency publishes an annual *Vacation Guide* for the entire state that summarizes everything of the remotest possible interest in a sentence or so. The publication contains a pull-out map, but also ask for the better State Highway Commission map.

For Santa Fe information, call the Convention & Visitors Bureau (800-777-CITY or 505-984-6760) or stop by the office at 201 West Marcy, downtown. In Taos the city contact is the Chamber of Commerce (800-732-TAOS or 505-758-3873) and in Albuquerque the Convention and Visitors Bureau (800-284-2282, 505-842-9918) handles the role. All three bodies will send you an official, sanitized guide to attractions and accommodations.

You may learn more from the local newspapers. Santa Fe's

New Mexican covers events of the coming week in its Friday "Pasatiempo" section, the *Albuquerque Journal* and the *Albuquerque Tribune* do the same right before the weekend, and in Taos, the weekly *Taos News* and *Sangre de Cristo Chronicle* review the northernmost scene on Thursday. Each of the papers issues occasional tourism supplements as well, the most thorough of which is the *New Mexican's* "Bienvenidos" (505-984-0363).

For current information on art galleries and exhibitions, get copies of the *Collector's Guide* and the quarterly *Collector's Calendar* from the Wingspread publishing company (800-873-4278 or 505-292-7537). The best single source of information about Pueblo activities is the Indian Pueblo Cultural Center in Albuquerque (505-843-7270).

Transportation

Obviously you can drive to New Mexico, or take a bus or train, but most visitors coming a substantial distance fly into the Albuquerque airport. The small airports in Santa Fe and Taos cater primarily to private planes and offer only limited and fluctuating commercial service.

Taxis and hotel shuttles provide transportation from the Albuquerque airport locally and several bus companies carry visitors north to Santa Fe and Taos. Shuttlejack (800-452-2665 or 505-982-4311) manages the job for Santa Fe, and Faust Transportation (505-758-3410) and Pride of Taos (800-273-8340 or 505-758-8340) compete on the route to Taos.

The best plan, however, is to rent a car. All the major national rental agencies have offices at the Albuquerque airport and toll-free numbers for reservations. Though you can enjoy much of Santa Fe and Taos on foot, you'll miss a lot without a car. Neither town has taxi stands or anything approaching regular urban service, and the bus system in Santa Fe is geared to the needs of residents rather than visitors.

Climate and Clothing

Although Albuquerque gets a little warmer and muggier than Santa Fe and Taos, particularly in midsummer, all three towns enjoy an appealing combination of intense sunshine and cooling mountain air. In the summer the sun dominates the day by 10:00, but as soon as it disappears the heat begins to dissipate. Even though shorts are comfortable most of the time, you might want a light sweater or jacket in the evening and early morning. The experienced take blankets or heavy coats for late nights at the Santa Fe Opera. While the sun reigns during the day—frying a sunbather in half the time required at sea level—the humidity usually stays low, making the heat much less oppressive than in some places far to the north.

Winter days get cold and often snowy but seldom frozen over. Ski jackets or the equivalent are needed from at least November through March. The sun stays strong, however, and is considerably more effective at snow removal than the mechanical methods. Even in the depths of winter, northern New Mexico remains the dancing ground of the sun.

Index